# EU Socio-Economic Governance since the Crisis



This book is the first to be dedicated entirely to the European Semester—a new framework for policy coordination across European Union (EU) member states. The semester represents a major advancement in EU governance. Created in 2010 in the wake of the financial and sovereign debt crises and revamped in 2015, it was intended to provide a new socio-economic governance architecture to coordinate national policies without transferring legal sovereignty to EU level. The chapters in this book are written by authors who have already contributed to this literature and have conducted original research for their studies. The book offers an empirical and theoretical assessment of the European Semester, examining its implications along three critical axes, running respectively between the economic and the social, the supranational and the intergovernmental, and the technocratic and democratic poles of EU governance. The book concludes that the European Semester challenges established theoretical understandings of EU governance, as it is a prime example of the complexity that supersedes simple polar oppositions.

The chapters in this book were originally published in a special issue of the *Journal of European Public Policy.*

**Jonathan Zeitlin** is Distinguished Faculty Professor of Public Policy and Governance at the University of Amsterdam, the Netherlands, and Scientific Director of the Amsterdam Centre for Contemporary European Studies (ACCESS EUROPE).

**Amy Verdun** is Professor of Political Science, Jean Monnet Chair Ad Personam, and the Faculty of Social Science Lansdowne Distinguished Fellow in European Integration Studies at the University of Victoria, Canada.

## Journal of European Public Policy Series

Edited by
Jeremy Richardson, *Nuffield College, Oxford University, UK, and National Centre for Research on Europe, University of Canterbury, New Zealand*

Berthold Rittberger, *International Relations at the Geschwister Scholl Institute of Political Science, University of Munich, Germany*

This series seeks to bring together some of the finest edited works on European Public Policy. Reprinting from special issues of the *Journal of European Public Policy*, the focus is on using a wide range of social sciences approaches, both qualitative and quantitative, to gain a comprehensive and definitive understanding of public policy in Europe.

For more information about this series, please visit: https://www.routledge.com/Journal-of-European-Public-Policy-Special-Issues-as-Books/book-series/JEPPSPIBS

**EU Socio-Economic Governance since the Crisis**
The European Semester in theory and practice
*Edited by Jonathan Zeitlin and Amy Verdun*

**Innovative Approaches to EU Multilevel Implementation**
Moving beyond legal compliance
*Edited by Eva Thomann and Fritz Sager*

**Transforming Food and Agricultural Policy**
Post-exceptionalism in public policy
*Edited by Carsten Daugbjerg and Peter Feindt*

**European Union Enlargement and Integration Capacity**
*Edited by Tanja Börzel, Antoaneta L. Dimitrova and Frank Schimmelfennig*

**Governance by International Public Administrations**
Bureaucratic influence and global public policies
*Edited by Christoph Knill and Michael Bauer*

**The European Union at an Inflection Point**
(Dis)integrating or the new normal
*Edited by Alasdair Young*

**Federal Challenges and Challenges to Federalism**
*Edited by John Erik Fossum and Markus Jachtenfuchs*

**Political Budgeting Across Europe**
*Edited by Christian Breunig, Christine S. Lipsmeyer and Guy D. Whitten*

**Ideas, Political Power, and Public Policy**
*Edited by Daniel Béland, Martin B. Carstensen and Leonard Seabrooke*

**The European Union as a Global Regulator**
*Edited by Alasdair Young*

**Differentiated Integration in the European Union**
*Edited by Benjamin Leruth and Christopher Lord*

**Legislative Lobbying in Context**
The policy and polity determinants of interest group politics in the European Union
*Edited by Jan Beyers, Caelesta Braun and Heike Klüver*

# EU Socio-Economic Governance since the Crisis

## The European Semester in Theory and Practice

***Edited by***
**Jonathan Zeitlin and Amy Verdun**

Routledge
Taylor & Francis Group
LONDON AND NEW YORK

First published 2018
by Routledge

2 Park Square, Milton Park, Abingdon, Oxfordshire OX14 4RN
52 Vanderbilt Avenue, New York, NY 10017

*Routledge is an imprint of the Taylor & Francis Group, an informa business*

First issued in paperback 2020



*British Library Cataloguing in Publication Data*
A catalogue record for this book is available from the British Library

ISBN 13: 978-1-138-49471-8 (hbk)
ISBN 13: 978-0-367-59121-2 (pbk)

Typeset in MyriadPro
by diacriTech, Chennai

**Publisher's Note**
The publisher accepts responsibility for any inconsistencies that may have arisen during the conversion of this book from journal articles to book chapters, namely the possible inclusion of journal terminology.

**Disclaimer**
Every effort has been made to contact copyright holders for their permission to reprint material in this book. The publishers would be grateful to hear from any copyright holder who is not here acknowledged and will undertake to rectify any errors or omissions in future editions of this book.

# Contents

# Citation Information

The chapters in this book were originally published in the *Journal of European Public Policy*, volume 25, issue 2 (2018). When citing this material, please use the original page numbering for each article, as follows:

**Introduction**

*Introduction: the European Semester as a new architecture of EU socioeconomic governance in theory and practice*
Amy Verdun and Jonathan Zeitlin
*Journal of European Public Policy*, volume 25, issue 2 (2018) pp. 137–148

**Chapter 1**

*Socializing the European Semester: EU social and economic policy co-ordination in crisis and beyond*
Jonathan Zeitlin and Bart Vanhercke
*Journal of European Public Policy*, volume 25, issue 2 (2018) pp. 149–174

**Chapter 2**

*Flexicurity in the European Semester: still a relevant policy concept?*
Sonja Bekker
*Journal of European Public Policy*, volume 25, issue 2 (2018) pp. 175–192

**Chapter 3**

*Deciding on the European Semester: the European Council, the Council and the enduring asymmetry between economic and social policy issues*
Adina Maricut and Uwe Puetter
*Journal of European Public Policy*, volume 25, issue 2 (2018) pp. 193–211

**Chapter 4**

*Enforcing the European Semester: the politics of asymmetric information in the excessive deficit and macroeconomic imbalance procedures*
James D. Savage and David Howarth
*Journal of European Public Policy*, volume 25, issue 2 (2018) pp. 212–230

**Chapter 5**

*Cherry-picking external constraints: Latvia and EU economic governance, 2008–2014*
Edgars Eihmanis
*Journal of European Public Policy*, volume 25, issue 2 (2018) pp. 231–249

**Chapter 6**

*Explaining the evolving role of national parliaments under the European Semester*
Mark Hallerberg, Benedicta Marzinotto and Guntram B. Wolff
*Journal of European Public Policy*, volume 25, issue 2 (2018) pp. 250–267

**Chapter 7**

*Parliamentary accountability in multilevel governance: what role for parliaments in post-crisis EU economic governance?*
Ben Crum
*Journal of European Public Policy*, volume 25, issue 2 (2018) pp. 268–286

# Notes on Contributors

**Sonja Bekker** is Associate Professor of European Social Policy at Tilburg University, the Netherlands.

**Ben Crum** is Professor of Political Science at the Vrije Universiteit Amsterdam, the Netherlands.

**Edgars Eihmanis** is a PhD researcher at the European University Institute in Florence, Italy.

**Mark Hallerberg** is Professor of Public Management and Political Economy at the Hertie School of Governance in Berlin, Germany.

**David Howarth** is Professor of Political Economy at the University of Luxembourg.

**Adina Maricut** is Postdoctoral Researcher at the Center for European Union Research (CEUR) at the Central European University, Budapest, Hungary.

**Benedicta Marzinotto** is Assistant Professor of Economic Policy at the University of Udine, Italy, and Visiting Professor at the College of Europe.

**Uwe Puetter** is Professor of European Public Policy and Governance and Director of the Center for European Union Research at the Central European University, Budapest, Hungary.

**James D. Savage** is Professor of Political Science at the University of Virginia, USA.

**Bart Vanhercke** is Director of the European Social Observatory (OSE), Brussels, Belgium.

**Amy Verdun** is Professor of Political Science, Jean Monnet Chair Ad Personam, and the Faculty of Social Science Lansdowne Distinguished Fellow in European Integration Studies at the University of Victoria, Canada.

**Guntram B. Wolff** is the Director of Bruegel, the European think tank focussing on economics.

**Jonathan Zeitlin** is Distinguished Faculty Professor of Public Policy and Governance at the University of Amsterdam, the Netherlands, and Scientific Director of the Amsterdam Centre for Contemporary European Studies (ACCESS EUROPE).

# Introduction: the European Semester as a new architecture of EU socioeconomic governance in theory and practice

Amy Verdun and Jonathan Zeitlin

**ABSTRACT**
The 'European Semester', a new framework for policy co-ordination across European Union (EU) member states, represents a major step in EU governance. Created in 2010 in the wake of the financial and sovereign debt crises and revamped in 2015, it was intended to provide a new socioeconomic governance architecture to co-ordinate national policies without transferring full sovereignty to the EU level. This introduction offers a brief overview and assessment of the European Semester, examining its implications along three critical axes, running respectively between the economic and the social, the supranational and the intergovernmental, and the technocratic and democratic poles of EU governance. We introduce and briefly summarize the seven other contributions that make up this collection. Our conclusions are that the European Semester challenges established theoretical understandings of EU governance, as it is a prime example of the complexity that supersedes simple polar oppositions.

## 1. Introduction

The 'European Semester' (hereafter 'Semester') is a new governance architecture for socioeconomic policy co-ordination in the European Union (EU). Created in 2010 in the wake of the financial and sovereign debt crises, the Semester has been periodically revamped, most significantly by the Juncker Commission in 2015. Its procedures build on, but also reformulate, the EU's pre-existing processes of fiscal, economic, employment and social policy co-ordination, as these had developed during the 1990s and 2000s, including the Stability and Growth Pact (SGP), the Broad Economic Policy Guidelines

Supplemental data for this article can be accessed https://doi.org/10.1080/13501763.2017.1363807.

(BEPGs), the European Employment Strategy (EES), the Lisbon Strategy and the Social Open Method of Co-ordination (OMC). The Semester was introduced as part of a panoply of far-reaching measures aimed at reinforcing EU economic governance in response to the euro crisis: the so-called 'Six-Pack', 'Two-Pack' and 'Fiscal Compact'. These measures included stronger and more 'automatic' sanctions for the SGP's Excessive Deficit Procedure (EDP); a new Macroeconomic Imbalance Procedure (MIP) for detecting and correcting non-fiscal imbalances (e.g., in the housing market or current account) that could negatively affect other member states, based on a scoreboard of economic indicators, in-depth country reviews and recommendations, with financial sanctions for persistent non-compliance; *ex ante* review by the Commission of euro area national budgets; and Reverse Qualified Majority Voting (RQMV) for overturning Commission proposals under the excessive deficit and imbalance procedures. The Semester was also intended to serve as the governance architecture for 'thematic co-ordination' of member state policies towards the 'smart, sustainable and inclusive growth' objectives of the Europe 2020 Strategy, which was explicitly designed to have a stronger social dimension than the preceding Lisbon Strategy, including specific guidelines and targets on poverty and social inclusion.[1]

The Semester brings together within a single policy co-ordination cycle a variety of EU governance instruments with different legal bases, from the SGP, MIP and Fiscal Compact to the Europe 2020 Strategy and the Integrated Economic and Employment Policy Guidelines. In this cycle, the Commission, the Council of the EU (hereafter: Council) and the European Council set priorities for the Union; review national performance, budgets and reform programmes; and issue Country-Specific Recommendations (CSRs), backed up in some cases by possible financial sanctions. Each member state receives a single integrated set of CSRs, except for those under a bailout programme (as in the case of Greece). The CSRs cover a wide range of policy fields, including issues such as wage determination, education and health care, which fall under the primary competence of member states and where the Union's legislative powers are severely limited. Although the Semester involves no legal transfer of sovereignty from the member states to the EU level, it has given the EU institutions a more visible and authoritative role than ever before in monitoring, scrutinizing and guiding national economic, fiscal and social policies, especially within the euro area.

The Semester in its current form begins each November with the Commission's Annual Growth Survey (AGS), which identifies the key reform priorities for the EU and offers general policy guidance to the member states for the coming year. The 'autumn package' includes the Commission's Alert Mechanism Report, which designates member states for MIP In-Depth Reviews (IDRs), its opinion on euro area draft budgets and proposed recommendations for the euro area as a whole, as well as the Joint Employment Report (which also covers social issues). In February, the Commission publishes detailed Country Reports laying out its analysis of the key challenges and reform progress of each member state, including the conclusions of the MIP IDRs, which are preceded and followed by intensive dialogue with national governments and stakeholders. Based on the AGS and subsequent Council conclusions, the March European Council adopts socioeconomic priorities and policy orientations for the Union. By early April, the member states submit their National Reform Programmes (NRPs) and fiscal Stability or Convergence Programmes. In May, the Commission assesses these programmes and proposes CSRs, which in turn are reviewed and sometimes amended by committees of member state officials preparing the work of the Council, based on multilateral implementation reviews of national reforms. The revised CSRs are then endorsed by the European Council and adopted by the Council in late June/early July. The European Parliament (EP) adopts resolutions and reports on the AGS and the CSR each year, and may invite the Presidents of the Commission, Council, European Council and Eurogroup to discuss the Semester through the so-called 'Economic Dialogue'.[2] For a schematic depiction of this process, see the Online Appendix.

Many observers believe that the European Semester represents a fundamental shift in EU socioeconomic governance. This collection analyses the changes introduced by the Semester and considers their consequences for the evolution of EU governance along three critical axes: the economic and the social; the supranational and the intergovernmental; and the technocratic and the democratic. Questions addressed under these rubrics include whether the Semester is leading to the subordination of EU social objectives and actors to economic imperatives of fiscal consolidation and competitiveness; whether EU socio-economic governance is becoming more supranational or more intergovernmental; and whether the Semester is promoting technocratic expert-based governance at the expense of democratic deliberation and accountability.

The contributions in this collection assess these critical dimensions of the Semester based on first-hand empirical research into its practical operation, without adopting a single unified theoretical perspective. Some focus primarily on the socioeconomic axis (Zeitlin and Vanhercke, Bekker, Eihmanis), others more on the supranational–intergovernmental axis (Maricut and Puetter, Savage and Howarth), and still others on the technocratic–democratic axis (Hallerberg *et al.*, Crum), though many deal with more than one axis and all address the Semester's impact on the changing governance relationship between the EU institutions and the member states. The contributors employ a variety of conceptual lenses, including new/deliberative intergovernmentalism (Maricut and Puetter), principal–agent analysis (Savage and Howarth), actor-centred constructivism and the 'usages of Europe' (Zeitlin and Vanhercke, Eihmanis), Europeanization (Hallerberg *et al.*), two-level games and normative democratic theory (Crum). The contributions also adopt different methodological and data-gathering approaches, from original surveys (Hallerberg *et al.*) to semi-structured interviews with key policy actors and content analysis of primary documents (at both EU and national levels). Taken together, they offer an authoritative state-of-the-art analysis of the Semester's implications for the evolution of EU socioeconomic governance since the crisis. In what follows, we review the literature on the Semester, introduce the individual contributions, and highlight the collection's most salient findings.

## 2. Literature review

The existing literature on the European Semester has focused on a number of major issues. One key theme in the early literature was how to characterize the balance within the Semester between 'hard', rules-based elements derived from the SGP and 'softer', more deliberative forms of policy co-ordination associated with the OMC, with authors such as Armstrong (2013) and Bekker (2013) emphasizing the hybrid character of the emerging governance architecture. Another preoccupation has been to assess the Semester's effectiveness, especially by looking at national implementation of the CSRs. A number of authors have criticized the member states' limited response to the CSRs, with Darvas and Leandro (2015) claiming that their annual rate of implementation declined over time (from 40 per cent to 29 per cent) and was lower than the unilateral recommendations of the Organization for Economic Co-operation and Development (OECD) (*cf.* also EP 2017; Hallerberg *et al.* 2011). Other studies, notably by the Commission, find a higher cumulative rate of implementation, with two-thirds of CSRs showing at least 'some progress' by 2016, reflecting the longer time horizon needed for major structural reforms (Deroose and Griesse 2014; European Commission 2017a: 4–7). But more thorough assessments of the Semester's causal influence on national reforms require a different research approach, based on comparative process tracing of the interplay between EU and domestic policy-making, as in Eihmanis's pioneering study of Latvia (2017).

Many scholars have argued that the Semester's governance architecture inherently privileges economic goals and actors over their social counterparts (e.g., Copeland and Daly 2015; Crespy and Menz 2015; de la Porte and Heins 2015). Others have found instead that this more integrated socioeconomic co-ordination process offers new opportunities for defending and 'mainstreaming' EU social objectives (e.g., Bekker [2015]; Gómez Urquijo [2017]; Jessoula [2015]; for a fuller review, see Zeitlin and Vanhercke 2017). The coming of the Semester and other economic and financial governance innovations adopted in response to the euro crisis has likewise triggered a major debate about whether these should be characterized as primarily intergovernmental or supranational. Scholars such as Bickerton *et al.* (2015) point to increased European integration in these areas without transferring powers to supranational institutions, which they term 'new' intergovernmentalism (*cf.* also Puetter 2014). Others point instead to the emergence of a 'new supranationalism' (Dehousse 2016), resulting from the enhanced role of the Commission and the ECB in the EU's post-crisis economic governance (Bauer and Becker [2014]; Savage and Verdun [2016]; for a fuller review of the debate, see Schmidt [2016]).

Finally, many authors have expressed deep concern about the European Semester as part of a broader set of measures introduced by the EU during the sovereign debt crisis which have shifted governance responsibilities away from democratic institutions, such as parliaments, into the hands of unelected and unaccountable technocrats (e.g., Chalmers *et al.* [2016]; Crum and Curtin [2015]; Dawson [2015]; Scharpf [2013]; for a fuller review, see Crum 2017). Ironically, however, careful process-tracing research shows that it was the EP rather than the Commission that pushed hardest for the inclusion of the Semester and RQMV in the Six-Pack legislation (Chang 2013: 264–5; Laffan and Schlosser 2016: 240).

## 3. Our contribution

The next contribution in this collection, by Jonathan Zeitlin and Bart Vanhercke 2017, provides a detailed analysis of the 'socialization' of the Semester since 2011, defined as a growing emphasis on social objectives in its substantive policy messages (including the CSRs) and an enhanced role for social and employment actors in its monitoring, review and decision-making procedures. Drawing on 'actor-centred constructivism' and the 'usages of Europe' approaches, the authors show how EU social and employment actors – especially committees of national officials advising the Employment, Social Policy, Health and Consumer Affairs (EPSCO Council) – have helped to change the 'rules of the game' and influence the positions of their economic policy interlocutors within the Semester. These actors have reflexively revised their own working methods and styles of argument to gain traction in 'evidence-based' deliberation, while successfully pushing back against the Commission's perceived efforts to impose uniform, over-prescriptive recommendations. As a result, the authors argue, not only has the integration of EU social and economic policy co-ordination within the Semester become more balanced, but its governance has also become more interactive and less hierarchical.

The third contribution, by Sonja Bekker 2017, examines the role within the Semester of 'flexicurity' as a leading EU policy concept developed before the crisis aimed at reconciling flexibility and security in labour markets. Many commentators have claimed that austerity measures adopted during the crisis led to the abandonment of flexicurity for a one-sided emphasis on flexibility in EU labour-market policies. Based on a systematic content analysis of key policy documents and CSRs, Bekker shows instead that flexicurity is not only alive and well within the Semester, but has been revitalized by incorporating a wider range of social concerns (such as a lifecycle approach to social security and improving transitions into stable jobs), in line with Zeitlin and Vanhercke's 'socialization' thesis. This redefinition of the concept, in her view, demonstrates the Semester's adaptability over time to changing policy priorities, alongside its capacity to tailor CSRs to the variety of challenges facing member states through different combinations of flexicurity elements.

The fourth contribution, by Adina Maricut and Uwe Puetter 2017, investigates the relationship between the economic and social dimensions of the Semester. Drawing on new/deliberative intergovernmentalist approaches, they argue that the uneven evolution of the Semester's co-ordination infrastructure has produced an asymmetry between economic and social issues. Not only are finance ministers better placed to build consensus through informal policy dialogue than their social and employment policy colleagues, but they also have better access to the European Council and greater control of the Semester's policy priorities. Yet the authors also find that the Commission and the committees advising social and employment ministers have managed to gain a greater expert role in the Semester and to integrate more social issues into the CSRs, even if this did not always lead to stronger political endorsement by the European Council. Their analysis suggests that ongoing asymmetries between economic and social issues within the Semester are rooted less in their different Treaty bases than in contingent and corrigible differences in the organization of the actors in the two domains, notably the more fragmented structure of the EPSCO Council, its less frequent meetings, and its insistence on conducting policy debates in televized public meetings rather than behind closed doors.

The fifth contribution, by James D. Savage and David Howarth 2017 employs a principal–agent approach to analyse the politics of asymmetric information in the EDP and MIP. The authors examine how the Commission and the Council have sought to enforce the requirements of the Semester as an information-driven surveillance system reliant on national budgetary and economic statistics. They show that while the Six-Pack legislation gave the Commission the right to investigate the compilation of member state fiscal statistics and to impose financial sanctions for misconduct, the European Central Bank and the EP have so far blocked efforts to give Eurostat similar 'police patrol' powers to ensure the reliability of MIP statistics. The contribution focuses particularly on the imposition of financial penalties on Spain for the misrepresentation of fiscal statistics by the Autonomous Community of Valencia, the first such case in the history of Economic and Monetary

Union (EMU), whose distinctive circumstances provide insight into the rare conditions under which the Commission may be prepared to use its sanctioning powers over member states.

The sixth contribution, by Edgars Eihmanis 2017, examines the fascinating case of Latvia, which experienced severe economic difficulties during the financial crisis. Between 2008 and 2014, the country was simultaneously subject to three EU economic governance frameworks – the European Semester, a Balance-of-Payments programme and the euro convergence criteria. Eihmanis finds that the Latvian government 'cherry-picked' and instrumentalized EU fiscal and economic targets, which it often exceeded. In contrast to the literature portraying the Commission as a neoliberal actor pushing austerity at the expense of social protection, he shows that in this case it played the role of social policy advocate, repeatedly pressing the Latvian authorities for stronger measures to help the poor – with some eventual success. The case study thus sheds valuable light on the Semester's influence on the relationship between the Commission and member state governments, as well as between economic and social policy objectives.

The seventh contribution, by Mark Hallerberg *et al.* 2017, analyses the role of national parliaments in the Semester. Based on original survey data, the authors trace whether national parliaments discuss and vote on national stability/convergence and reform programmes, as well as how their involvement has changed over time. They find considerable variation among national parliaments as to whether debates on the Semester take place at all, and if so in which committees at which stage of the process. Their research shows that between 2012 and 2015, Budget/Finance committees played an increasingly promising role in *ex ante* scrutiny of national planning documents as they became more aware of the Semester's impingement on their core business. Counter-intuitively, however, it was parliaments in non-euro area member states not subject to potential financial sanctions which were most active in ex post review of the CSRs, suggesting that they were motivated more by the pursuit of electoral advantage through symbolic contestation of EU involvement in domestic reforms than by democratic concerns with the policy recommendations themselves.

Finally, the eighth contribution, by Ben Crum 2017, examines how the new economic governance of the euro area has affected the ability of parliaments (national and European) to scrutinize and control economic policy. It analyses the specific challenges to parliamentary accountability that emerge when executive power is shared between the national and the supranational levels. It argues that such accountability has been compromised in EU post-crisis economic governance because governments' budgetary decisions are constrained by the Semester and national parliaments find themselves on the losing side of a reinforced two-level executive game, while the European Parliament lacks effective powers to control the decisions of the European

Council and the Commission in this field. The contribution concludes by proposing guidelines for safeguarding parliamentary accountability in multilevel settings like that of EU post-crisis economic governance, which the author believes would reinforce the Semester's character as a dialogical rather than hierarchical process.

## 4. Conclusion

This collection has sought to assess the European Semester as a new architecture of EU socioeconomic governance by examining its consequences along three critical axes: the economic and the social; the intergovernmental and the supranational; and the technocratic and the democratic. Taking the contributions together, we find that that changes introduced by the Semester cannot easily be captured by such polar oppositions, thereby challenging established theoretical understandings of EU governance.

With regard to the economic–social axis, our contributions show that these two poles of EU policy co-ordination have become increasingly closely intertwined within the Semester. Social objectives and actors have become more prominent and influential over time in the Semester's substantive policy orientations and governance procedures, including the drafting, review and adoption of the CSRs. But major national reforms in interdependent policy fields like pensions, health care, labour-market regulation and social security have both economic and social dimensions, which need to be taken into account in framing EU recommendations, even if officials from each domain might prefer to take decisions independently. While jurisdictional struggles persist around overlapping issues, especially those linked to the SGP and MIP, the contributions in this collection suggest that the Semester provides a workable, if still imperfect framework for integrating EU social and economic policy co-ordination, without sacrificing the objectives of either process.

On the intergovernmental–supranational axis, the contributions likewise show that there is no simple winner. Member states do not control the European Semester, nor have supranational institutions become all-powerful. Although the European Council formally remains the political master of the Semester, it cannot and does not run the process itself. The Commission plays a pivotal role in steering the Semester, having gained new powers and developed new capacities to set priorities, review national policies and performance, draft CSRs and propose sanctions under the EDP and MIP. But the Commission does not exercise these powers and capacities in isolation from national actors. Sectoral committees of member state officials, whose detailed knowledge of national policy challenges and developments far exceeds that of the Commission, have numerous opportunities to feed in their views at key moments in the Semester process and have demonstrated their ability to amend the Commission's draft CSRs, drawing on evidence from their own complementary monitoring and review procedures. To enhance national ownership of proposed reforms, the Commission now engages in an increasingly intense bilateral and multilateral dialogue with a multiplicity of actors from the member states at each stage in the Semester cycle. Taken together, these developments have blurred the boundaries between 'European' and 'national' actors in EU policy co-ordination, and made it increasingly difficult – and perhaps even irrelevant – to characterize the Semester as either intergovernmental or supranational.

Criticism of the Semester has perhaps been harshest in relation to the technocratic–democratic axis. Such criticism has concentrated on the limited role of national and European parliaments in its decision-making processes. Yet the contributions in this collection show that national parliaments, especially within the euro area, have by no means fully exploited the opportunities available to them to debate the Semester's policy orientations or to scrutinize its recommendations. The EP, as previously noted, fought for the legislative codification of the Semester in its present form, as well as for the introduction of RQMV for financial sanctions. Given limitations of time and expertise, as well as the electoral incentives facing their members, it seems unrealistic to expect most national parliaments to play a more active part in scrutinizing the Semester process. While there is a stronger case for extending the EP's codecision role in setting the Semester's policy priorities and orientations, it could hardly be expected to participate effectively in reviewing and adopting the CSRs. Here, as the contributions in this collection show, it is within the apparently 'technocratic' components of the Semester – the 'core group' of Commission DGs and the sectoral committees of member state officials advising the Council – that much of the real contestation and debate about EU policy recommendations and the implementation of national reforms actually takes place. Hence, as with the other two axes, a sharp polarization between the Semester's democratic and the technocratic dimensions seems both empirically and conceptually misplaced.

The European Semester, like EU post-crisis governance more generally, is a work in progress. The Semester's policy content and decision-making procedures have evolved considerably since its creation in 2010, and further revisions have been mooted. The Five Presidents' Report (Juncker *et al.* 2015) envisaged using reinforced monitoring of national reforms within the Semester to drive convergence towards agreed binding standards, including in the social field, a proposal which reappears in the Commission's recent Reflection Paper on Deepening EMU (European Commission 2017b). It remains unclear for now how such arrangements would work in practice, and still more so how far member states would be prepared to embrace them. But our assessment of its first seven years suggests that the Semester has already reshaped the architecture of EU governance in ways that challenge established theoretical understandings, by integrating the pursuit of social and economic objectives into an interactive cycle of deliberation between national and supranational actors in which peer review by expert officials enhances rather than restricts the scope for democratic debate.

## Notes

1. For an overview of the Semester's place in the evolution of EU socioeconomic governance, see Zeitlin and Vanhercke (2014: 15–27); on the evolution of EU pre-crisis economic governance, see also Verdun (2009).
2. See: https://ec.europa.eu/info/strategy/european-semester/european-semester-timeline_en; http://www.consilium.europa.eu/en/policies/european-semester/how-european-semester-works/; http://www.europarl.europa.eu/legislative-train/theme-deeper-and-fairer-economic-and-monetary-union/file-european-semester-improvement (accessed 26 July 2017).

## Acknowledgments

The authors are pleased to acknowledge the generous support of the Amsterdam Centre for Contemporary European Studies (ACCESS EUROPE) for two workshops on the European Semester at which most of the contributions in this collection were originally presented and discussed.

## Disclosure statement

No potential conflict of interest was reported by the authors.

## Funding

This work was supported by the Amsterdam Centre for Contemporary European Studies (ACCESS EUROPE), University of Amsterdam/VU University Amsterdam; Social Sciences and Humanities Research Council of Canada: [Grant Number 435-2015-0943].

## References

Armstrong, K. (2013) 'The new governance of EU fiscal discipline', *European Law Review* 38(5): 601–17.

Bauer, M.W. and Becker, S. (2014) 'The unexpected winner of the crisis: the European Commission's strengthened role in economic governance', *Journal of European Integration* 36(3): 213–29.

Bekker, S. (2013) *The EU's Stricter Economic Governance: A Step Towards More Binding Coordination of Social Policies*, WZB Discussion Paper SP IV 2013-501, Berlin: Social Science Research Center.

Bekker, S. (2015) *European Socioeconomic Governance in Action: Coordinating Social Policies in the third European Semester*, OSE Research Paper No. 19, Brussels: European Social Observatory.

Bekker, S. (2017) 'Flexicurity in the European Semester: still a relevant policy concept?', doi:10.1080/13501763.2017.1363272

Bickerton, C., Hodson, D. and Puetter, U. (2015) 'The new intergovernmentalism: European integration in the Post-Maastricht era', *JCMS: Journal of Common Market Studies* 53(4): 703–22.

Chalmers, D., Jachtenfuchs, M. and Joerges, C. (eds) (2016) *The End of the Eurocrats' Dream*, Cambridge: Cambridge University Press.

Chang, M. (2013) 'Fiscal policy coordination and the future of the community method', *Journal of European Integration* 35(3): 255–69.

Copeland, P. and Daly, M. (2015) 'Social Europe: from 'add-on' to 'dependence-upon' economic integration', in A. Crespy and G. Menz (eds), *Social Policy and the Euro Crisis: Quo Vadis Social Europe*, Houndmills: Palgrave Macmillan, pp. 140–60.

Crespy, A. and Menz, G. (2015) 'Commission entrepreneurship and the debasing of Social Europe before and after the Eurocrisis', *JCMS: Journal of Common Market Studies* 53(4): 753–68.

Crum, B. (2017) 'Parliamentary accountability in multi-level governance: what role for parliaments in EU post-crisis economic governance', doi:10.1080/13501763.2017.1363270

Crum, B. and Curtin, D. (2015) 'The challenge of making European Union executive power accountable', in S. Piattoni (ed.), *The European Union: Democratic Principles and Institutional Architectures in Times of Crisis*, Oxford: Oxford University Press, pp. 63–87.

Darvas, Z.M. and Leandro, Á. (2015) *The Limitations of Policy Coordination in the Euro Area Under the European Semester*, Policy Contribution 2015/19, Brussels: Bruegel.

Dawson, M. (2015) 'The legal and political accountability structure of 'post-crisis' EU economic Governance', *JCMS: Journal of Common Market Studies* 53(5): 976–93.

de la Porte, C. and Heins, E. (2015) 'A new era of European Integration? Governance of labour market and social policy since the sovereign debt crisis', *Comparative European Politics* 13(1): 8–28.

Dehousse, R. (2016) 'Why has EU macroeconomic governance become more supranational?', *Journal of European Integration* 38(5): 617–631.

Deroose, S. and Griesse, J. (2014) 'Implementing economic reforms–are EU Member States responding to European Semester recommendations?' *ECFIN Economic Brief*, Issue 37, October.

Eihmanis, E. (2017) 'Cherry-picking external constraints: Latvia and EU economic governance, 2008–2014', doi:10.1080/13501763.2017.1363267

European Commission (2017a) *2017 European Semester: Country-Specific Recommendations*, COM(2007) 500 final, Brussels, 22 May.

European Commission (2017b) *Reflection Paper on the Deepening of the Economic and Monetary Union*, Brussels, 31 May.

European Parliament (2017) *Country Specific Recommendations for 2016 and 2017: A Comparison and An Overview of Implementation*, Directorate-General for Internal Policies, Economic Governance Support Unit, PE 602.081, 23 May.

Gómez Urquijo, L. (2017) 'The Europeanisation of policy to address poverty under the new economic governance: the contribution of the European Semester', *Journal of Poverty and Social Justice*, doi:10.1332/175982716X14822521840999

Hallerberg, M., Marzinotto, B. and Wolff, G.B. (2011) *How Effective and Legitimate is the European Semester? Increasing the Role of the European Parliament*, Working Paper No. 2011/09, Brussels: Bruegel.

Hallerberg, M., Marzinotto, M.B. and Wolff, G.B. (2017) 'Explaining the evolving role of national parliaments under the European Semester', doi:10.1080/13501763.2017.1363273

Jessoula, M. (2015) 'Europe 2020 and the fight against poverty—beyond competence clash, towards 'hybrid' governance solutions?', *Social Policy & Administration* 49(4): 490–511.

Juncker, J.-C., Tusk, D., Dijsselbloem, J., Dragi, M. and Schulz, M. (2015) *Completing Europe's Economic and Monetary Union*, Brussels: European Commission.

Laffan, B. and Schlosser, P. (2016) 'Public finances in Europe: fortifying EU economic governance in the shadow of the crisis', *Journal of European Integration* 38(3): 237–49.

Maricut, A. and Puetter, U. (2017) 'Deciding on the European Semester: The European Council, the council and the enduring asymmetry between economic and social policy issues', doi:10.1080/13501763.2017.1363271

Puetter, U. (2014) *The European Council and the Council: New Intergovernmentalism and Institutional Change*, Oxford: Oxford University Press.

Savage, J.D. and Howarth, D. (2017) 'Enforcing the European Semester: the politics of asymmetric information in the Excessive Deficit and Macroeconomic Imbalances Procedures', doi:10.1080/13501763.2017.1363268

Savage, J.D. and Verdun, A. (2016) 'Strengthening the European Commission's budgetary and economic surveillance capacity since Greece and the euro area crisis: a study of five directorates-general', *Journal of European Public Policy* 23(1): 101–18.

Scharpf, F.W. (2013) 'Monetary Union, fiscal crisis and the disabling of democratic accountability', in A. Schäfer and W. Streeck (eds), *Politics in the Age of Austerity*, Cambridge: Polity, pp. 108–42.

Schmidt, V. (2016) 'The "new" EU governance: "new" intergovernmentalism versus "new" supranationalism plus "new" parliamentarism', in *Cahiers du CEVIPOL* 5/2016, Université Libre de Bruxelles, pp. 5–31.

Verdun, A. (2009) 'Regulation and cooperation in European monetary and economic policy', in I. Tömmel and A. Verdun (eds) *Innovative Governance in the European Union: The Politics of Multilevel Policy-Making*, Boulder: Lynne Rienner, pp. 75–86.

Zeitlin, J. and Vanhercke, B. (2014) *Socializing the European Semester: Economic Governance and Social Policy Coordination in Europe 2020*, SIEPS Report 2014:7, Stockholm: Swedish Institute for European Policy Studies.

Zeitlin, J. and Vanhercke, B. (2017) 'Socialising the European Semester: EU economic and social policy coordination in crisis and beyond', doi:10.1080/13501763.2017.1363269

OPEN ACCESS

# Socializing the European Semester: EU social and economic policy co-ordination in crisis and beyond

Jonathan Zeitlin and Bart Vanhercke

**ABSTRACT**
This contribution analyses how EU social objectives and policy co-ordination have been integrated into the Union's post-crisis governance architecture. It argues that between 2011 and 2016, there was a partial but progressive 'socialization' of the 'European Semester' of policy co-ordination, in terms of increasing emphasis on social objectives in its priorities and key messages, including the Country-Specific Recommendations; intensified social monitoring and review of national reforms; and an enhanced decision-making role for EU social and employment actors. In explaining these developments, the contribution highlights the contribution of strategic agency, reflexive learning and creative adaptation by social and employment actors to the new institutional conditions of the Semester, building on recent theoretical work on 'actor-centred constructivism' and the 'usages of Europe'.

## Introduction

Since the onset of the euro crisis, the European Union (EU) has introduced a series of far-reaching changes in its socio-economic governance architecture (see the introduction to this collection). At its core is the 'European Semester' of policy co-ordination, through which the Commission, the Council and the European Council set priorities for the Union; review national performance and reform programs; and issue Country-Specific Recommendations (CSRs) to member states, backed up in some cases by possible financial sanctions. The European Semester (henceforth 'Semester') brings together within a single annual policy co-ordination cycle a wide range of EU governance instruments with different legal bases and sanctioning authority. This process has

Supplemental data for this article can be accessed at https://doi.org/10.1080/13501763.2017.1363269.

given the EU institutions a more prominent role than ever before in scrutinizing and guiding national economic, fiscal and social policies, especially within the euro area.

The advent of the Semester has raised a set of contested questions about the relationship between social and economic policy co-ordination within the EU's new post-crisis governance architecture. Has the integration of EU social policy co-ordination, as developed through the Open Method of Coordination on Social Protection and Social Inclusion ('Social OMC'), into the Europe 2020 Strategy and the Semester resulted in its subordination to fiscal discipline and budgetary austerity objectives imposed by the main economic policy actors?[1] Or has such integration instead offered new opportunities for social and employment policy actors[2] to defend and mainstream EU social objectives, such as the adequacy and accessibility of pensions and health care or the fight against poverty and social exclusion, throughout the Semester process?

Critiques of the Semester's social dimension have revolved around three interrelated empirical claims. The first concerns the subordination of social objectives to higher-order economic goals within the EU's post-crisis governance architecture. Thus Crespy and Menz (2015a: 762) contend that 'the slippage of Europe 2020 into the European Semester ... has meant the further absorption of social policy into macroeconomic policy'. Hence, in their view, EU 'social policy is becoming increasingly ... subsumed to economic objectives focused on competitiveness, narrowly defined as low labour costs ... and stringent fiscal discipline' (Crespy and Menz 2015b: 199–200). For Degryse *et al.* (2014: 70), similarly, 'the CSRs reflect a particular concept of the European economic model ... focused on growth and competitiveness, while neglecting ... the principal role of social policies ... '. More strongly still, Copeland and Daly (2015: 150) assert that 'the European Semester has served as a focal point to organize a form of economic governance in which national budgetary discipline and the correction of macroeconomic imbalances ... have been made the principles on which all other policy objectives are dependent'.

The second claim advanced by the Semester's critics concerns the dominance of EU economic policy actors over their social and employment policy counterparts within its decision-making procedures. Thus as de la Porte and Heins (2014: 169–70) contend, 'Europe 2020 is dominated by DG ECFIN and the ECOFIN Council with a very marginal role for the European social policy actors' (cf. also Degryse *et al.* 2014). Such power imbalances within the Semester, they argue, reflect the fact that the economic actors 'operate in areas where the EU has strong jurisdiction', unlike their social counterparts, who are responsible for fields 'where the EU has only weak legislative competence' (de la Porte and Heins 2015: 12). For Copeland and Daly (2015: 150, 153), likewise, the structure of the Semester privileges economic policy actors and 'formalizes the historically disadvantaged position within the EU's political hierarchy of social actors'.

The third claim underpinning the social critique of the Semester concerns its coercive and prescriptive character. Many commentators have seen the process as a centralized mechanism for imposing structural reforms on member states, including in areas of primary national competence such as social and employment policy, through CSRs underpinned by the threat of sanctions under the Stability and Growth Pact (SGP) and Macroeconomic Imbalance Procedure (MIP). Dawson (2015: 984), for example, asserts that the new 'post-crisis economic governance in many ways entails a return to "command-and-control" regulation', whereby 'national diversity ... is often placed within strict limits with high levels of supra-national policy prescription'. While Dawson (2015: 984–6) and Degryse *et al.* (2014: 72, 76) highlight the uniform 'one-size-fits-all' message embodied in the CSRs, other critics such as Scharpf (2013: 137–8) decry instead their discretionary application, involving 'a radical extension of hierarchical European controls over national policy choices'. Either way, however, de la Porte and Heins (2014: 170) contend that 'the European Semester and the instruments designed to re-enforce it are highly intrusive along the dimensions of policy interference, surveillance, as well as coercion'. Within the Semester, they conclude, fiscal and budgetary governance instruments 'have become more precise in terms of objectives, and stricter in terms of surveillance and enforcement', while social and labour market policy instruments remain weaker on these dimensions and thus in their 'potential impact' (de la Porte and Heins 2015: 10).

By contrast, a second body of recent research has drawn attention to the gradual evolution of the Semester in a more socially balanced direction in relation to each of the preceding empirical claims. Thus Bekker has analysed the changing content of the CSRs, finding not only an increasing emphasis on social and employment issues, but also that even recommendations issued under the SGP and the MIP sometimes promote EU social objectives such as accessibility of health care and the fight against poverty and social exclusion (Bekker 2015; Bekker and Klosse 2013). Coding the policy measures contained in the CSRs between those promoting 'social investment' as opposed to austerity or 'social retrenchment', Crespy and Vanheuverzwijn (2016: 77–8, 85–6) estimate that the proportion of the former has increased from 50 per cent to 64 per cent between 2011 and 2016.[3] Focusing on poverty and social inclusion, Jessoula (2015: 496) observes that the growing number of CSRs on this issue was 'the result of the process whereby DG EMPL learnt how to defend and support the Europe 2020 social dimension in inter-DGs bargaining at the various stages of the Semester'. Finally, Bekker has examined the CSRs and National Reform Programs (NRPs) of France, Germany, Poland and Spain between 2009 and 2014, concluding that while the degree of flexibility varies across countries and over time, 'the European Semester, including the SGP, allows for developing alternative socio-economic policies' (Bekker 2016: 62).

Building on this latter body of work, along with two earlier research reports of our own (Zeitlin and Vanhercke 2014; Vanhercke et al., 2015), this contribution analyses the evolution and dynamics of the Semester from its inception in 2010 through the 2016 cycle, bringing new evidence to bear on the main disputed questions about the relationship between social and economic policy co-ordination in the EU's post-crisis governance architecture. The contribution makes two major contributions to this debate. The first is empirical: drawing on 76 interviews with key policy players as well as a systematic analysis of EU documents, we demonstrate that over this period there was a partial but progressive 'socialization' of the Semester, both in terms of its substantive content and its governance procedures. This socialization, as we define it, comprises: 1) a growing emphasis on social objectives in the Semester's policy orientations and messages, embodied in the AGS and especially the CSRs; (2) intensified monitoring, surveillance, and review of national reforms by EU social and employment policy actors and (3) an enhanced role for these actors relative to their economic policy counterparts in drafting, reviewing and amending the CSRs. Finally, regarding the Semester's prescriptive and coercive character, the contribution shows that a concerted pushback by the Employment, Social Policy, Health and Consumer Affairs (EPSCO) Council and its advisory committees against the Commission's perceived efforts to impose uniform, over-detailed recommendations on social and employment issues resulted in significant revisions to the Semester's decision-making arrangements, including the CSRs themselves, which have made them less hierarchical and more interactive. The second major contribution is explanatory and theoretical. In accounting for the empirical developments traced in the contribution, we highlight the contribution of strategic agency, reflexive learning and creative adaptation to the new institutional conditions of the European Semester by the key actors, especially on the social and employment side.

The remainder of the contribution is organized as follows. Section 2 presents the theoretical approach, building on 'actor-centred constructivism' and the 'usages of Europe', along with the data and methods supporting the empirical analysis. Section 3 examines the relationship between social and economic policy co-ordination from the Lisbon Strategy to Europe 2020 and the inception of the Semester. Section 4 analyses the socialization of the Semester under the Barroso Commission (2012–2014), in terms both of policy orientations and governance procedures. Section 5 shows how this socialization was further institutionalized under the Juncker Commission. The final section summarizes the empirical evidence and revisits our contribution to the ongoing academic debate.

## Theoretical approach, data and methods

In explaining the partial but progressive socialization of the European Semester between 2010 and 2016, this contribution focuses on the strategic agency and creative adaptation to changing institutional conditions of the key actors concerned. Here we draw on and extend recent theoretical work on 'sociological approaches' to European integration and policy-making, notably 'actor-centred constructivism' (Saurugger 2009, 2016) and the 'usages of Europe' (Jacquot and Woll 2003; Woll and Jacquot 2010). These approaches provide valuable conceptual resources for understanding how apparently weaker players, such as the EU social and employment policy actors, can advance their substantive goals and decision-making influence in complex multi-level governance processes like the European Semester, despite the institutional asymmetries and structural power imbalances emphasized by the critical literature discussed in the previous section.

As presented by Saurugger, 'actor-centred constructivist' approaches to the EU diverge from standard rationalist and historical institutionalist analyses that overstate the weight of structural constraints and path dependence on actors' choices, while underestimating the 'possibilities for actors to modify the rules and institutions in which they act'. Such actor-centred approaches, in her formulation, likewise differ from classic constructivist and sociological institutionalist accounts that emphasize how dominant cognitive frames and taken-for-granted norms shape actors' behaviour, thereby downplaying their 'room for manoeuvre in power struggles and social conflicts'. In this view, too, actors' capacities for action are not 'entirely predefined' either by their resource endowments or by the structure of the field in which they operate; instead actors 'are able to adapt and to change their environment' (Saurugger 2016: 73–5).

Work on the 'usages of Europe' gives concrete form to actor-centred constructivism as defined above by analysing how different types of actors identify and strategically exploit opportunities within EU multi-level governance processes to advance their own preferences and objectives. The concept of usages 'highlights how actors engage with, interpret, appropriate or ignore the dynamics of European integration'. This means that actors can fail to seize opportunities for action identified by external observers, either because they do not perceive them as such or because they are more concerned with the possible risks than the potential benefits involved. Moreover, while actors intentionally make use of the opportunities and resources they find in EU institutions and policies to pursue their own goals, the outcome may not be identical to the original objective, since 'the effects of an action are often not entirely predictable or controllable'. Finally, 'as strategic as usages may be initially', in the longer term, as Woll and Jacquot (2010: 115–6) observe, they 'entail cognitive and/or normative adaptation by actors and their political environment, which in turn affects their subsequent behaviour and positioning'. Just as there is 'no impact of Europe without usage' by the actors (Jacquot and Woll 2003: 5–6), so too as another scholar working within this approach remarks, there are 'no usages of Europe without impact' (Sanchez Salgado 2014: 203).

Although the usages of Europe, like actor-centred constructivism, has been conceived as a general conceptual approach to European integration and policy-making, it has mainly been applied to the strategic identification and 'creative appropriation' of opportunities arising from EU governance processes (including both the OMC and the Lisbon Strategy) by national-level actors to advance their own domestic objectives and agendas (Barcevičius *et al.* 2014; Graziano et. 2011; Jacquot and Woll 2003; Woll and Jacquot 2010). But as their proponents explicitly envisage, these approaches can also be used to illuminate the evolution and dynamics of EU governance processes themselves. Thus, for example, the 'usages of Europe' approach draws attention to how actors situated at the intersection between national and supranational policy-making (such as EU committees of member-state officials) may strategically exploit the ambiguities of European concepts, rules and procedures in order to reframe policy issues, build political coalitions, enhance their institutional influence, and justify decisions taken at the EU as well as the domestic level (Woll and Jacquot 2010: 116–7).

In this contribution, we extend the insights of these agency-focused and possibility-orientated approaches by tracing how reflexive learning from past experience by key actors, especially on the social and employment side, together with creative adaptation of their own organization and practices to the new institutional conditions of the EU's post-crisis governance architecture, has contributed to the partial but progressive socialization of the Semester. Here we focus on how EU social and employment policy actors have deliberately revised their working methods and styles of argument to gain traction in 'evidence-based' deliberation with their economic policy counterparts. At the same time, we analyse how the arguments and demands advanced by the social players through the Semester process have helped to change the broader 'rules of the game' and influence the positions of their economic policy interlocutors.

In terms of data sources, this contribution draws on six rounds of elite interviews, conducted between 2010 and 2016, with current and former members of the European Commission (multiple DGs); Council advisory committees (EMCO, SPC, EPC, EFC); EU social partners and NGO networks; the European Council and Council Secretariat; and the European Parliament. A total of 76 interviews were conducted with 61 separate individuals. Some interviews involved multiple participants, while 17 people were interviewed two to four times in light of their key role in the development of the Semester. Nearly all interviewees agreed to be quoted, provided that the source could not be identified, e.g., by naming only their institutional affiliation rather than their specific position. Interviews cited in the text are referred to by a unique code, the key to which is presented in Online Appendix Section 1, along with a complete list of interviews by date.

This contribution is also based on near-complete access to the papers of the Employment Committee (EMCO) and the Social Protection Committee (SPC) during this period. These papers, which include documents from the EU economic policy actors, allow a fine-grained process tracing of decision-making within each Semester cycle, and were used to triangulate information from the interviews. For reasons of space, we have supported empirical claims in the main text with more extensive quotations from interviews and EU documents in Online Appendix Section 4.[4]

Given the nature of our sources, the analysis in this contribution focuses on the evolution and dynamics of the European Semester at EU level, rather than its causal influence in the member states, which requires a different research approach, based on comparative process tracing of national policy-making.

## The European Semester and the Europe 2020 strategy: advancing or subverting Social Europe?

The relationship between social and economic policy co-ordination has been a hot-button issue at EU level since the late 1990s. A key impetus for the creation of the OMC processes on pensions and health/long-term care in the early 2000s came from EU social policy actors' efforts to ensure that the social objectives of these fields were not eclipsed by the fiscal and budgetary focus of EU economic policy co-ordination. Hence the objectives of the pensions and healthcare OMCs included social adequacy, quality and accessibility as well as financial sustainability (Barcevičius *et al.* 2014: ch. 2).

The Europe 2020 Strategy, adopted in 2010, was designed to have a stronger social dimension, compared to the preceding Lisbon Strategy, which had focused primarily on growth and jobs after its 2005 relaunch. Europe 2020 featured 'inclusive growth', by 'fostering a high employment economy delivering economic, social and territorial cohesion', as one of three overarching priorities, along with an EU-wide headline target, aimed at lifting 'at least 20 million people out of the risk of poverty and exclusion'. It also incorporated for the first time a separate guideline on 'Promoting social inclusion and combating poverty', which highlighted the contribution to social cohesion of pensions, healthcare and public services. At the same time, however, there was a founding ambiguity within the Strategy about the relationship between fiscal and macroeconomic surveillance by the ECOFIN Council and 'thematic co-ordination' by the other Council formations of progress towards the Europe 2020 goals, targets and guidelines (Barcevičius *et al.* 2014: 31–4).

Initial experiences under the Semester seemed to confirm critics' worst fears that the new integrated EU policy co-ordination framework would result in the subordination of social objectives to fiscal consolidation, budgetary austerity and welfare retrenchment imposed by economic policy actors (Pochet 2010). The first Annual Growth Survey (AGS) and CSRs[5] focused primarily on fiscal consolidation, while pushing for financial reform of pension and healthcare systems, tax and benefit shifts to 'make work pay', revision of employment protection legislation and measures to contain wage growth (Bieling 2012: 264). Only three countries received CSRs explicitly addressing poverty and social inclusion, despite weak national targets, which the Commission acknowledged would not together meet the EU-wide poverty target by 2020 (European Commission 2011: 5). But many member states also received recommendations urging them to enhance the effectiveness of active labour market policies for vulnerable groups (10); expand childcare provision (5); reduce school drop-out rates, improve access to education and training and encourage lifelong learning (9). Ten of the fifteen countries receiving CSRs on reducing early labour-market exit and linking the statutory retirement age to life expectancy were likewise urged to ensure the adequacy of pension benefits, especially through active ageing measures aimed at maintaining the employability of older workers (own analysis based on European Parliament 2013;[6] cf. Clauwaert 2014: 11; Gómez Urquijo 2017: 7.) Overall, Crespy and Vanheuverzwijn (2016: 77–8) estimate that the social and employment policy measures recommended in the 2011 CSRs were evenly divided between those promoting social retrenchment and social investment.

Procedurally, the first Semester cycle followed a prescriptive 'one-size-fits-all' approach, with limited adaptation of the CSRs to the specific situation of individual Member States (Bekker 2013: 15–16). The EU institutions explicitly sought to use multilateral surveillance by Member States of each other's policies and performance to exert peer pressure for implementation of structural reforms (EMCO 2012; President of the European Council 2011). Social actors at both EU and national level conversely found themselves largely excluded from preparation and review of the National Reform Programmes (NRPs) and CSRs (SPC 2011b).

At the same time, the Commission withdrew its support for the Social OMC as an autonomous process. Member states were no longer requested to produce National Social Reports (NSRs), while the Commission also withdrew from the production of the annual Joint Report on Social Protection and Social Inclusion. A key motivation in both cases was the insistence by the Commission, particularly its Secretariat-General (SECGEN), that there should be no parallel policy co-ordination processes outside Europe 2020, which one high-ranking Commission official called 'the only game in town' for Social Europe, and that social reporting should be channelled exclusively through the Semester (Barcevičius *et al.* 2014: 34–5; SPC 2011a; COM-COORD6; COM-EMPL7).

## Socializing the Semester 2012–2014

### *Policy orientations*

As the sovereign debt crisis within the eurozone morphed into a broader economic downturn, leading to a rapid erosion of public support for the EU, a significant rebalancing between social, economic and employment objectives became visible in the policy orientation of successive European Semesters.

The 2011 AGS had set three overarching priorities for the EU: 'rigorous fiscal consolidation for enhancing macroeconomic stability', 'labour market reforms for higher employment' and 'growth enhancing measures'. The 2012 AGS replaced these with a more socially balanced set of priorities, including 'tackling unemployment and the social consequences of the crisis', which were reaffirmed in 2013 and 2014.

As EU institutions came under increasing pressure to tackle the deepening economic and employment crisis, the Commission and particularly DG EMPL responded by launching a succession of socially orientated 'pacts' and 'packages'. Foremost among these were the Employment Package (April 2012), the 'Compact for Growth and Jobs' (June 2012), the Youth Employment Package (December 2012) and the Social Investment Package (February 2013). Alongside specific policy measures (notably the Youth Guarantee) and EU recommendations (on child poverty and active inclusion), a key feature of these pacts and packages was that implementation of the proposed measures should be reported on, monitored and reviewed within the Semester.

As the Semester's policy priorities, expressed through the AGS and other Commission initiatives, shifted towards a more socially balanced stance, so too did the CSRs, whose social orientation expanded steadily between 2012 and 2014. For reasons of space, we do not analyse the 2012 and 2013 CSRs here, but jump directly to those for 2014, the final year of the Barroso Commission.[7]

In 2014, twelve member states received recommendations on poverty and social inclusion, of whom nine were urged to ensure the adequacy and coverage of their social assistance and unemployment benefits. Nineteen received recommendations on reform of their healthcare and/or pension systems, whose purpose according to the Commission was to ensure that they 'continue to be socially adequate' and 'to provide universal access to high-quality care', as well as to be cost-effective and financially sustainable (European Commission 2014a: 8–10). Five countries were specifically urged to safeguard the accessibility and quality of health and long-term care, while eleven were exhorted to promote the employability of older workers, e.g., by expanding lifelong learning. As in previous years, however, not all CSRs dealing with social and employment issues could be considered 'socially orientated', and a number of countries continued to receive recommendations to reform their wage determination systems to improve competitiveness (6), reduce employment protection for insiders (4) or strengthen job search requirements for unemployment benefits (1).

Such recommendations were largely outnumbered by CSRs urging member states to improve their education, training, and activation systems (all except the Netherlands); reduce early school leaving (8); improve skills and training (21); implement the youth guarantee (8); enhance educational outcomes and access to the labour market for disadvantaged groups (12); increase the availability, accessibility and quality of childcare (9) and public social services (6) (own analysis based on European Parliament 2014; cf. European Commission 2014a: 17; SPC 2014; Clauwaert 2014: 14; Gómez Urquijo 2017: 7–8).

Other systematic analyses of the Semester's evolution largely confirm this trend towards a progressive expansion in the number and scope of socially orientated CSRs from 2011 to 2014. Thus, a report by the European Trade Union Institute found that the number of specific recommendations within the CSRs addressing social and employment policy issues rose steadily from 95 in 2011 to 140 in 2014, accounting in each year for 40–47 per cent of the total (Clauwaert 2015: 11). Bekker's (2015) more comprehensive content analysis of the 2013 CSRs, which includes education and health care, concluded that 67 of the 141 recommendations contained at least one item addressing employment or social policies, while 11 more requested recipients to adopt a 'growth friendly approach' to fiscal consolidation. Using an expansive definition of anti-poverty policies (including 'improving social transfers', 'accessibility to social services', 'improving the employability of at-risk-of-poverty' groups' and 'specific measures to alleviate poverty of vulnerable groups'), Gómez Urquijo (2017: 5–8) found that the number of countries receiving recommendations under one or more of these headings increased from four in 2011 to six in 2012, twenty in 2013 and eighteen in 2014. Finally, Crespy and Vanheuverzwijn (2016: 77–8) estimate that the proportion of social and employment policy measures in the CSRs promoting social investment rather than retrenchment expanded year by year from 50 per cent in 2011 to 60 per cent in 2014.

### *Governance procedures*

The substantive reorientation of the European Semester towards a more socially balanced policy stance from 2011 to 2014 was accompanied by a set of procedural developments, which have reinforced the role of social and employment policy actors in its governance.

The progressive opening up of the CSRs to social issues reflects the fact that the process of drafting them became increasingly collaborative within the Commission itself. The groundwork for the CSRs is prepared by Country Teams led by SECGEN, with bottom-up input from desk officers and support from horizontal policy units across a wide range of DGs, including those responsible for health, education, enterprise and justice, as well as the other 'core' DGs: ECFIN, EMPL and (until 2015) Taxation and Customs Union (TAXUD). The CSRs themselves are drafted by the Country Team leaders, drawing on 'intelligence, ideas, and some wording' supplied by the various DGs, which are then discussed by the Directors of the core DGs, before being approved by the College of Commissioners, which often makes final changes. Our interviewees argued that this process has become increasingly deliberative and 'evidence-based'. DG EMPL officials involved in the process underlined how this emphasis on evidence and argument could overturn any implicit hierarchy among the participating units. A clear case in point was the 2014 CSRs on implementation of the youth guarantee scheme, which were initially opposed by both DGs ECFIN and SECGEN, but where DG EMPL eventually succeeded in getting them through based on evidence from the Country Teams and Staff Working Documents (COM-COORD4; COM-EMPL2, 6, 8, 10; EPC4) **[1]**.

The other major developments that reinforced the role of social and employment policy actors during the Barroso era were driven by the EPSCO Council and especially its advisory committees. The first of these changes was the 2011 SPC initiative, subsequently endorsed by EPSCO, to 'reinvigorate' the Social OMC (SPC 2011a). Member states were invited to prepare regular National Social Reports, to be submitted alongside the NRPs, while the SPC also took over responsibility for the production of an annual Social Europe Report, replacing the previous Joint Report with the Commission.

In addition to reinvigorating the Social OMC, the SPC established itself as a significant player in monitoring, reviewing and assessing national reforms within the European Semester, alongside EMCO, EPC and EFC. At the EPSCO Council's request, EMCO and the SPC developed a Europe 2020 Joint Assessment Framework (JAF) for monitoring the Employment Guidelines (European Commission-EMCO-SPC 2010), which since 2013 has been extended to healthcare (SPC 2013; Baeten and Vanhercke 2016: 14). The results of the JAF feed into the Employment and Social Protection Performance Monitors (EPM, SPPM) developed by the two committees. These Monitors include visual representations of member states' comparative performance against a battery of indicators, along with detailed country profiles summarizing key challenges or negative 'trends to watch', as well as good outcomes (EMCO 2016a; SPC 2012b). Both EMCO and the SPC are committed to using their Monitors as analytical tools to underpin multilateral surveillance and support member states in setting reform priorities, identifying good practices and stimulating mutual learning, while also feeding into the broader EU policy debate. They likewise serve as an important point of reference for discussions within the committees about amendments to the Commission's proposed CSRs (COM-EMPL3, 6; EMCO1, 3; SPC2, 3) **[2]**.

This extended social and employment policy monitoring was accompanied by intensified multilateral surveillance and peer review within both committees. By all accounts, multilateral surveillance in EMCO has become progressively more critical, more focused, and more evidence-based (EMCO Chair 2012; EMCO1-5, 7; COM-COORD4) **[3]**. Whereas until 2012 SPC peer reviews occurred once a year, focused rather superficially on the NSRs, now multilateral surveillance activities are conducted throughout the year, with in-depth thematic and country reviews focused on member states' responses to past CSRs and negative 'trends to watch' in their social performance. SPC members were asked in 2012 if they were ready to make country surveillance 'less descriptive, more critical' and more analytical (SPC 2012a), which subsequent interviewees confirmed has in fact occurred (COM-EMPL6; SPC3, 4) **[3]**. On overlapping issues like employment and healthcare, SPC reviews of CSR implementation are conducted jointly with EMCO and (since 2013) with the Working Party on Public Health at Senior Level (WPPHSL) (Baeten and Vanhercke 2016: 13). As in EMCO, the written conclusions of these multilateral reviews are submitted to the Council and contribute to discussions on proposed CSRs.

Both EMCO and the SPC have thus been seeking to combine 'tougher' multilateral surveillance in employment and social policies with increased opportunities for deliberation and mutual learning. Commission officials as well as committee members see this mutual surveillance process as a 'game changer', making exchanges within the committees less 'cozy' and more incisive than in the past, while transforming 'the bilateral discussion on the CSRs between Member States and the Commission into a multilateral decision making process' (COM-COORD4; EMCO3, 5; SPC3) **[4]**.

Such intensified monitoring, multilateral surveillance and peer review in turn has formed the basis for enhanced input by EMCO and the SPC into the adoption of the CSRs. In the 2011 Semester, the SPC and the EPSCO Council were largely excluded from the review and adoption of the CSRs. From 2012, however, the SPC began to acquire a more influential place in the process, drawing on the expertise gained through its monitoring, surveillance and review activities, as well as through explicit political challenges by the EPSCO Council to the jurisdiction of economic policy actors over social and employment issues. The 2012 Semester catalysed a vigorous pushback by member states against the Commission's increasingly prescriptive approach to the CSRs, along with its reluctance to deliberate over proposed amendments with national representatives (SPC 2012a; Cypriot Presidency 2012; EMCO Chair 2012; EMCO4, 5, 7; SPC5; Zeitlin and Vanhercke 2014: 43–4) **[5]**.

The mounting pressure for reorientation of the Semester and revision of its governance procedures gained momentum and political salience through the EU-wide debate on the social dimension of Economic and Monetary Union initiated by the President of the European Council in 2013. EPSCO Ministers responded by calling for a strengthening of the governance role of the Social OMC, building on the employment guidelines, together with the monitoring instruments, peer reviews and multilateral surveillance procedures developed within EMCO and the SPC. They also demanded the development of mechanisms to facilitate 'more effective interaction' between the EPSCO and ECOFIN Councils, 'especially as regards the adoption and review of the implementation of country specific recommendations' (EPSCO 2013).

These conflicts resulted in a substantially revised procedural framework for the Semester, based on a clearer allocation of responsibilities and co-ordination in reviewing and amending the CSRs in areas of overlapping competences between the committees and Council formations involved (Irish Presidency 2012; Zeitlin and Vanhercke 2014: 46–9). Underlying this framework were new decision-making arrangements within as well as between the participating committees. In each case, amendments to the CSRs were supported by 'reinforced' qualified majority voting (rQMV) to test the support for changes to the Commission's proposals.[8] As explained above, multilateral surveillance within the committees has likewise become crucial to the review and amendment of the CSRs. Since under the 'comply or explain' rules of the European Semester, the Council is expected to provide a written explanation of its reasons for modifying the Commission's recommendations, both committees also refer explicitly to these multilateral reviews in the formal reports justifying their amendments (EMCO2-6; COM-EMPL7; COM-COORD4) **[6]**.

The revised procedural arrangements for reviewing and adopting the CSRs had a significant impact on the success rate of amendments. In 2012, an EMCO source estimated that proposed social and employment policy amendments had no more than a ten per cent chance of success (EMCO7). In 2013, interviewees estimated that one-third of all such proposed amendments to the CSRs were adopted without objection by the Commission, while the success rate for contested amendments had reached 50 per cent (EMCO4-5; SPC5). In 2013, there were fourteen contested amendments to the CSRs, of which ten concerned social and employment issues, compared to eleven in 2012 of which eight concerned social and employment issues. In 2014, contested revisions to the CSRs on social and employment issues continued at a similar rate, accounting for ten of eleven amendments successfully adopted over the Commission's opposition (own calculations from Council of the EU 2012, 2013, 2014).

Most of these amendments concerned better contextualization of individual CSRs in relation to national challenges and reform measures. But even when amendments concerned only a single country, they could nonetheless involve policy issues of EU-wide significance, as in the case of a 2012 recommendation to Sweden on improving the employment participation of youth and vulnerable groups, which was revised to focus on enhancing the effectiveness of labour market policies rather than wage flexibility, while underlining the responsibility of the social partners for wage determination (Council of the EU 2012). It was also sometimes possible to obtain 'horizontal' amendments to multiple CSRs addressing broader issues, as in the case of pension reform, where the comply-or-explain text emphasized the need to allow Member States to choose among alternative paths to reaching the common objective of raising the effective retirement age (Council of the EU 2013). This message was endorsed by successive Council Presidencies, which concluded that 'Member States need some leeway to choose the implementation path that best suits their national conditions, in particular in areas which remain in [their] competence', urging the Commission accordingly to 'ensure that its CSR proposals are sufficiently precise as regards policy outcomes but not overly prescriptive as regards policy measures so as to leave sufficient space for ... national ownership ....' (Cypriot Presidency 2012; Lithuanian Presidency 2013).

## The Juncker Commission: streamlining and further socializing the Semester

In a speech to the European Parliament in October 2014, where Commission President-Elect Juncker enunciated his ambition for the EU to achieve a 'Social Triple A' rating, he stated that the Semester is not just an economic and financial process, but should necessarily take into account the social dimension, including the CSRs (Juncker 2015). The new Commission promptly introduced a series of significant innovations to the organization of the Semester. Building on plans initiated by its predecessor and responding to member state demands, the Juncker Commission sought to 'streamline' the Semester process by integrating the MIP In-Depth Reviews with the Staff Working Documents supporting the CSRs into a single Country Report, setting out its analysis of the main national reform challenges and measures taken to address them. These Country Reports were the subject of intensive bilateral discussions with member states both before and after publication. The Commission also released both the Country Reports and CSRs earlier in the Semester cycle, thereby leaving more time for review and debate within the Council advisory committees. But the most fundamental change was the Commission's decision to reduce drastically the number and scope of the CSRs, focusing on 'key priority issues of macro-economic and social relevance' identified as actionable and monitorable within a twelve--eighteen month timescale. In most cases, these streamlined CSRs focused more on challenges and outcomes than on specific policy measures, 'putt[ing] the focus on what to achieve instead of prescribing how to achieve it, in order to guide Member States while leaving the necessary room for manoeuvre'. Countries further advanced in the Excessive Deficit and Imbalance Procedures tended, however, to receive more numerous and sharply targeted recommendations (European Commission 2014b; 2015a; 2015b: 3; 2016b: 4–5; COM-COORD1, 3; COM-EMPL3) **[7]**.

The 'streamlining' of the Semester by the Juncker Commission was accompanied by a further socialization of both its substantive policy content and its governance procedures, which became increasingly visible in the 2016 cycle.

### *Policy orientations*

While 'tackling unemployment and the social consequences of the crisis' no longer featured explicitly among the overarching priorities proposed by the Commission, the 2015 AGS emphasized the need for measures aimed at 'improving the dynamics in labour markets and tackling the high level of unemployment'; 'pension reforms ... to ensure both sustainability and adequacy'; and 'modernising social protection systems' to 'be efficient and adequate at all stages of a person's life', through better targeting, 'affordable quality childcare and education, prevention of early school leaving, training and job assistance, housing support and accessible health care' (European Commission 2014b: 10–13).

Inclusive social and employment policy objectives figured even more prominently in the 2016 AGS. Central to its policy orientations was a renewed focus on social investment, including not only education and training systems, but also healthcare, childcare and housing; and flexicurity, including measures to foster transitions to permanent contracts, as well as 'well-designed income support systems' and 'policies to ... equip job seekers with the right skills and better match them with vacancies' (European Commission 2015c: 4–5, 7–8, 11–12). Compared to the EU's earlier common principles on flexicurity, which were widely criticized for neglecting the security dimension, Bekker (2017) argues that the revised version of this concept has become more socially orientated, acknowledging the need to reduce flexibility in some areas. Another significant development concerned the future of the Europe 2020 Strategy, where the Commission affirmed its commitment 'to make the best use of the existing strategy and its tools' – including the headline targets – 'by improving its implementation and monitoring in the context of the European Semester'. Hence member states were requested in preparing their NRPs 'to make sure that the Europe 2020 Strategy continues to play a prominent role' (European Commission 2015b: 5–6).

In 2015, the number of CSRs on social and employment issues fell substantially compared to 2014. Using the Commission's classification scheme, the drop was particularly evident in the fields of poverty and social exclusion (from 12 to 6 member states), education and skills (from 25 to 13) and health and long-term care (from 16 to 11 and 7 to 2 respectively) (European Commission 2014a: Annex 1; European Commission 2015a: Annex 1). This development was a direct consequence of the Juncker Commission's decision to reduce the total number of recommendations and focus their content more sharply, while cutting down their length and scope. Considered in relative rather than absolute terms, however, the proportion of social CSRs did not decline (Clauwaert 2015: 10–14). Looking beneath the surface, a striking feature of the 2015 CSRs, as Commission interviewees emphasized, was their more integrated character, whereby social objectives were 'mainstreamed' into recommendations formally focused on other issues, such as labour market policy, education and taxation (COM-EMPL2-3; COM-COORD1-2). Thus, while only six CSRs were coded by the Commission as addressing poverty and social inclusion, a further six member states received recommendations to improve the educational participation and achievement of disadvantaged groups, with particular emphasis on Roma inclusion. Four countries also received recommendations to improve the adequacy, quality and accessibility of their pension or healthcare systems (European Commission 2015a, Annex 1; cf. Gómez Urquijo 2017: 7).[9]

In 2016, despite a further reduction in the number of CSRs (to 89 from 102 in 2015), the number of discrete employment and social recommendations contained within them remained nearly stable (114 vs. 118), resulting in an increased relative 'social' prominence. On the employment side, the most frequent recommendations received by member states concerned skills, education and training (16) and activation and employment services (14). In other policy areas, like taxes and undeclared work, youth employment and wage determination, the number of CSRs fell sharply, reflecting perceived progress in these domains. On the social side, eleven countries received recommendations on poverty and social inclusion according to the Commission's classification. Only two CSRs explicitly mentioned poverty reduction, despite limited progress towards the Europe 2020 target and increases in the risk and depth of poverty in more than one-third of member states. But as the SPC observed, 'poverty reduction can also be achieved through policy recommendations on improving the effectiveness of social protection systems', on which fourteen member states received CSRs, including the coverage of social assistance schemes and the adequacy of benefits, as well as access to and quality of social services. While the number of countries receiving CSRs on health and long-term care remained stable, six received recommendations explicitly addressing quality and accessibility challenges, more than in previous years. The number of member states receiving recommendations on pensions, extending working lives and employability of older workers fell from fifteen in 2015 to ten in 2016, reflecting the reforms carried out in this domain, though few CSRs explicitly addressed adequacy and sustainability issues. As in previous years, the vast majority of CSRs specifically focused on poverty and social exclusion were directed to Eastern and Southern countries where the absolute problems were perceived to be most urgent, while social inclusion concerns in Northern and Western countries were more likely to be expressed through recommendations to enhance employment and educational participation of disadvantaged groups, facilitate transitions from precarious to standard forms of employment and improve the tax and benefit position of low-wage earners (European Commission 2016b; EMCO 2016a; SPC 2016). Crespy and Vanheuverzwijn (2016: 77–8) conclude that the proportion of 2016 CSRs promoting social investment rather than retrenchment policy measures rose to 64 per cent, the highest rate since the Semester's inception.

### *Governance procedures*

Already under the Barroso Commission, the production of the CSRs had become an increasingly collaborative process, in which DG EMPL played a key role in both the teams preparing the country analyses and the Core Group responsible for drafting the recommendations themselves. Beginning in 2015, this process was carried a step further, as DG EMPL was charged with drafting the chapter on social and employment policy in the new Country Reports, which incorporated the MIP In-Depth Reviews previously written by DG ECFIN alone. DG EMPL also played an even more prominent part within the Core Group itself, as one of three line DGs working under SECGEN's lead. In so doing, DG EMPL could draw on substantial in-house policy and country expertise built up over the preceding years, as well as on key units dealing with Labour Market Policy and Training and Skills transferred by the Juncker Commission from DGs ECFIN and Education and Culture (EAC) respectively. In healthcare, DG Health and Food Safety (SANTE) contributed both to the Country Reports and CSRs, drawing on detailed country knowledge developed in recent years along with an indicator-based analytical tool for assessing the performance of national systems (COM COORD1; COM-EMPL2-4; COM-ECFIN1-2; COM-OTHER1-2).

A key objective behind the streamlining of the Semester, including both its revised timetable and the refocusing of the CSRs, was to increase national 'ownership' of recommended reforms and thereby improve their implementation (European Commission 2015a: 3, 10). Our interviewees and EU committee documents together confirm that these changes have been broadly welcomed by the member states, especially the opportunity to discuss and sometimes correct the Commission's analysis of national reform challenges and implementation progress in both bilateral and multilateral settings. There was broad agreement that as a result, the quality and accuracy of the analysis in the Commission's Country Reports was much higher than in previous years. National representatives also largely approved of the sharper focus of the CSRs on a reduced number of key priorities, together with the Commission's greater emphasis on outcomes rather than specific policy measures in responding to national challenges, though some recommendations (e.g., on pensions) were still considered overly prescriptive (SPC2; EMCO1; EPC1; COM-EMPL3; COM-ECFIN1; COM-COORD3; EMCO 2016b; SPC 2016) **[8]**.

Streamlining appears to have improved the relationship between the EPSCO and ECOFIN Councils, as well as between the Commission and the member states. The revised Semester timetable gave EMCO and the SPC more time to discuss and review both the Commission's Country Reports and the CSRs, enriching the process of multilateral surveillance and contributing to the formation of internal consensus on proposed reforms. It also allowed for enhanced co-ordination of views across national delegations, which had previously been a major source of tension between social and economic policy actors. Compared to earlier years, there was better co-ordination between the EPSCO and ECOFIN advisory committees, ensuring 'a coordinated and balanced preparation of the CSRs' adoption by the Council', according to the SPC's own 2016 assessment. The main outstanding complaint of the EPSCO committees was the high proportion of social and employment policy CSRs issued under the SGP and MIP, which fall under the formal jurisdiction of the ECOFIN Council (SPC1-2; EMCO1; EPC1; COM-EMPL4; EMCO 2016b; SPC 2016; cf. Maricut and Puetter 2017) **[9]**.

But even where EU economic policy actors formally retain a leading role, they appear to have internalized some of the objectives and concerns championed by their social interlocutors. Thus DG ECFIN's 'Horizontal Assessment Framework for Age-Related Fiscal Sustainability Challenges' included indicators for quality and accessibility of healthcare in 2016 for the first time, leading directly to the multiplication of CSRs on these issues (European Commission 2016a). And the Eurogroup itself has begun to discuss how pension reforms can be made 'more acceptable, socially viable and lasting' through flanking policies aimed at extending working lives such as lifelong learning, workplace adaptations and flexible working arrangements for older employees (European Commission 2015d).

Given the reduced number of CSRs, member states managed to obtain in 2015 a similar proportion as in previous years of contested amendments on social and employment issues, which accounted for six of nine successful amendments opposed by the Commission (own calculations from Council of the EU 2015a). In two of these cases (Finland and Italy), the CSRs were amended to recognize explicitly the autonomous role of the social partners in wage bargaining. In 2016, the improved accuracy of the CSRs resulting from intensified dialogue with member states around the Country Reports appear to have reduced demand for amendments, while the Commission also seems to have been more willing than in previous years to accept revisions proposed by EMCO and the SPC based on evidence from their multilateral surveillance reviews. The only contested social amendment adopted over the Commission's objections was to the euro area CSRs, where the EPSCO Council successfully insisted that national reforms should promote 'adequate and sustainable social protection systems that contribute effectively throughout the lifecycle both to social inclusion and labor market integration', rather than focusing more narrowly on work incentives and targeted support for those in need (Council of the EU 2015b; European Parliament 2016; Bekker 2017).

## Conclusions

Between 2011 and 2016, a partial but progressive socialization of the Semester occurred. This shift was visible at the level of substantive policy orientations, in terms of a growing emphasis on social objectives in the AGS and especially the CSRs. The latter expanded considerably from year to year in social scope and ambition, placing increasing stress on the need for member states to ensure the adequacy, accessibility, and effectiveness of their social security, pension and healthcare systems; to combat poverty and social exclusion on a variety of dimensions; and to improve their education, training, childcare, employment and social services, especially for vulnerable groups – even if the growing volume and coverage of these social CSRs was still counterbalanced by recommendations to many countries on fiscal consolidation and competitiveness.

The socialization of the Semester was equally visible at the level of governance procedures, in terms of an enhanced role for EU social and employment policy actors in monitoring, reviewing and amending the CSRs. Jurisdictional struggles continued with EU economic policy actors about overlapping issues, especially those linked to the SGP and MIP. But revisions to the Semester's procedural framework, coupled with the detailed knowledge of the social and employment situation in the member states built up through intensified monitoring, mutual surveillance, and peer review, made it possible for EMCO and the SPC, as well as for DG EMPL, to feed their views into the process at key moments. These developments also enabled the EPSCO committees to push through amendments of the Commission's draft CSRs on both larger and smaller issues, despite the high rQMV threshold.

Member state representatives were able to push back against what they perceived as 'over-prescriptive', 'one-size-fits-all' recommendations from the Commission, which sought to lay down not only reform objectives, but also the specific way of reaching them, without taking sufficient account of national contexts and competences. By demonstrating their ability to amend the draft CSRs, these committees compelled the Commission to engage more deliberatively with member states in both multilateral and bilateral forums. Responding to persistent criticisms of its limited social dimension and weak national ownership, the incoming Juncker Commission strategically revamped the Semester process, 'by giving more time for dialogue with the Member States and mainstreaming social considerations alongside economic goals', as the 2017 AGS (European Commission 2016c: 4) proudly proclaims, leading to a further socialization of both its substantive policy content and governance procedures. The governance of the Semester has likewise become less hierarchical and more interactive, while the CSRs, especially in the social and employment field, have become less uniform, less prescriptive, and better adapted to national circumstances. Thus, since its inception in 2011, the Semester has slowly but steadily evolved in a more socially balanced direction in relation to each of the three critical empirical claims discussed in the introduction.

This progressive socialization of the Semester can be interpreted as a response by the Commission and other EU institutions to external developments, notably rising social and political discontent among European citizens with austerity policies, demonstrated by falling levels of public support for the EU and electoral defeats for incumbent governments in many countries. But it should also be understood as the product of strategic agency, reflexive learning and creative adaptation by EU social and employment actors of their own organization and practices in response to the new institutional conditions of the Semester.[10] This process began with the employment policy actors within EMCO and DG EMPL, who were already familiar with the challenges of debating their positions with the economic policy actors under the Integrated Guidelines of the Lisbon Strategy and took the first steps to strengthen their intelligence-gathering and analytical capacities through the development of new monitoring instruments, the intensification of multilateral surveillance, and the introduction of rQMV on amendments to the Commission's draft CSRs. Their example was quickly emulated by the social policy actors within the SPC and DG EMPL, who not only followed suit in developing new instruments to monitor and analyse the Semester's social dimension, deepening multilateral surveillance of CSR implementation and adopting rQMV for amending the CSRs, but also proactively used the institutional *acquis* and flexibility of the Social OMC to introduce new social reporting initiatives at both national and EU level and to foster mutual learning on promising approaches to tackling common policy challenges beyond those flagged in the CSRs. These innovations in turn helped EU social and employment policy actors not only to gain ground in 'evidence-based' negotiations over the CSRs, but also to revise the rules of the Semester game and influence the positions of their economic policy interlocutors on some key issues. 'Puzzling' and 'powering' (Heclo 1974) thus went hand-in-hand in socializing the European Semester.

In understanding how such apparently weaker actors can advance their substantive goals and decision-making influence despite the institutional asymmetries and structural power imbalances underlined by the Semester's social critics, 'actor-centred constructivism' and the 'usages of Europe' approach provide valuable conceptual resources. Complex governance processes like the European Semester, as these approaches emphasize, do not narrowly predetermine the outcome of political struggles, but typically offer multiple opportunities and resources for strategic agency by contending groups of actors, whose effective exploitation depends on the latter's ability and willingness to identify and act upon them. By seizing such opportunities and creatively adapting their own organization and practices, these actors may be able to reshape pre-existing power balances and procedural rules even where the overarching institutional framework remains formally unchanged. The socialization of the European Semester demonstrates in turn the power of these theoretical approaches to illuminate the evolution and dynamics of EU governance processes, along with the usage of such processes by national actors to which they have mainly been applied in previous research.

An outstanding empirical issue remains the domestic implementation and causal influence of the European Semester on national social and employment policies. This issue, as observed at the outset, requires a different research approach, based on comparative process tracing of national policy-making, similar to that developed in empirical studies of the OMC (Barcevičius *et al.* 2014). Here, too, 'actor-centred constructivism' and the 'usages of Europe' approach are of great potential value, by emphasizing the scope for creative appropriation of EU targets and recommendations, as initial research like that of Eihmanis (2017) on 'cherry-picking external constraints' and the implementation of social CSRs in Latvia illustrates. In the absence of more such empirical studies, however, scholars should not assume the existence of a direct relationship between the formal legal basis of the CSRs and their national influence, as much of the critical literature on the social dimension of the Semester discussed earlier appears to do, especially since no sanctions have yet been imposed on member states for non-compliance with either the MIP or the SGP.[11]

## Notes

1. Notably the Commission's Directorate-General for Economic and Financial Affairs (DG ECFIN), the Economic and Financial Affairs (ECOFIN) Council, the Eurogroup, the Economic and Financial Committee (EFC) and the Economic Policy Committee (EPC).
2. Especially the Commission's Directorate-General for Employment and Social Affairs (DG EMPL), the Employment and Social Affairs (EPSCO) Council and the Employment and Social Protection Committees (EMCO and SPC).

3. Crespy and Verheuverzwijn suggest that this trend could stem from higher implementation rates of retrenchment-orientated recommendations, but do not provide supporting evidence for this interpretation.
4. References to this Appendix are indicated in the body of the text by bold numbers in square brackets.
5. AGSs, proposed CSRs, and CSRs as adopted by the Council are available for 2011-2014 at http://ec.europa.eu/europe2020/making-it-happen/index_en.htm. Countries covered by an Economic Adjustment Programme or Memorandum of Understanding do not receive CSRs under the European Semester.
6. For a country key to this and subsequent CSR analyses, see Online Appendix Section 2. Figures in the text refer to numbers of member states receiving recommendations on a particular topic, not to numbers of CSRs or recommended measures. The number of member states receiving CSRs varies from year to year, as countries subject to an Economic Adjustment Programme are excluded.
7. For a discussion of the 2012-2013 CSRs, along with a country key to socially orientated recommendations referred to in the text, see Online Appendix, Section 2.
8. Under the Lisbon Treaty, when the Council takes a decision not based on a Commission proposal, this must be supported by a 'reinforced' qualified majority comprising 72 per cent of member states accounting for 65 per cent of the Union's population (http://eur-lex.europa.eu/summary/glossary/reinforced_qualified_majority.html).
9. For an analysis of 'hidden' social recommendations in the 2015 CSRs, see Online Appendix Section 3.
10. For reasons of space, we do not discuss in this contribution EU social NGOs and social partner organisations, who played a limited role in the evolution and dynamics of the European Semester during this period. For extended analyses, see Zeitlin and Vanhercke (2014: 54–5); Vanhercke et al. (2015: 15–17); Sabato et al. (2017).
11. Apart from a small fine levied on Spain for fraudulent fiscal reporting by one of its autonomous regions, exposed by the national statistical office itself (Savage and Howarth 2017).

## Acknowledgments

This contribution draws on two previous reports prepared for the Swedish Institute of European Policy Studies (SIEPS) and the Luxembourg Parliament respectively. We are grateful to these bodies for supporting our research, as well as to our many generous interviewees, without whose cooperation this contribution would not have been possible. For valuable comments on earlier drafts, we would also like to thank Sigrid Quack, Amy Verdun, two anonymous reviewers, and the participants in two workshops organized by the Amsterdam Centre for Contemporary European Studies (ACCESS EUROPE), along with a variety of other academic and policy meetings, too numerous to list here.

## Disclosure statement

No potential conflict of interest was reported by the authors.

## References

Baeten, R. and Vanhercke, B. (2016) 'Inside the black box: the EU's economic surveillance of national healthcare systems', *Comparative European Politics*, doi:10.1057/cep.2016.10.

Barcevičius, E., Weishaupt, J.T. and Zeitlin, J. (eds) (2014) *Assessing the Open Method of Coordination: Institutional Design and National Influence of EU Social Policy Coordination*, Houndmills: Palgrave Macmillan.

Bekker, S. (2013) *The EU's stricter economic governance: a step towards more binding coordination of social policies*, WZB Discussion Paper SP IV 2013–501, Berlin: Social Science Research Center.

Bekker, S. (2015) *European socioeconomic governance in action: coordinating social policies in the third European Semester*, OSE Research Paper No. 19, Brussels: European Social Observatory.

Bekker, S. (2016) *Is there flexibility in the European Semester process? Exploring interactions between the EU and member states within post-crisis socio-economic governance*, SIEPS Report 2016: 1, Stockholm: Swedish Institute for European Policy Studies.

Bekker, S. (2017) 'Flexicurity in the European Semester: still a relevant policy concept?', *Journal of European Public Policy*, doi:10.1080/13501763.2017.1363272.

Bekker, S. and Klosse, S. (2013) 'Eu governance of economic and social policies: chances and challenges for social Europe', *European Journal of Social Law* 2: 103–120.

Bieling, H.-J. (2012) 'Eu facing the crisis: social and employment policies in times of tight budgets', *Transfer: European Review of Labour and Research* 18(3): 255–71.

Clauwaert, S. (2014) *The country-specific recommendations in the social field: an overview and comparison. Update including the CSRs 2014–2015*, Background Analysis 2014.01, Brussels: European Trade Union Institute.

Clauwert, S. (2015) *The country-specific recommendations in the social field: an overview and comparison. Update including the CSRs 2015–2016*, Background Analysis 2015.02, Brussels: European Trade Union Institute.

Copeland, P. and Daly, M. (2015) 'Social Europe: from 'add-on' to 'dependence-upon' economic integration', in: A. Crespy and G. Menz (eds), *Social Policy and the Euro Crisis: Quo Vadis Social Europe*, Houndmills: Palgrave Macmillan, pp. 140–60.

Council of the EU. (2012) *Explanations of modifications to Commission recommendations for the Country Specific Recommendations*, 11941/12, 6 July.

Council of the EU. (2013) *Explanatory note accompanying document to Council Recommendations to Member States under the European Semester 2013*, 11336/13, 8 July.

Council of the EU. (2014) *Explanations of modifications to Commission Recommendations for the Country Specific Recommendations: Accompanying document to Council Recommendations to Member States under the European semester 2014*, 10810/1/14 REV 1, 18 June.

Council of the EU. (2015a) *Explanation of modifications to Commission Recommendations for the Country Specific Recommendations*, 9305/1/15 REV 1, 17 June.

Council of the EU. (2015b) *Explanatory note accompanying document to the Council Recommendation on the economic policy of the euro area*, 14860/15 ADD 1 REV 1, 3 December.

Crespy, A. and Menz, G. (eds) (2015a) *Social Policy and the Euro Crisis: Quo Vadis Social Europe*, Houndmills: Palgrave Macmillan.

Crespy, A. and Menz, G. (2015b) 'Commission entrepreneurship and the debasing of Social Europe before and after the Eurocrisis', *JCMS: Journal of Common Market Studies* 53(4): 753–68.

Crespy, A. and Vanheuverzwijn, P. (2016) 'What "Brussels" means by structural reforms', in: *Cahiers du CEVIPOL 5/2016*, Brussels: Université Libre de Bruxelles, pp. 57–88.

Cypriot Presidency (2012) *European Semester 2012 – Lessons Learned*, Council of the EU 13439/12, 18 September.

Dawson, M. (2015) 'The legal and political accountability structure of "post-crisis" EU economic governance', *JCMS: Journal of Common Market Studies* 53(5): 976–93.

de la Porte, C. and Heins, E. (2014) 'Game change in EU social policy: towards more European integration', in M.J. Rodrigues and E. Xiarchogiannopoulou (eds), *The Euro Crisis and the Transformation of EU Governance*, Farnham: Ashgate, pp. 157–70.

de la Porte, C. and Heins, E. (2015) 'A new era of European integration? governance of labour market and social policy since the sovereign debt crisis', *Comparative European Politics* 13(1): 8–28.

Degryse, C., Jepsen, M. and Pochet, P. (2014) 'A worrying prospect: towards a more imbalanced European social governance?' in D. Natali (ed.), *Social Developments in the European Union 2013*, Brussels: European Trade Union Institute/European Social Observatory, pp. 57–83.

Eihmanis, E. (2017) Cherry-picking external constraints: Latvia and EU economic governance, 2008–2014', *Journal of European Public Policy.*

EMCO (2012) *EMCO's programme of multilateral surveillance*, 2 March.

EMCO (2016a) *Europe 2020 Employment Performance Monitor*, INDIC/11/17052016/EN, 17 May.

EMCO (2016b) *Horizontal opinion on the 2016 country specific recommendations including the results of the multilateral surveillance on the 2015 CSRs*, Council of the EU 9684/16, Annex 1, 9 June.

EMCO Chair (2012) 'Speaking notes for EPSCO as delivered', 4 October.

EPSCO (2013) *The social dimension of the Economic and Monetary Union*, annex to Irish Presidency letter to President of the European Council, 15 May.

European Commission (2011) *Concluding the first European semester of economic policy coordination: Guidance for national policies in 2011–2012*, COM(2011) 400 final, 7 June.

European Commission (2014a) *2014 European Semester: Country Specific Recommendations*, COM(2014) 400 final, 2 June.

European Commission (2014b) *Annual Growth Survey 2015*, COM(2014) 902 final, 28 November.

European Commission (2015a) *2015 European Semester: country-specific recommendations*, COM (2015) 250 final, 13 May.

European Commission (2015b) *On steps towards completing Economic and Monetary Union*, COM(2015) 600 final, 21 October.

European Commission (2015c) *Annual Growth Survey 2016: strengthening the recovery and fostering competitiveness*, COM(2015) 690 final, 26 November.

European Commission (2015d) *Pensions – implications for fiscal sustainability in the euro area*, DG ECFIN/C2, Note for the attention of the Eurogroup, Ref. Ares(2015)5578474, 4 December.

European Commission (2016a) *Age-related fiscal sustainability challenges: a horizontal assessment framework for pension, health care, long-term care policies for the 2016 European Semester*, DG ECFIN/C2, Note to the Economic Policy Committee, February.

European Commission (2016b) *2016 European Semester: country-specific recommendations*, COM(2016) 321 final, 18 May.

European Commission (2016c) *Annual Growth Survey 2017*, COM(2016) 725 final, 16 November.

European Commission, EMCO and SPC (2010) *Foundations and structures for a Joint Assessment Framework (JAF) to monitor the Employment Guidelines under Europe 2020*, Council of the EU 16984/10 ADD 1, 26 November.

European Parliament (2013) *Country Specific Recommendations (CSRs) under the European Semester Cycles 2011, 2012 and 2013*, DG for Internal Policies, Economic Governance Support Unit, IPOL-ECON_NT(2013)497730_EN, 30 August.

European Parliament (2014) *Country Specific Recommendations (CSRs) for 2014: A comparison of Commission and Council texts – 'comply or explain'*, DG for Internal Policies, Economic Governance Support Unit, IPOL-ECON ET(2014)528746_EN, 8 July.

European Parliament (2016) *Country Specific Recommendations for 2016: a comparison of Commission and Council recommendations (the 'comply or explain' principle')*, DG for Internal Policies, Economic Governance Support Unit, IPOL STU (2016)574422_EN, 29 June.

Gómez Urquijo, L. (2017) 'The Europeanisation of policy to address poverty under the new economic governance: The contribution of the European Semester', *Journal of Poverty and Social Justice*, doi:10.1332/175982716X14822521840999.

Graziano, P.R., Jacquot, S. and Palier, B. (eds) (2011) *The EU and the Domestic Politics of Welfare State Reforms: Europa, Europae*, Houndmills: Palgrave Macmillan.

Heclo, H. (1974) *Modern Social Politics in Britain and Sweden*, New Haven: Yale University Press.

Irish Presidency (2012) *Incoming Presidency note for the Chairs of Committees involved in the process leading to the adoption of Country-Specific Recommendations (CSRs) by the Council under the European Semester*, Council of the EU, December.

Jacquot, S. and Woll, C. (2003) 'Usage of European integration – europeanisation from a sociological Perspective', *European Integration Online Papers* 7(12): 1–18.

Jessoula, M. (2015) 'Europe 2020 and the fight against poverty - beyond competence clash, towards 'hybrid' governance solutions?' *Social Policy & Administration* 49(4): 490–511.

Juncker, J.-C. (2015) 'Setting Europe in Motion: Main Messages, opening statement in the European Parliament Plenary Session', Strasbourg, 22 October.

Lithuanian Presidency (2013) *Lessons from 2013 and way forward*, Council of the EU 14618/13, 16 October.

Maricut, A. and Puetter, U. (2017) 'Deciding the European Semester: The European Council, the Council and the enduring asymmetry between economic and social policy issues', *Journal of European Public Policy*, doi:10.1080/13501763.2017.1363271.

Pochet, P. (2010) *What's wrong with EU2020?* European Trade Union Institute Policy Brief, European Social Policy 2.

President of the European Council (2011) 'Speech by Herman Van Rompuy at the European Parliament', EUCO 134/11, 16 November.

Sabato, S. and Vanhercke, B., with Spasova, S. (2017) *Listened to, but not heard? Social Partners' multilevel involvement in the European Semester*. OSE Paper Series no. 35, Brussels: European Social Observatory.

Sanchez Salgado, R. (2014) *Europeanizing Civil Society: How the EU Shapes Civil Society Organizations*, Houndmills: Palgrave Macmillan.

Saurugger, S. (2009) 'Sociological approaches in EU studies', *Journal of European Public Policy* 16(6): 935–49.

Saurugger, S. (2016) 'Sociological approaches to the European Union in times of turmoil', *JCMS: Journal of Common Market Studies* 54(1): 70–86.

Savage, J. and Howarth, D. (2017) 'Enforcing the European Semester: the politics of asymmetric information in the Excessive Deficit and Macroeconomic Imbalance Procedures', *Journal of European Public Policy*, doi:10.1080/13501763.2017.1363268

Scharpf, F.W. (2013) 'Monetary union, fiscal crisis and the disabling of democratic accountability', in A. Schäfer and W. Streeck (eds), *Politics in the Age of Austerity*, Cambridge: Polity, pp. 108–42.

SPC (2011a) *Reinvigorating the Social OMC in the context of Europe 2020*, SPC Opinion, 17 May.

SPC (2011b) *Analysis of the SPC experience in the first European Semester*, SPC/2011.09.03, 7 September.

SPC (2012a) *SPC evaluation of the second European Semester: preparing for the 2013 European Semester*, SPC/2012.09.1b, 7 September.

SPC (2012b) *Social protection performance monitor (SPPM) – methodological report*, Indicators Sub-Group, 17 October.

SPC (2013) Developing an assessment framework in the area of health based on the Joint Assessment Framework methodology: final report to the SPC on the first stage of implementation, Indicators Sub-Group, 19 November.

SPC (2016) *SPC assessment of the 2016 CSRs package and the implementation of the 2015 Council CSRs in the area of social protection and social inclusion*, Council of the EU 9684/16, Annex 2, 9 June.

Vanhercke, B. and Zeitlin, J., with Zwinkels, A. (2015) *Further socializing the European Semester: Moving forward for the Social Triple A?*, report for the Luxembourg Parliament and Presidency of the European Union, Brussels: European Social Observatory.

Woll, C. and Jacquot, C. (2010) 'Using Europe: strategic action in multi-level politics', *Comparative European Politics* 8(1): 110–26.

Zeitlin, J. and Vanhercke, B. (2014) *Socializing the European Semester: Economic Governance and social policy coordination in Europe 2020*, SIEPS Report 2014:7, Stockholm: Swedish Institute for European Policy Studies.

OPEN ACCESS

# Flexicurity in the European Semester: still a relevant policy concept?

Sonja Bekker

**ABSTRACT**

Before the crisis, flexicurity was a leading European Union (EU) policy concept, which aimed to balance labor-market flexibility and security. The recent focus on austerity measures to reduce public deficits might be thought to have reduced attention to the 'security' component of flexicurity. Accordingly, a 'farewell to flexicurity' has been claimed to have occurred. This paper challenges that claim and explores the role of flexicurity within the European Semester. It analyses the European Semester's policy goals between 2007 and 2016, as well as the country-specific recommendations (CSRs) to member states between 2009 and 2015. The analysis shows that the EU flexicurity concept has been revitalized, while its definition changed to encompass more social concerns. Even at the peak of the crisis, CSRs continued to devote attention to elements of both flexibility and security, although the precise details differed across countries and have changed over time.

## Flexicurity in a European context

The flexicurity concept has been a key orientation for the European Commission's social policy agenda for the past two decades. However, lately, a 'farewell to flexicurity' has been claimed to have occurred, not only in national policies, but also at the EU level (compare Barbier 2015; Bolton *et al.* 2016; Hastings and Heyes 2016; Heyes 2013). This paper answers the question whether and how the flexicurity concept still plays a role within the European Semester's co-ordination activities. It establishes to what extent the term flexicurity and its key elements is still used within the European Semester. In order to judge how flexicurity plays a role, the paper builds on the different conceptualisations of the European Social Model (ESM) (Jepsen and Serrano Pascual 2005). The ESM's basic idea of interacting social and economic goals

Supplemental data for this article can be accessed https://doi.org/10.1080/13501763.2017.1363272.

(Hemerijck 2002) resembles the double goal flexicurity tries to serve: offering both labor-market flexibility and labor-market security to all types of workers (Wilthagen and Tros 2004). Moreover, debates on flexicurity reflect issues that recall the four ways in which the ESM is construed: as an entity, an ideal model, a European project and a political project (Jepsen and Serrano Pacual 2005). The ESM as an entity, meaning the common institutions, values or forms of regulations, may resemble some of the elements of original academic notion of flexicurity, including providing security to employees, preserving social cohesion in European societies and valuing social dialogue (Wilthagen and Tros 2004). Moreover, along the lines of the second conceptualization of the ESM, flexicurity found its ideal types in the Danish and Dutch models, which had attracted attention due to their high employment rates (Madsen 2008; Wilthagen and Tros 2004). After 2006, the term 'flexicurity' became prominent in EU policy debates. The EU's initial search to combine flexibility and security was set in the context of maintaining the ESM whilst responding to fundamental challenges such as globalization, technological innovation and the ageing of society (Bekker 2012; European Commission 1997; Tsarouhas and Ladi 2013). This resembles the third way of understanding the ESM: as a dynamic and evolving European project, reacting to exogenous developments. Indeed, including wider welfare state challenges such as changes in family structures and gender balances at the labor market and changing political landscapes (Hemerijck 2012), flexicurity attempts to find ways to deal with 'new' labor market risks, including offering security to new types of workers: part-timers and flex workers who may face risks of social exclusion in and outside the labor market.

The EU flexicurity concept, as adopted by the Council (2007), received a good deal of criticism, mainly from academic and trade union circles (Mailand 2010). These criticisms not only dealt with the norms constituting flexicurity and its (in)ability to lead to balanced practices, but also with (hidden) political agendas. This latter resembles the fourth conceptualization of the ESM as a politically constructed project: flexicurity as a concept fed by political proposals for joint EU solutions (Jepsen and Serrano Pascual 2005: 243). One of the criticisms of flexicurity was that its broad definition made the concept rather ambiguous (Burroni and Keune 2011). Also, its promise of a balanced perspective on flexibility and security was contentious, most notably in cases where the concept was used to justify specific policy reforms (Keune and Jepsen 2007; Veille and Bovin 2008; Viebrock and Clasen 2009). In addition, the flexicurity concept had not yet matured into an elaborated theory and therefore lacked a solid foundation to convert ideas into balanced practices and to measure progress appropriately (Auer 2010; Bredgaard *et al.* 2008; Burroni and Keune 2011; Keune and Serrano 2014). Subsequent academic studies paid more attention to these aspects, proposing indicators to measure the components of flexicurity (Chung

2012; Muffels and Wilthagen 2013; Viebrock and Clasen 2009). National reforms were assessed in terms of how far they pursued a balanced approach to flexibility and security, while also incorporating the effects of the crisis (Andersen 2012; Gwiazda 2011; Heyes 2011; Madsen 2013). National-level developments were generally judged as moves towards greater flexibility whilst forgetting the 'security' part (Lopez *et al.* 2014). For example, national reforms flexibilized the rules on fixed-term contracts, extending the maximum period during which an individual can be employed on a fixed-term contract by the same employer (in CZ, EL, PT, RO, ES),[1] increased the maximum number of renewals of fixed-term contracts (NL, PL) or combined both changes (SK) (for an overview see Clauwaert and Schömann 2012). Moreover, many countries reduced social expenditure, for instance by cutting spending on unemployment benefits and pensions (Hermann 2014). The assumed demise of the flexicurity model has been linked to the EU's crisis focus on austerity measures, which lowered the fiscal space of countries to guarantee suitable social security (Barbier 2015; Heyes 2013). Moreover, EU-level attention has been viewed as being biased towards structural reforms that favor flexibility over security (Hermann 2014; Woolfson and Sommers 2016). Some predict that the EU will continue to try to exit the crisis by stimulating flexibility policies at the expense of employee security (Tsarouhas and Ladi 2013). Findings about one-sided structural reforms may not only point at a weak normative anchor of a balanced flexicurity concept. They may also point at rather uniform, constant and one-sided policy messages. Current claims of the demise of the EU flexicurity model have not taken systematically into account more recent developments in socio-economic governance within the European Semester. A longitudinal perspective is however relevant to assess whether there has been a 'socialization' of the European Semester or a certain resilience of the values and regulations constituting the ESM (Barnard 2014; Zeitlin and Vanhercke THIS ISSUE).

## Methodology

The paper explores EU-level developments around flexicurity, taking a longitudinal approach. First, it looks at changes in the pre and post-crisis definitions of flexicurity. Secondly, it analyses the presence of flexicurity in the CSRs of 2009, 2011, 2013 and 2015. The methodology of qualitative content analysis and close reading has been used to extract flexicurity elements from the CSRs. Relevant phrases and text segments have been tagged, using a priori coding (Taylor and Gibbs 2010; White and March 2006). The four flexicurity elements adopted by the EU in 2007 and furthered in 2016 have formed the basis for selecting the appropriate text segments that identify either flexicurity, or one of its elements. These elements are flexible and reliable contractual arrangements, comprehensive lifelong learning strategies, effective active labor market policies (ALMP), and modern, adequate and sustainable social protection systems. Thus, whenever a CSR included a term such as 'ALMP', or referred to the government or the public employment services to bring back (groups of) unemployed to the labor market, this has been tagged as a flexicurity element. Likewise, the element of contractual arrangements includes job quality, labor market transitions and segmentation issues, while the social security ingredient includes sustainable pensions, childcare and social transfers. Flexicurity elements have been taken into account, following the notion that countries have different starting points when it concerns flexicurity (Muffels and Wilthagen 2013). This means that the absence of a CSR on one of the flexicurity elements does not automatically imply that the EU takes an unbalanced approach. For example, a country with a well-established lifelong-learning system (LLL) is unlikely to get a CSR on this. Section 4 further explains these considerations. As the data do not contain information about existing national policies, the study cannot draw a conclusion on whether CSRs might support national-level flexicurity outcomes. However, the study can illustrate which flexicurity elements are part of the recommendations, whether these favor certain messages over others and whether these messages are stable over time.

In a semi-quantitative approach, segments of the textual data have been converted into numerical counts so as to expose trends. The text segments are thus converted into variables that can be counted and employed as quantitative data sets (Johnson *et al.* 2010). All CSRs addressed to member states in the three European Semesters of 2011, 2013 and 2015, were included in the analysis, as well as the 2009 CSRs, which were part of the Lisbon Strategy (2000–2010). When counting the number of references to flexicurity elements, it is relevant to note that a single CSR often addresses several different policies, for instance combining issues of lifelong learning, unemployment and social exclusion. Therefore, the observed number of flexicurity elements is larger than the number of CSRs that have been addressed to a particular country in a given year. Although this semi-quantitative approach allows distillation of trends, the method at times loses precision. In the process of converting the close-reading findings into semi-quantitative calculations, a number of choices had to be made. A first choice is based on the fact that most CSRs only address part of a flexicurity element. Especially the flexicurity elements 'contractual arrangements' and 'social security' consist of many different items. Whereas some of these items have been included in CSRs, there are fewer cases in which all items belonging to social security or contractual arrangements have been addressed. For instance, partial CSRs on contractual arrangements may suggest combating the negative consequences of labor market segmentation, without mentioning job quality. A CSR that partially addresses a flexicurity element is coded as a CSR addressing this particular flexicurity element. Moreover, pension reforms are included as a flexicurity element, but only if they refer to the sustainability of the pension system. This interpretation follows the line of recent reasoning by the Council (2015a), relating such reforms to the sustainability of social protection over the life course and for instance minding intergenerational solidarity (see section 3). If the CSRs did not clearly mention sustainability, then the Commission's background documents, such as the Country Reports, were consulted in order to establish whether or not the proposed pension reforms should support sustainability. If this was not the case, it was not counted as supporting flexicurity. Excluded are CSRs addressing initial education (education for children, teenagers and students) and CSRs referring to health care. A second methodological choice relates to the fact that parts of each flexicurity element may be addressed in several CSRs. For instance, parts of social security may be addressed in CSR 1 referring to the pension system and CSR 3 addressing childcare. These scattered observations have been grouped together as addressing social security and are thus counted only once. Moreover, the number of countries receiving CSRs varies per year. In 2009 there were member states without a CSR, or with CSRs that did not refer to flexicurity elements. In later years the so-called program countries stopped receiving CSRs. Instead, these countries, for example Greece and Portugal, got more forceful policy prescriptions via Memoranda of Understanding as a condition for receiving financial assistance. Most of these countries returned to the Semester's co-ordination activities once they exited the program and consequently started receiving CSRs again.

The first part of the analysis shows the number of times flexicurity elements have been addressed in each of the four years. In a second stage, the analysis incorporates a more dynamic view, showing whether or not specific flexicurity elements have received decreasing or increasing attention. CSRs reflect the degree of tailored policy advice to countries on how to improve their policy efforts and thus offer the opportunity to mind the specific national situation and challenges when judging the 'survival' of the flexicurity concept within the European Semester. Because countries have different flexicurity starting points, it cannot be assumed that CSRs should be the same for each member state. For the dynamic analysis, the year 2009 serves as a benchmark. Around 2009 there was still ample attention to flexicurity, including in the CSRs. The benchmark year helps to hypothesize the likelihood that flexicurity elements will be part of surveillance in later years. An example hypothesis is that if ALMP is part of a CSR in 2009, then this item will reappear in the CSRs of subsequent years. Possible dynamics in data have been coded as follows:

- Stable or equal level of attention if a CSR in 2009 is drafted again in subsequent years (yes in 2009/yes in later years).
- Reduced attention if a CSR in 2009 is not repeated in later years (yes/no).

- Increased attention if there was no CSR in 2009, but if there was a CSR in later years (no/yes).
- No attention in case of the absence of a CSR in 2009 and an absence in later years (no/no).

Such hypotheses have a rather static approach, suggesting that messages to member states are constant over time. Taking a longitudinal and dynamic approach enables the detection of pluriform and changing messages. However, due to data limitations, it is not possible to explain why such dynamics occur. The assumption is that all policy priorities are included in the CSRs, perhaps reducing the complexity of the actual co-ordination system as found elsewhere (Zeitlin and Vanhercke THIS ISSUE). If a 2009 CSR is not repeated in later years, this could first of all be explained by a national reform that has made EU-level attention obsolete. However, CSRs do not contain information on national reforms. Studies linking CSRs to national reforms have established that such reforms sometimes explain the disappearance of topics in subsequent CSRs (Bekker 2016). A second explanation is that the EU still finds an issue relevant, but chooses to prioritize other topics, for instance because new challenges have emerged (see section 4). Prior research demonstrated that the disappearance of a topic from the CSRs does not necessarily mean that the particular national policy challenge has been resolved (Bekker 2016). Therefore, findings based on CSRs alone need to be interpreted carefully. In spite of the data limitations, this paper makes a valuable contribution by demonstrating dynamics in policy messages, based on all member states that were part of the four co-ordination cycles explored, illustrating changes in the balance between social and economic goals and variety across member states.

## Towards a post-crisis EU flexicurity policy concept

The origins of the flexicurity concept may be traced back to the early 1990s and gradually advanced through EU-level discussions during the 2000s (Barbier 2015). The Council codified the ideas emerging from these discussions into the 2007 common principles of flexicurity (see Online Appendix table 1). In essence, Principle 1 emphasizes that flexicurity is not the end goal, but rather a means to reach the goals of the European Employment Strategy (EES), which was part of the Lisbon Strategy at that time. Principle 2 defines flexicurity as the deliberate combination of four ingredients, some of which appeal to certain norms and institutions constituting the ESM, such as providing social security. Likewise, flexicurity Principle 6 on gender equality and Principle 7 on social dialogue refer to norms and institutions that might relate to parts of the ESM. Flexicurity received a great deal of criticism, however, especially on its ability to really develop a strong social dimension. Particularly the ingredient of contractual arrangements provoked heated arguments about employment protection legislation (EPL) (Bekker 2012). It reflected worries that flexicurity would ultimately be about more flexibility without paying much attention to developing security as well. Flexicurity Principle 3 refers to the tailor-made approach of social and employment policy co-ordination, which suggests that countries should not necessarily implement uniform policies. This also means that CSRs should vary across countries.

Soon after the adoption of the flexicurity common principles, the economic and financial crisis began impacting the EU's socio-economic debate. Around the same time the Lisbon Strategy was replaced by the Europe 2020 Strategy. The flexicurity concept remained part of the new EU's ambitions and was among others included in the new Integrated Guidelines of Europe 2020. Employment guideline 7 on increasing labor market participation and reducing structural unemployment calls on member states to integrate the flexicurity principles into their labor market policies, so as to increase labor market participation, combat segmentation and inactivity, lower gender inequality and reduce structural unemployment. Furthermore, flexicurity formed part of the EU's flagship initiative to create new skills for new jobs. Also, in 2008 flexicurity missions were organized to five member states, and a subsequent report of the findings emphasized its key role in promoting jobs and growth in times of economic downturn. The term was moreover used in a Commission evaluation assessing whether flexicurity could survive the crisis (European Commission 2013). Nevertheless, the concept seemed to fade into the background while economic and fiscal issues gained priority (Barbier 2015). This development left little room for the 'security' part of flexicurity (Hastings and Heyes 2016), at least in the early years of the European Semester. A similar conclusion was drawn by the Commission, which observed that during the crisis, more flexibility at the national level was hardly compensated by more security (European Commission 2013). In this respect, the weight of flexicurity Principle 8 on sustainable public budgets might have been larger during the crisis, than those referring to the social dimension.

The latest EU policy documents show that the crisis years have not led to a permanent disappearance of the flexicurity concept. On the contrary, flexicurity seems to have undergone a kind of revival. Its recurrence coincides with a (re)fit of the concept to new societal challenges and political preferences to deal with these challenges, resembling the third and fourth conceptualization of the ESM. In 2015 the term was carefully re-introduced in the Five Presidents' Report. The concern for how to maintain the ESM given Europe's socio-economic challenges was a reason for reintroducing flexicurity on the policy agenda. The Five Presidents' Report called for a common standard for labor markets, which should be developed as part of the completion of the

Economic and Monetary Union (EMU). This proposal involved elements which are quite similar to the 'old' flexicurity ingredients, expanding the latter by including among others a fifth ingredient on open markets and supportive labor taxation. The subsequent Commission Communication on steps towards completing the EMU confirmed this idea (European Commission 2015a). The Annual Growth Survey 2016 provided more details on the renewed concept (European Commission 2015b). It explained that flexicurity reforms should simultaneously address reducing labor market segmentation, supporting adequate wage developments, ensuring well-designed income support systems, introducing policies to ease transitions to new jobs, and equipping jobseekers with the right skills and better match them with vacancies. Moreover, as was also stressed in the 'old' flexicurity Principle 7, the social partners should be included in the design of reforms. These concerns have been followed up in the recent CSRs for the Eurozone countries. The Commission's argument for reviving flexicurity was that countries with flexicurity policies have resisted the crisis better in terms of safeguarding employment and fairness (European Commission 2015c). Flexicurity is also mentioned in relation to the Commission's 2016 public consultation on the European Pillar of Social Rights.

This paper takes the 2016 Euro Area recommendations as a starting point for exploring the CSRs. These call on member states to implement reforms that combine:

(I) flexible and reliable labor contracts that promote job quality and smooth labor market transitions and avoid a two-tier labor market;
(II) comprehensive lifelong learning strategies;
(III) effective policies to help the unemployed re-enter the labor market,
(IV) adequate and sustainable social protection systems that contribute effectively and efficiently throughout the life cycle both to social inclusion and labor market integration;
(V) open and competitive product and services markets. Reduce the tax wedge on labor, particularly on low-earners, in a budgetary-neutral way to foster job creation (European Commission 2015c: 9).

Flexicurity elements 1 and 4, addressing contractual arrangements and social protection systems, have changed significantly, compared to the old flexicurity ingredients. Overall, the amendments seem to improve the attention to the social aspects of flexicurity, at times even acknowledging the need to lower flexibility. The new flexicurity element on contractual arrangements includes the fight against labor market segmentation. This issue was also mentioned as an aim of the old flexicurity Principle 4, yet has now been inserted in the first flexicurity element itself, thus gaining a more prominent position. This prominence fits progressive concerns about labor market segmentation, including in the flexicurity 'model' country, the Netherlands.

Some of the changes in the flexicurity definition were proposed by the Commission (see the Commission's proposal in Council 2015a). Other suggestions came from the Employment Committee (EMCO) and Social Policy Committee (SPC), in their contribution to the Employment, Social Policy, Health and Consumer Affairs Council (EPSCO) discussion (SPC and EMCO 2015). In the draft euro area CSR, the Commission already proposed to extend the old flexicurity element on flexible and reliable contractual arrangements by adding that these should promote labor market transitions and avoid two-tier labor markets. The Council supported some of these changes, while adding new elements, whose rationale it set out in a comply-or-explain procedure. Regarding the first flexicurity element, the Council included the phrase 'promote job quality and smooth labor market transitions'. The Council (2015a: 3) stated that 'the main goal of labor market reforms is to promote quality jobs, contributing to a stronger inclusion and supporting economic growth', making it necessary to highlight the aspect of inclusiveness. On the third flexicurity ingredient, EMCO and SPC suggested to amend the part on helping the unemployed by adding 'and particularly the long-term unemployed' (SPC and EMCO 2015: 1–2). This suggestion, however, did not appear in the final version of the CSRs endorsed by the Council.

Regarding the fourth flexicurity element, the Commission proposed to change the original wording of 'modern, adequate and sustainable social protection systems' into 'modern social protection systems that support those in need and provide incentives for labour market integration'. EMCO and SPC suggested significant amendments to this formulation, proposing 'adequate and sustainable social protection systems that contribute effectively and efficiently throughout the lifecycle both to social inclusion and labor market integration' (SPC and EMCO 2015: 2). The Council adopted this revision, thus agreeing to add a lifecycle approach to social security. In its explanation, the Council (2015a) argued that it is inappropriate to limit social protection to those in need. Rather, the objective should be to have comprehensive social protection for all citizens. Moreover, social protection systems should ensure an adequate level of social protection for the population more broadly and perform a preventative function. The Council argued that men and women face various types of risks throughout the life course. Moreover, risks vary from one cycle of life to another, meaning that there is no age where risks are absent and where social protection is not needed. It also referred to the EPSCO Council conclusions of 9 March 2015, which endorsed key messages of the SPC (2015), emphasizing the need for a proper social dimension of the EU, in order to recover from the crisis. Reform strategies should underpin inclusive economic growth by adequate and sustainable social protection systems. The amendments to the flexicurity elements followed from such considerations.

These 2015 EU policy documents demonstrate that the flexicurity concept is indeed subject to change, yet not necessarily towards more flexibility. Rather, the changing definition supports claims of a progressive 'socialization' of the European semester (Zeitlin and Vanhercke THIS ISSUE). The changes could thus be seen as more supportive of the norms constituting the ESM, while also the notion of the ESM as a European project plays a role: adapting the ESM to fit the needs of modern labor markets, for instance including a life cycle approach to the social security element of flexicurity. The question how CSRs have addressed flexicurity will be answered in the next section.

## Flexibility and security in the CSRs

In 2009, 12 countries received a CSR using the term 'flexicurity'. For instance, the CSR to Germany recommended to

> proceed with planned measures that enhance the efficiency and effectiveness of job placement services and promote the integration of the low-skilled and long-term unemployed into the labour market through a flexicurity approach which combines better access to qualifications with improved incentives to work. (European Commission 2009: 16)

The year 2009 was also the last in which the term flexicurity appeared in a CSR to a specific country. In 2016 flexicurity became part of the Euro area CSRs. Flexicurity elements were also addressed in 2009, mostly referring to LLL. This strong attention to lifelong learning has shifted in later years to social security and ALMP (Online Appendix, figure 1).

The fact that flexicurity elements have frequently been part of CSRs means that there has been consistent attention to each of the elements, although after 2009 the term itself was no longer used in the CSRs to specific countries. While the latter supports the thesis of the demise of the concept, its reappearance in the euro area CSRs of 2016 indicates a careful come-back. Also the CSRs' consistent attention to all four flexicurity elements, including at the peak of the crisis, suggests that flexicurity has survived at least partially. The greatest attention to all four flexicurity elements came in 2013. This peak relates to the increasing precision of the CSRs after 2009, as the Commission started including more and more policy areas and policy reforms into its CSRs. The subsequent lower attention to flexicurity elements in 2015 relates to the decision of the Juncker Commission to focus CSRs on key priorities only. It has limited the number of CSRs as well as narrowed down the number of policy areas per CSR (Zeitlin and Vanhercke THIS ISSUE). Overall, all four flexicurity elements have received relatively consistent attention over the years, with social security clearly getting the most attention, whereas contractual arrangements have received the least attention.

Some countries only received recommendations on one or two flexicurity elements. In 2009, 2011, 2013 and 2015 together, there were 24 cases in which countries received CSRs that covered all four flexicurity elements. This pattern suggests that the separate reform recommendations at times covered a large part of the flexicurity concept, which could result in integrative or balanced reform approaches. Obviously, the validity of such conclusion depends on the specific content of the CSRs, which might not support the balanced 'spirit' of flexicurity. Therefore, in the Online Appendix figure 2 shows a more detailed content analysis. The Commission's definition of the four flexicurity elements contains both policy messages that support social goals and policy suggestions that support flexibility or economic values. For instance, the growing attention to social security does not necessarily mean more focus on developing social policies, but rather relates to the numerous recommendations to make pension systems more sustainable. This occurred 47 times during the years studied, often involving recommendations to increase the pension age. Obviously, such measures are debatable and sometimes seen as a way to dismantle the social security of older workers and pensioners. Thus, one could question to what extent their inclusion reflects a 'security' element of flexicurity. A counter-argument could be that a sustainable pension system improves intergenerational solidarity, which could then support the long-term security of younger generations. Again, only pension CSRs have been included in the calculations that aimed to make pension systems more sustainable. Apart from these 47 references to pension reforms, the social-security component includes 12 suggestions on improving child-care facilities and 21 on other forms of social security, including suggestions to improve social transfers. These latter recommendations support social-security facilities over the life course, for instance in a part of the second CSR to Estonia in 2015: 'Ensure high-quality social services and availability of child-care services at local level' (Council 2015b: 41). Thus, social security addresses the security component of flexicurity, at least partially, but at times also includes fiscal concerns.

Contractual arrangements are another broadly defined flexicurity element. This has begun to include job quality and good labor market transitions since 2015. One of the critiques of the flexicurity concept has been its drive for greater flexibility on the labor market, for instance advising governments to lower EPL. Figure 2 shows, however, that within the CSRs a wider range of contractual arrangement issues is addressed: labor law, the reduction of labor-market segmentation, including calls for improve transitions into stable jobs and fighting the shadow economy. The latter two suggestions may be viewed as supporting the social or protective aspect of labor law rather than stimulating flexibility. Amending labor law has been associated more often with meeting employers' demands, and includes in this study suggestions to lower EPL, suggestions to make labor law more flexible so as to make better use of fixed-term contracts, as well as recommendations to install a new labor law package, monitor effects of recent labor law reforms and revise contractual arrangements. Breaking down the variable of contractual arrangements means that the number of observations goes up, as some countries have received more than one suggestion about contractual arrangements in a given year.

Overall, EPL changes received the most attention in 2009, after which it has been mentioned only three times in 2011 and in 2013, while only being part of one CSR in 2015. Reducing segmentation has received more stable attention over time, being mentioned four or three times in the years explored. Tackling undeclared work shows a more oscillating trend, being mentioned most often in 2013, whereas in 2015 it was still mentioned two times. Thus, while there was attention to greater flexibility, especially in the early crisis years, attention has also been paid to the social aspects of contractual arrangements. It indicates that the European Semester's balancing of social and economic goals is dynamic, meaning also that the European Semester is able to adapt to new challenges. Figures 1 and 2 (in the Online Appendix) indirectly also show that the European Semester still tailors its CSRs to specific country challenges. The next section presents the second-stage analysis, dealing with the trend of increasing or reducing attention to (elements of) flexicurity.

## *Dynamics: changing attention to flexibility and security*

In 2009, 23 member states received CSRs. Four member states (Denmark, Finland, Luxembourg and Sweden) did not receive a CSR. Moreover, Ireland did receive CSRs, yet neither referring to flexicurity nor to one of its components. Overall 12 countries received a CSR with explicit reference to the flexicurity concept (BE, BG, CZ, FR, DE, EL, IT, LV, NL, PL, PT, SL).[1] The most frequently mentioned flexicurity element was that of developing LLL. For each flexicurity aspect, the benchmark year 2009 hypothesizes whether or not a flexicurity element will be addressed in subsequent years. Data show that after 2009, there has been growing attention to the separate elements of flexicurity: there are 87 observations of increasing attention and 64 observations of stable attention (not in figure). There are only 43 cases of reduced attention to a specific flexicurity element in CSRs. These trends underline the adaptability of the European Semester goals and also demonstrate that countries do not necessarily receive the same policy messages each year. Consistent with findings in former sections, interest has grown in social security, especially in countries that did not receive a CSR on flexicurity in 2009. Getting reduced or increased attention to a given flexicurity element strongly depends on the country under scrutiny. Germany, Belgium and Spain, for example, show quite different trends, ranging from a constant attention or the constant absence of attention to a certain topic in the CSRs to what comes across as a quite random inclusion of a topic, alternating from year to year. For example, whereas the CSRs for Belgium conform to the hypothesis for contractual arrangements (no CSRs in all years), lifelong learning was not mentioned in 2009 and 2011, but has become an item in the 2013 and 2015 CSRs. Conversely, ALMP has ceased to be an issue in Belgium in 2015. Social security develops along yet another trend, not being a CSR item in 2009, while receiving continuous attention in later years. For Germany, based on the 2009 CSRs, the expectation was that ALMP would be an issue for later CSRs, yet this has only been the case in 2013. Conversely, contractual arrangements were no issue in 2009 and 2011, yet have become part of a CSR in 2013 and 2015. For Spain, LLL only forms part of a CSR every once in a while, but shows no consistent pattern. It demonstrates that the European Semester contains many different dynamics, and that a linear reasoning of it containing uniform and constant policy messages is not supported by the data employed in this study.

## Conclusion

This paper answers the question if and how the flexicurity concept still plays a role within the European Semester. The EU's crisis emphasis on austerity measures and structural reforms might be thought to have reduced attention to the 'security' component of flexicurity, thus leading to a demise of the concept. Looking at the goals of the Lisbon Strategy and the European Semester between 2007 and 2016, the conclusion is that whereas the flexicurity concept seemed to receive less attention through 2013, the term has been used more frequently in the 2015 EU policy documents. Comparing the CSRs of 2009, 2011, 2013 and 2015, the term flexicurity was explicitly used in the 2009 recommendations to specific countries and in the 2016 Euro area recommendations only. However, between 2011 and 2015, the CSRs address the four flexicurity elements separately. They do so rather frequently, also at the peak of the crisis. This finding suggests that the European Semester has paid constant attention to all flexicurity elements, whether security-supporting or flexibility-supporting. A first answer to the research question is thus that flexicurity still plays a role within the European Semester. To judge how the concept played a role, the paper related the flexicurity concept to the four conceptualisations of the ESM. The first two conceptualisations take a relatively static approach, looking at certain norms that serve as a foundation of the ESM and its reflections in certain ideal-typical models. This is similar to some of flexicurity's elements, for instance those advocating the importance of social security, whereas the Danish and Dutch flexicurity models served as ideal types. However, the changing definition of the EU's flexicurity concept as well as its deliberate positioning in the context of maintaining the ESM while responding to fundamental challenges might also resemble the conceptualisations of the ESM as a European project and as a political project (Jepsen and Serrano Pascual 2005). Compared to 2007, the EU definition of flexicurity has undergone some changes, giving more attention to the social aspects of flexicurity policies. For instance, contractual arrangements, which were a much contested aspect during the development of the EU's flexicurity concept around 2007, now include more consideration of the negative aspects of labor market segmentation and moreover support job quality and smooth labor market transitions. The social security element has been strengthened by adding a life-cycle approach and by paying attention to social inclusion.

Within the CSRs, we do see evolutions in the popularity of certain flexicurity elements. This pattern seems dependent on the country receiving the CSRs as well as on the year of scrutiny. One relevant change is the increasing number of flexicurity-related CSRs in 2011 and 2013, which corresponds to the overall expansion in the number of CSRs in those years. Conversely, in 2015 the number of CSRs decreased, and refocused on policy priorities. This change has led especially to reduced attention to contractual arrangements and lifelong learning. Social security in particular has received much greater attention since 2009, much but not all of which reflects CSRs on increasing the sustainability of pension systems. Other social security CSRs requested certain member states to improve social transfers or childcare facilities. CSRs on contractual arrangements at times include a flexibility-enhancing recommendation, especially in the first years of the crisis. However, security-enhancing suggestions also form part of the European Semester, including CSRs on reducing labor market segmentation and improving transitions into stable jobs. However, the evolution of the CSRs shows no clear overall pattern. In some years and in some countries the CSRs appear to have been more biased towards flexibility and austerity than in others. Identifying how the CSRs complement existing national policies, and whether these jointly lead to balanced flexicurity practices at the national level, lies beyond the scope of the data. However, based on key policy documents of the European Semester, combined with analyses of the CSRs, the analysis supports a dynamic view of flexicurity which should assist to cope with new social and economic challenges. Moreover, the changes in the definition of flexicurity might reflect to some extent the changing political preferences, for instance the installation of a new Commission that developed an agenda to better mind the social dimension.

Thus, it seems that the flexicurity concept is still part of the EU policy agenda, and claims of a demise of the concept should at least be nuanced. The concept has been redefined and pays greater attention to social concerns. Relating views on flexicurity to the different conceptualisations of the ESM, flexicurity may be seen as part of a European project and perhaps even a political project; however, its redefinition feeds into norms and institutions as well. The new definition reemphasizes the relevance of certain social concerns that were already part of the old flexicurity definition, yet also brings new social concerns to the fore. The redefinition of flexicurity moreover illustrates the adaptability of the European Semester. Looking at the variety in CSRs across countries, the European Semester seems to combine this adaptability with a tailor-made approach to countries. In addition, a policy message to a country might change over time. Jointly, these assets open up space for the European Semester to continue to find an appropriate balance between social and economic goals.

## Note

1. BE = Belgium, BG = Bulgaria, CZ = Czech Republic, DE = Germany, EL = Greece, ES = Spain, FR = France, IT = Italy, LT = Lithuania, LV = Latvia, NL = Netherlands, PL = Poland, PT = Portugal, RO = Romania, SK = Slovakia, SL = Slovenia.

## Disclosure statement

No potential conflict of interest was reported by the author.

## References

Andersen, T.M. (2012) 'A flexicurity labour market in the great recession: the case of Denmark', *De Economist* 160(2): 117–40.

Auer, P. (2010) 'What's in a name? The rise (and fall?) of flexicurity', *Journal of Industrial Relations* 52(3): 371–86.

Barbier, J.C. (2015) '*Aktivering, flexicurity*, the surface europeanization of employment?' *Cuadernos de Relaciones Laborales* 33(1): 357–95.

Barnard, C. (2014) 'EU employment law and the European social model: the past, the present and the future', *Current Legal Problems* 67: 199–237.

Bekker, S. (2016) 'Is there flexibility in the European Semester process?', *SIEPS paper No. 2016:1*, Stockholm: SIEPS.

Bekker, S. (2012) *Flexicurity: the Emergence of a European Concept*, Antwerp: Intersentia.

Bolton, S., Laaser, K., Mcguire, D. (2016) 'Quality work and the moral economy of european employment Policy', *JCMS: Journal of Common Market Studies* 54(3): 583–98.

Bredgaard, T., Larsen, F. and Madsen, P.K. (2008) 'Flexicurity: in pursuit of a moving target', *European Journal of Social Security* 10(4): 305–23.

Burroni, L. and Keune, M. (2011) 'Flexicurity: a conceptual critique', *European Journal of Industrial Relations* 17(1): 75–91.

Chung, H. (2012) 'Measuring flexicurity: precautionary notes, a new framework, and an empirical example', *Social Indicators Research* 106(1): 153–71.

Clauwaert, S. and Schömann, I. (2012) 'The crisis and national labour law reforms: a mapping exercise', *ETUI Working Papers No. 2012:4*, Brussels: ETUI.

Council of the European Union (2007) 'Towards common principles of flexicurity - Council conclusions', *Council Document No.16201/07*, 6 December, Brussels: Council of the European Union, available at http://register.consilium.europa.eu/doc/srv?l=EN&f=ST%2016201%202007%20INIT (accessed July 2016).

Council of the European Union (2015a) 'Document from the Permanent Representatives Committee (Part 1) to the Council on the recommendation for a Council recommendation on the economic policy of the euro area', *Council Document No. 14860/15 1 REV 1*, 3 December, Brussels: Council of the European Union, available at http://data.consilium.europa.eu/doc/document/ST-14860-2015-ADD-1-REV-1/en/pdf (accessed July 2016).

Council of the European Union (2015b) 'Council Recommendation of 14 July 2015 on the 2015 National Reform Programme of Estonia and delivering a Council opinion on the 2015 Stability Programme of Estonia', *Council Document No. 2015/C 272/11*, 18 August, Brussels: Council of the European Union, available at http://ec.europa.eu/europe2020/pdf/csr2015/csr2015_council_estonia_en.pdf (accessed July 2016).

European Commission (1997) 'Partnership for a new organization of work; Green Paper', *COM(97)128 Final*, 22 November, Brussels: Commission of the European Communities, available at http://eur-lex.europa.eu/legal-content/EN/TXT/?uri=CELEX%3A52006DC0708 (accessed July 2016).

European Commission (2009) 'Recommendation for a Council recommendation on the 2009 up-date of the broad guidelines for the economic policies of the Member States and the Community and on the implementation of Member States' employment policies', *COM(2009) 34/2*, Brussels: Commission of the European Communities.

European Commission (2013) 'Flexicurity in Europe, administrative agreements', *JCR Number 31962-2010-11 NFP ISP-FLEXICURITY 2 Final report*, Brussels: European Union, available at http://ec.europa.eu/social/BlobServlet?docId=10227&langId=en (accessed July 2016).

European Commission (2015a) 'Communication from the Commission on steps towards completing Economic and Monetary Union', *COM(2015) 600 Final*, 21 October, Brussels: Commission of the European Communities, available at http://eur-lex.europa.eu/legal-content/EN/TXT/?uri=CELEX%3A52015DC0600 (accessed July 2016).

European Commission (2015b) 'Annual Growth Survey 2016: strengthening the recovery and fostering convergence', *COM(2015) 690 Final*, 26 November, Brussels: Commission of the European Communities, available at http://eur-lex.europa.eu/legal-content/en/TXT/?uri=CELEX%3A52015DC0690 (accessed July 2016).

European Commission (2015c) 'Recommendation for a Council recommendation on the economic policy of the euro area', *COM(2015) 692 Final*, 26 November, Brussels: Commission of the European Communities, available at http://eur-lex.europa.eu/legal-content/EN/TXT/?uri=CELEX%3A52015DC0692 (accessed July 2016).

Gwiazda, A. (2011) 'The europeanization of flexicurity: the Lisbon strategy's impact on employment policies in Italy and Poland', *Journal of European Public Policy* 18(4): 546–65.

Hastings, T. and Heyes, J. (2016) 'Farewell to flexicurity? austerity and labour policies in the european Union', *Economic and Industrial Democracy*, First Published 2 March, doi:10.1177/0143831X16633756.

Hemerijck, A. (2012) *Changing Welfare States*, Oxford: Oxford University Press.

Hemerijck, A. (2002) 'The self-transformation of the European social model(s)', in G. Esping-Andersen (ed.), *Why we Need a New Welfare State*, Oxford: Oxford University Press, pp. 173–214.

Hermann, C. (2014) 'Crisis, structural reform and the dismantling of the european social model(s)', *Economic and Industrial Democracy*, First Published 17 December, doi:10.1177/0143831X14555708.

Heyes, J. (2013) 'Flexicurity in crisis: European labour market policies in a time of austerity', *European Journal of Industrial Relations* 19(1): 71–86.

Heyes, J. (2011) 'Flexicurity, employment protection and the jobs crisis', *Work, Employment and Society* 25(4): 642–57.

Jepsen, M. and Serrano, A. (2005) 'The European social model: an exercise in deconstruction', *Journal of European Social Policy* 15(3): 231–45.

Johnson, B.D., Dunlap, E. and Benoit, E. (2010) 'Structured qualitative research: organizing "mountains of words" for data analysis, both qualitative and quantitative', *Substance Use & Misuse* 45(5): 648–70.

Keune, M. and Serrano, A. (2014) *Deconstructing Flexicurity and Developing Alternative Approaches: Towards new Concepts and Approaches for Employment and Social Policy*, London: Routledge.

Keune, M. and Jepsen, M. (2007) 'Not balanced and hardly new: the european commission's quest for flexicurity', in H. Jørgensen P.K. Madsen (eds), *Flexicurity and Beyond. Finding a new Agenda for the European Social Model*, Copenhagen: DJØF Publishing, pp. 189–214.

Lopez, J., de le Court, A. and Canalda, S. (2014) 'Breaking the equilibrium between flexibility and security: flexiprecarity as the spanish version of the model', *European Labour Law Journal* 5: 18–42.

Madsen, P.K. (2013) '"Shelter from the storm?"- danish flexicurity and the crisis', *IZA Journal of European Labor Studies* 2(6): 1–19.

Madsen, P.K. (2008) 'The danish road to 'flexicurity': where are we compared to others? and how did we get there?', in R. Muffels (ed.), *Flexibility and Employment Security in Europe: Labour Markets in Transition*, Cheltenham: Edward Elgar, pp. 341–62.

Mailand, M. (2010) 'The common European flexicurity principles: how a fragile consensus was reached', *European Journal of Industrial Relations* 16(3): 241–57.

Muffels, R. and Wilthagen, T. (2013) 'Flexicurity: a new paradigm for the analysis of labor markets and policies challenging the trade-off between flexibility and security', *Sociology Compass* 7(2): 111–22.

SPC (2015) 'Social Europe: aiming for inclusive growth 2014 annual report of the SPC on the social situation in the EU', *SOC 78, 6194/15*, 24 February 2015, Brussels, available at http://register.consilium.europa.eu/doc/srv?l=EN&f=ST%206194%202015%20INIT (accessed December 2016).

SPC and EMCO (2015) 'Letter by the Chairs to the Ministers' Date 30 November 2015.

Taylor, C. and Gibbs, G.R. (2010) 'How and what to code', *Online QDA Web Site*, available at onlineqda.hud.ac.uk/Intro_QDA/how_what_to_code.php (accessed March 2016).

Tsarouhas, D. and S. Ladi (2013) 'Globalisation and/or europeanisation? The case of flexicurity', *New Political Economy* 18(4): 480–502.

Veille, P. and Bovin J.M. (2008) 'Putting security at the heart of the European social pact – proposals to make flexicurity more balanced', *Transfer: European Review of Labour and Research* 14(3): 419–33.

Viebrock, E., and Clasen, J. (2009) 'Flexicurity and welfare reform: a review', *Socio-Economic Review* 7(2): 305–31.

White, M.D. and March, E.E. (2006) 'Content analysis: a flexible methodology', *Library Trends* 55: 22–45.

Wilthagen, T. and Tros, F. (2004) 'The concept of 'flexicurity': a new approach to regulating employment and labour markets', *Transfer: European Review of Labour and Research* 10(2): 166–86.

Woolfson, C. and Sommers, J. (2016) 'Austerity and the demise of social Europe: the baltic model versus the European social model', *Globalizations*, 13(1): 78–93.

Jonathan Zeitlin & Bart Vanhercke (2017) Socializing the European Semester: EU social and economic policy co-ordination in crisis and beyond, Journal of European Public Policy, 25:2, 149–174, DOI: 10.1080/13501763.2017.1363269

# Deciding on the European Semester: the European Council, the Council and the enduring asymmetry between economic and social policy issues

Adina Maricut and Uwe Puetter

**ABSTRACT**

This contribution investigates the asymmetrical relationship between economic and social aspects under the European Semester by looking at the roles of the European Council and the Council between 2010 and 2016. Drawing on the theories of deliberative and new intergovernmentalism, this asymmetry is associated with an uneven evolution of the co-ordination infrastructure, notably the varying degree to which key policy issues are subject to informal policy dialogue. Not only are finance ministers better placed to conduct policy dialogue, they also control the European Semester policy priorities more effectively than their colleagues in the Employment, Social Policy, Health and Consumer Affairs Council (EPSCO). Finance ministers also are more closely linked to discussions at the highest political level, the European Council. Social affairs committees and the Commission managed to gain a greater role at the expert level and to integrate more social issues into policy recommendations. Yet, these successes are not matched by higher level political endorsement.

## Introduction

This contribution investigates the roles of the European Council and Council in relation to the European Union's (EU) central socioeconomic governance framework – the European Semester. The European Semester is seen to follow the tradition of the two variants of the Lisbon process and its open method of co-ordination (OMC) approach. It is a vehicle for the horizontal and vertical co-ordination of Economic and Monetary Union (EMU) economic governance, employment policies and areas of social policy in which the EU has no legislative competences. Two closely related questions guide the research behind this contribution. First, what are the institutional mechanisms which help to

Supplemental data for this article can be accessed https://doi.org/10.1080/13501763.2017.1363271.

generate consensus among member state representatives and the Commission on the European Semester? Second, is there evidence for a persisting asymmetry between the economic and social policy domains with more emphasis being given to the former in the co-ordination process?

Building on recent theoretical contributions on deliberative and new intergovernmentalism (Bickerton *et al.* 2015a, 2015b; Puetter 2012, 2014), the viability of the European Semester as a co-ordination device is understood as being dependent on the generation of self-commitment to EU-level guidelines and to implementation among the most senior decision-makers at the national and EU levels. The analysis of the years immediately before the launch of the European Semester as well as thereafter, a period which saw a series of institutional and policy responses to the euro crisis, reveals that the European Semester suffers from an asymmetry in favour of finance ministers, on the one hand, at the expense of employment and social affairs ministers, on the other hand. Moreover, oversight on the part of the European Council is lacking, despite the initiating role the heads played in setting up the co-ordination framework and the annual routine of so-called Spring European Council meetings. There is evidence that policy dialogue related to the European Semester intensified across institutional settings, yet euro crisis management, the oversight of financial assistance programmes and excessive deficits deviate attention from the European Semester as a broader socioeconomic governance device. Whether the European Semester constitutes a framework within which concerns about sound public finances and broader social policy objectives can be considered in relation to each other or whether economic governance is strengthened at the expense of social issues remained a concern for many analysts (Costamagna 2013), though there is evidence that social and employment policy issues have received greater attention in the context of country-specific recommendations (CSRs) in the aftermath of the peak period of euro crisis management (Bekker 2015; Zeitlin and Vanhercke 2014). However, the European Semester is also seen to receive only lukewarm political support by member states, albeit it remains without alternatives (Darvas and Leandro 2015). With its focus on lead EU institutional actors, this contribution offers a complementary perspective. It points to the relevance of high-level policy deliberation which may crucially influence how other core components, such as written and publicly stated policy recommendations and procedural requirements, commit member states to co-ordinated policies.

The contribution examines agenda data from European Council, Council and Eurogroup conclusions and press statements, as well as media reports. Interviews with senior officials who are in charge of preparing the meetings of the relevant forums substantiate information on working practices and inter-institutional relations. The analysis unfolds as follows. First, the applicability of deliberative and new intergovernmentalism as analytical frameworks for studying post-Maastricht EU policy co-ordination is discussed in relation to the European Semester. Second, the analysis turns to the role of the European Council as the initiator of the European Semester framework and as an oversight institution. Third, the institutional trajectories and working practices of the three main groupings of ministers – the Eurogroup as well as the Economic and Financial Affairs Council (ECOFIN) and the Employment, Social Policy, Health and Consumer Affairs Council (EPSCO) – are identified. Finally, the analysis turns to what is referred to as the bureaucratization of the European Semester, namely the central roles of the Commission and senior expert committees in the co-ordination process.

## Deliberative and new intergovernmentalism and the European Semester

Students of the original Lisbon OMCs noted the reliance of the new governance framework on Council and European Council decision-making early on (Borrás and Jacobsson 2004: 188; 198; 200). Notably the European Council empowered itself in the context of the Lisbon process. Policy initiative increasingly came from member states. The Commission, albeit it played a central role in providing expertise and surveillance, relied on political backing from ministers and the European Council. The European Semester is not different in this regard. This contribution follows the analytical frameworks of deliberative and new intergovernmentalism (Bickerton *et al.* 2015a, 2015b; Puetter 2012, 2014), which embed the centrality of the European Council and Council in EU policy-making into a broader discussion about contemporary EU governance and formulate specific hypotheses on institutional trajectories, roles and inter-institutional relations. Two hypotheses are relevant for this contribution: firstly, deliberation and consensus have become the guiding norms at *all* levels of decision-making. Consensus generation is not restricted to the level of expert committees but is required at the highest political level, as policy issues have repercussions for domestic politics. It is thus important to complement existing research on committees with a focus on the interplay of the different levels of decision-making. Only in areas where these processes are closely intertwined new intergovernmentalism would expect wider political impact. Secondly, member states are reluctant to delegate decision-making authority to supranational institutions, notably the Commission, which in turn is not hard-wired to seek ever-closer union according to the classic community method. The key argument is that institutional change within the European Council and the Council in the post-Maastricht period is marked by a series of attempts at enhancing the consensus generation capacity of high-level intergovernmental forums in areas outside the classic community method – namely economic governance, foreign policy, employment and social affairs. Collective EU action in these areas is essentially constituted by constantly renewed political agreement among national governments and the Commission. Even written policy guidelines rely on continuing political support on the part of member states because the Commission lacks unilateral enforcement powers. The trajectory of the Stability and Growth Pact since the late 1990s is perhaps the most blatant illustration of this dilemma, which is also inherent to the European Semester. The emphasis on consensus is not trivial, as consensus generation is a complex and iterative process. It is not sufficient to agree on common rules, but it matters that senior political representatives of the member states remind themselves of the need for common action and continue to support policy paths against the background of constant contestation. The European Semester implies deep interferences with domestic policy paths. It is unlikely to gain clout without strong political endorsement throughout the annual cycle. The euro crisis revealed the politicization of EU economic governance. This aspect is unlikely to go away, as the co-ordination process has become more ambitious.

As forums for collective decision-making, the European Council and the Council are in principle well positioned to address this dilemma. Yet, how they do this requires closer inspection. Deliberative intergovernmentalism as a theory of micro-level institutional change is well placed to investigate differences in institutional performance when it comes to studying different decision-making settings. The key argument behind deliberative intergovernmentalism is that consensus is not a foregone conclusion, but needs to be engineered. Institutional practices and working methods vary when it comes to their potential to generate consensus and maintain it over a longer period of time and in relation to difficult controversies around the application of common rules. Deliberative intergovernmentalism considers the Council to be a heterogeneous environment in which policy co-ordination and legislative decision-making coexist. Co-ordination in the field of socioeconomic governance requires consensus generation well beyond the instance of rule setting, whereas the latter marks the successful conclusion of legislative decision-making. Since the rollout of a broader EU policy co-ordination agenda in the fields of socioeconomic governance and foreign and security policy by the end of the 1990s, the EU's main forums for intergovernmental decision-making have witnessed important changes to their working methods, which mark the shift away from legislative decision-making. Yet, deliberative intergovernmentalism holds that such processes of institutional adjustment are unevenly pronounced.

Puetter (2014: 61–5) identifies the indicators for policy deliberation as being more frequent meetings in longer sessions, as well as informal and face-to-face debates with a reduced number of participants who make decisions under conditions of uncertainty. The argument is that informal deliberations on policy co-ordination in the new areas of EU activity have become routinized. This type of routine policy co-ordination is shown to play an important role in forums such as the Eurogroup, the ECOFIN Council, the Foreign Affairs Council and, indeed, the European Council itself. Can such focus on micro-level institutional change help to advance the discussion about the asymmetry between economic and social issues within the European Semester? The current literature offers two opposing interpretations of this asymmetry. One side argues that budgetary austerity and fiscal discipline have largely removed social concerns from current policy initiatives, as EU institutions effectively promoted 'lower levels of social assistance and employment protection' (Crespy and Menz 2015: 8). The point here is that structural reforms systematically undermine the so-called European Social Model (Hermann 2017; Pochet and Degryse 2012) through the support, for example, of a growth-friendly approach to taxation and social security which disregards national variations (Dawson 2015: 985). Some authors contend that euro crisis management in fact amplified an already declining trend to propose social policy at the EU level. This trend is also associated with the election of liberal and conservative governments starting in the mid-2000s (Graziano and Hartlapp 2015: 13). In contrast, the alternative interpretation finds a 'progressive "socialisation" of the European Semester' as a result of the empowerment of institutional actors who represent social and employment policies, notably the EPSCO Council and the European Commission's Directorate-General for Employment, Social Affairs and Inclusion (DG EMPL) (Vanhercke *et al.* 2015; Zeitlin and Vanhercke 2014). This perspective gives credit to preparatory bodies in particular – the Employment Committee (EMCO) and the Social Protection Committee (SPC) – for placing social objectives in the CSRs. Zeitlin and Vanhercke (2014) further argue that the socialization of the European Semester can be understood when examined over time 'as the product of strategic agency, reflexive learning and creative adaptation by EU social and employment policy actors' to a new institutional context.

Deliberative intergovernmentalism adds to this debate by providing evidence for asymmetrical institutional trajectories inside the Council, while at the same time appreciating that there is room for socially minded actors within the Council and the relevant expert committees to increase their influence in the European Semester process. Puetter's previous research finds that the institutional environment in economic governance is one which is most likely to foster the occurrence of consensus generation among key political actors. In particular, the Eurogroup is identified as 'the most developed infrastructure for informal policy dialogue' in the EU (Puetter 2014: 156). The work of finance ministers is also seen to be closely intertwined with the Economic and Financial Committee (EFC) and its Eurogroup Working Group (EWG) and Alternates (*ibid.*: 192–5), and even analytical work from the Economic Policy Committee (EPC) attracts the attention of finance ministers (*ibid.*: 223). Most importantly, finance ministers tend to align themselves with what is best referred to as the Eurogroup working consensus, which is a set of shared policy beliefs and priorities and which ministers advocate successfully in relation other actors (Puetter 2006: 151–6). In contrast, EPSCO is shown to have been dominated before the launch of the European Semester by legislative decision-making, which prevented a more radical transformation towards informal deliberation as observed in the cases of the Eurogroup and the ECOFIN Council. In fact, EPSCO working methods were considered to have failed to provide an institutional environment conducive to successful policy dialogue (*ibid.*: 181–2). This view echoes the findings of a comprehensive study on the EU's socioeconomic policy committees by Jacobsson and Vifell (2007), whose concept of deliberative transnationalism shares a number of similarities with Puetter's deliberative intergovernmentalism. These authors also consider deliberative features to be more pronounced in the EFC and EPC contexts, if compared to EMCO and SPC, because the former are more secretive and closed to outside actors (Jacobsson and Vilfell 2007: 178). Generally, greater transparency is seen to trigger bargaining rather than deliberation (*ibid.*: 183).

To conclude, previous research within the new intergovernmentalism framework provided evidence that high-level policy deliberation shapes key policy choices and empowers the European Council and specific groups of ministers in relation to other EU institutions and individual member states. The question is to what extent these deliberations focus on European Semester issues.

## The European Council

In June 2010, the European Council gave its explicit endorsement to the European Semester framework (European Council 2010a: 5) as an integral part of its initial set of institutional reforms in response to the escalating euro crisis. Endorsing the work of the so-called Van Rompuy Task Force (European Council 2010b), the European Council reacted to the crisis by intensifying and tightening the existing economic policy co-ordination regime rather than opting for a more centralized approach to euro area governance. The following adoption of the six-pack, which regulates the co-ordination process and provides a legal basis for the European Semester, relied on the European Council as main initiator of institutional reform despite Commission activism. The insistence of the European Council on the implementation of a revamped integrated co-ordination and surveillance framework reflects both the expansion of the scope of co-ordination, i.e., the inclusion of a wide range of socioeconomic governance issues, and its intensification, i.e., closer surveillance and enhanced peer pressure. Yet, the priority list of the Van Rompuy Task Force and the European Council conclusions at the time also show the predominance of concerns for fiscal stability.

This response to the crisis is consistent with European Council action in the post-Maastricht period. From 1992 to 2015, economic governance has been the most relevant agenda item, featuring in 104 out of its total 138 meetings (see Diagram 1 in the Online Appendix). While EMU economic governance has been on the agenda almost at each and every single European Council meeting since 1998, the escalation of the euro crisis in 2010 made economic governance issues even more dominant. Puetter (2014: 92–3) quotes qualitative interview data which show that the European Council normally allocates more than half of the time of each meeting to the economic governance portfolio. In contrast, employment and social affairs received less attention, featuring in 61 out of the total of 138 meetings examined for this contribution. There were a few landmark meetings which were dedicated to social matters, such as the Luxembourg European Council in 1997 on employment or the Lisbon European Council in 2000. These meetings underlined the European Council's support for a more integrated co-ordination agenda in relation to EMU economic governance, on the one hand, and social and employment policies, on the other hand. In the context of the Lisbon process, this more integrated approach was reflected in the institutionalization of annual Spring European Council meetings. At these meetings, the heads were supposed to dedicate extra time for discussing socioeconomic governance issues. In practice, the focus of these discussions, however, could vary substantially.

European Council agenda data (see Diagram 1 in Online Appendix) reveal a dramatically reinforced gap in political attention during the peak period of euro crisis management between economic governance, on the one hand, and social and employment affairs, on the other. Starting in 2010, employment and social affairs issues become less prominent on the European Council agenda. In 2011, for example, social issues were absent altogether from the conclusions, as the focus was primarily on immediate responses to the sovereign debt crisis such as financial assistance programs. The predominance of economic governance issues suggests a higher degree of routinization of high-level policy dialogue than with regard to any other policy area. This is an important indicator of an asymmetric institutional development.

Initial European Council endorsement of the European Semester as an integrative co-ordination mechanism is not matched by a close involvement of the heads in the co-ordination process, as it is true for some aspects of economic governance, as for example the provision of financial assistance. Such involvement, where it occurs, remains a formal exercise. European Council endorsements of the policy priorities of the annual European Semester cycle at the spring meetings in March and of the CSRs in June each year have not led so far to more extensive debates on specific issues among the heads (COM1).[1] They typically endorse what the ECOFIN and EPSCO Council formations have already agreed upon, as one official explains: 'The fact that the CSRs are endorsed by the European Council is a ritual' (EUCO). As of May 2016, there was only one CSR which was raised by Belgium at a European Council meeting on a highly politicized domestic issue (EPC). Not only are there no controversial cases discussed, but also general debates on CSRs are no longer of importance to the European Council, as another official explains: 'It has been a few years since CSRs have been raised during European Council meetings' (COUNCIL1). Moreover, another official expects the heads to react to potential future requests to raise CSR-related issues by saying: 'That's not for us, don't come to us, go to your [finance] minister' (EUCO).

With regard to the broader framing of the European Semester as an encompassing framework for EU socioeconomic governance, the role of the first European Council President Herman Van Rompuy is noteworthy. Van Rompuy played a significant role in increasing the profile of social affairs in the originally economic-centred EU response to the crisis. Specifically, Van Rompuy resorted to the unprecedented step of participating directly in the deliberations of the EPSCO Council. Van Rompuy took part in two gatherings of EPSCO (in 2010[2] and 2013[3] respectively), which dealt with the interrelatedness of the economic governance and social and employment policy co-ordination portfolios in the context of the Europe 2020 strategy and the future role of social and employment policy in a reformed EMU. In both cases, Van Rompuy declared his ambition to improve horizontal co-ordination between the two dossiers and the two responsible Council formations – EPSCO and ECOFIN. Van Rompuy himself referred to his February 2013 visit at the EPSCO Council as 'historic'[4] because there was now a direct discussion between the European Council President and ministers.

The situation changed under the succeeding president, Donald Tusk. During his first 18 months in office he did not establish direct connections to EPSCO ministers (COUNCIL2). Tusk is generally 'less interested in economic issues than Van Rompuy' (COUNCIL1) and emphasizes other policy matters such as the energy union or the relations with Russia (EUCO). Indeed, the Presidency of Van Rompuy coincided with the peak period of euro crisis management and was marked by European Council interventions into specific policy decisions. Tusk's cabinet is said to have changed this stance and insists that there 'should be little details discussed, that's not for the European Council', which instead 'is supposed to have a debate on the economic situation in a strategic manner.' (*ibid.*). It is difficult to say whether the lack of attention to social issues, which featured in only two European Council meetings in 2015, and the declining attention to economic aspects more generally, was simply related to developments such as the refugee crisis, terrorist attacks, Ukraine and Brexit, or whether it represented evidence of profound policy change.

## The ECOFIN and EPSCO councils and the Eurogroup

The three configurations of ministers working on EU socioeconomic governance issues are invested to varying degrees in the European Semester. Interviewees report that there is some competition between the ECOFIN Council and the meeting format of euro area finance ministers, the Eurogroup, on the one hand, and EPSCO, on the other hand, regarding their influence in the European Semester. Given the Treaty base of the co-ordination processes, this institutional rivalry is not surprising. The European Semester builds on the basic structures of economic and employment policy co-ordination respectively as enshrined in Title VIII, chapter 1, TFEU, the domain of ECOFIN and the Eurogroup, as far as euro area-specific issues are concerned, and Title IX, TFEU, the domain of the EPSCO Council. Also social affairs, as stipulated under Title X, TFEU, belong to EPSCO, although here the Treaty does not prescribe a single co-ordination mechanism and the situation is more complex, given that EPSCO acts both as a legislator and a co-ordinator of policy issues, depending on whether these are included or exempted from the catalogue of EU legislative competences. According to one interviewee, this double legal basis of the European Semester policy co-ordination process and the lack of EU legislative competences regarding many social policy issues fuels competition between finance ministers and EPSCO ministers. This is especially true for the recent phase of policy co-ordination related to the European Semester (COM3). While during the first decade of the 2000s EPSCO's legislative decision-making agenda was still detectable, member states became, over time, increasingly reluctant to agree on new social policy legislation. This has left EPSCO ministers searching for a new role of their Council formation and, thus, for a strengthened role in the European Semester.

Furthermore, data on the agenda of meetings retrieved from the Council's Register of Documents show that euro area finance ministers met 89 times within the Eurogroup during the six-year period 2010–2015 (see Diagram 2 in the Online Appendix). They attended another 81 meetings of the ECOFIN Council. Thus, euro area finance ministers not only attend the most frequently convened ministerial grouping within the EU – next to the Foreign Affairs Council – but they also have a double affiliation and spend more time together on the same set of policy issues than any other group of senior government representatives. In the same period, labour and social affairs ministers instead came together for 38 EPSCO Council meetings. During the peak period of euro crisis management, the Eurogroup was convened more than once per month and finance ministers from all EU member states, in addition to formal ECOFIN gatherings, met throughout 2010 within the context of the Van Rompuy Task Force, which was vital for establishing the European Semester framework as discussed in the previous section. During that period

EPSCO, in contrast, maintained on average its regular six meetings per year, four formal and two informal ones during each Presidency. These differences in the frequency of ministerial gatherings strikingly reveals the asymmetry between economic governance compared to social and employment policies as regards the role of EU intergovernmental institutional actors.

In relative terms, however, the European Semester was more central to the activities of EPSCO than it was for those of ECOFIN and the Eurogroup. Specifically, European Semester issues featured in about two-thirds of all EPSCO meetings, whereas finance ministers in ECOFIN dealt with this portfolio on average only at every second meeting (see Diagram 2 in the Online Appendix). Yet, this still means that they did so almost twice as often as EPSCO, because finance ministers met far more frequently. The Eurogroup debated European Semester issues on 25 occasions during the six-year period, which is similar to the absolute number of EPSCO meetings during which European Semester issues featured. Yet, Eurogroup debates complement the discussions of all EU finance ministers within ECOFIN and thus add to the time which, at least, euro area finance ministers devote to this subject.

Moreover, it is noteworthy that between 2010 and 2015 finance ministers devoted much attention to a set of institutional issues such as the creation of the European Stability Mechanism (2010), the Fiscal Compact (2012), the adoption of the Six-Pack (2011) and the Two-Pack (2013), the Single Supervisory Mechanism (2013) and the Single Resolution Mechanism (2014). Regular items on the agenda were also the assistance and adjustment programmes (Greece, Ireland, Portugal, Cyprus) and countries in the Excessive Deficit Procedure (EDP). All these issues implied time-consuming consensus-building efforts and received high-level political attention, including from the European Council. Many of these decisions had repercussions on the European Semester, either because they influenced CSRs or because they simply constituted political priorities of utmost importance and urgency which rendered other aspects of the co-ordination process less relevant.

The Eurogroup's key role in crisis management represented a test for its informal working method because pressure on finance ministers to find agreement within a relatively short period of time increased dramatically. Yet, Eurogroup discussions were considered to deliver consensus and frank informal debates from the early stages of crisis management onwards (COUNCIL1). Eurogroup discussions on the European Semester follow the standard practice of informal discussions within the group and take place behind closed doors. Such emphasis on informal debate can also be found in ECOFIN, which saw a revival of its so-called informal breakfast meetings as a key venue for policy dialogue with the beginning of EU crisis management (Interviews H, 7 April 2009, and L, 12 November 2009). European Semester issues are debated behind closed doors within the informal parts of ECOFIN meetings. Unlike the Eurogroup, the ECOFIN and EPSCO Council formations are obliged to have public debates about all legislative issues, which the European Semester is not.

However, the intensity of European Semester debates in ECOFIN declined over time. Ministers spent one to two hours in the first years compared to half an hour in 2015. In the words of an official who is familiar with ECOFIN debates:

> In the beginning, there was more excitement about this [the European Semester], but now everything is agreed by the committees below. [The] EFC endorses decisions without reopening them. ... At ministerial level this isn't an efficient discussion – to discuss the CSRs of 28 member states. What we try to identify are horizontal issues, those are more suitable for discussion. All this has become a bureaucratic routine, it is difficult to motivate ministers about it. (COUNCIL1)

As a result, most issues are dealt with at the committee level. It is rare that finance ministers discuss controversial matters (COM2). As another official puts it: 'Finance ministers debate and agree on Council conclusions, but if the committees have done their job, they just adopt the conclusions' (EPC). Nevertheless, the declining interest in active debate among finance ministers does not imply that they have conceded ground to other institutional actors, as one of the above-quoted officials explains further:

> I can still say that it is a very ECOFIN-centred process. The European Semester started out as a concrete, legal process of macroeconomic coordination. ... My feeling is that the whole process is ECOFIN-led, there's no denying that most issues are economic, or that the social aspects cannot be dissociated from the economic ones. (COUNCIL2)

The reverse image is detectable with regard to European Semester debates within the EPSCO Council. Here, ministers continued to pay more attention to this portfolio from 2010 onwards, yet they find it difficult to compete with finance ministers for influence and to mobilize political support at the highest level. As discussed in the above section on the European Council, except for the visits by the first European Council Herman Van Rompuy, EPSCO ministers rarely get attention for their work from the heads. An official familiar with EPSCO debates sees the European Semester as the central item on the EPSCO agenda:

> These days there's nothing else. The problem is the lack of competence, you cannot impose legislation, there is no common social policy, so the European Semester [i.e., policy coordination] is the best you can get. (COUNCIL2)

In recent years, the Juncker Commission's 'Better regulation agenda' (European Commission 2015) meant less or no legislation for discussion within EPSCO. For a Council formation that used to spend most of its time on legislative decision-making, the lack of legislative proposals brought a need for the reorganization of the meetings. Paradoxically, this motivated ministers to debate European Semester issues in public rather than behind closed doors, as it is normally done with non-legislative items. Typically, debate is guided by a Presidency paper. However, the public meeting format has a negative impact on deliberation. Controversial issues, such as pension reforms, are simply not put on the agenda in order to avoid heated discussions. In the words of the above-quoted official, EPSCO debates on the European Semester tend to get 'relatively sterile, excluding the June one, when CSRs are debated. During this meeting, member states might not necessarily say 'we don't want this CSR', but they will give a reason why this cannot be implemented/achieved at the domestic level.' (*ibid.*).

Another official highlighted that EPSCO cannot compete with the Eurogroup because there is no 'Euro Area EPSCO' and 'economic issues are overwhelmingly stronger in the Council.' (EUCO). However, in 2015 EPSCO decided unilaterally to discuss the euro area CSRs and amended one recommendation, which according to another official made ECOFIN 'furious because there was no coordination [between the Council formations].' (COUNCIL1). In general, EPSCO is trying to strengthen its role in the European Semester, while finance ministers take their lead role for granted and entrust decision-making to the EFC, EWG and EPC as their senior support committees, as the same official explains:

> Indeed, EPSCO has been pushing for something every year and they have managed to become more influential. ... In theory Council formations should be equal, but ECOFIN is clearly above others. (*ibid.*)

## The bureaucratization of the European Semester: senior expert committees and the Commission

The institutionalization of the European Semester has brought about routine involvement by several committees. On the economic side, the European Semester is discussed in the EPC, the EWG with regard to euro area recommendations, and the EFC Alternates' meeting; on the social side, the EMCO and the SPC are in charge. The EFC, as the most senior economic affairs committee, endorses everything decided at lower levels and discusses outstanding issues. The EFC and the EWG are the lead preparatory bodies for ECOFIN and the Eurogroup respectively, and their members usually sit next to their finance ministers in ECOFIN and Eurogroup meetings. The EFC/EWG president is also a close adviser of the European Council President on economic governance issues. The EPC is a less senior expert committee at the disposal of finance ministers, which concentrates on policy guidelines, peer review and analysis. Conversely, the EMCO and the SPC prepare portfolios for EPSCO. Yet, even EMCO, which can be considered to be more senior than the SPC, given its legal basis as the central committee for employment policy co-ordination, cannot claim to have an almost exclusive access to ministers as it is the case for the EFC/EWG duo.

The status of the EFC is further reflected in its relation with Committee of Permanent Representatives (COREPER) II. The ambassadors normally do not open issues coming from the EFC (COM3). Conversely, on the social side, one official familiar with EPSCO committees explained that COREPER I can play an important role, as it considers itself more senior to EMCO and SPC members (COUNCIL1). The official mentioned that COREPER I changed the wording of policy recommendations which were prepared by EMCO and SPC on several occasions. These practices have important repercussions for the policy dialogue among ministers. The committee process on the social side is relatively bureaucratic. The EMCO and the SPC, together with COREPER I and the Commission, deal with most of the substantial issues while direct access to the relevant ministers is more limited than in the case of the EFC/EWG tandem (Interview A, 23 May 2016).

Moreover, the biggest part of the European Semester – the Macroeconomic Imbalance Procedure (MIP) – is dealt with by the EPC, which also follows up on the CSRs drafted by the Commission. The EMCO and the SPC have both strengthened their role in monitoring and assessing social reforms within the Semester, by establishing different indicators such as the Europe 2020 Joint Assessment Framework for monitoring the Employment Guidelines, the Social Protection Performance Monitor, the Employment Performance Monitor, as well as the so-called Social Scoreboard developed in 2014 (Zeitlin and Vanhercke 2014: 37–8). There is huge joint EPC/SPC/EMCO meeting once a year, exclusively on the CSRs. One interviewee explained that in his/her experience the opinion of finance ministries tends to prevail in these situations 'for the simple fact that finance ministers have more power at the domestic level' (COUNCIL1).

In an effort to streamline the European Semester, the new Juncker Commission further strengthened the role of the EPC. The total number of CSRs in the MIP was reduced, including the ones on social issues (*cf.* Vanhercke *et al.* 2015). This meant that CSRs that used to be under the exclusive competence of the EMCO/SPC tandem are now under joint competence of EPC/EMCO or EPC/SPC. As a result, in the 2016 cycle, only 14 out of 152 CSRs were under exclusive EMCO/SPC competence, while the other 26 social CSRs were under joint purview (EPC). Some officials disagree with the inclusion of social issues in the MIP, which is a further indication of a profound asymmetry between different institutional actors: 'This is nonsense, the MIP was created for a purpose and social aspects have no place there, also if we are to consider subsidiarity rules. We should avoid transforming the nature of the procedure, but the Commission wanted to have a more social voice' (EUCO). One of the above-quoted officials believes that while CSRs under the Juncker Commission have become more social in terms of tone and proportion, the EMCO and the SPC are less, rather than more, influential with regard to discussions within the Council (EPC).

Finally, the Commission's role in the European Semester was strengthened. Yet, the Commission is complicit with member states when it comes to the overall approach of closer co-ordination instead of further legislative initiatives. Significant resources were allocated in recent years in relation to the European Semester, especially to DG EMPL, where approximately a third of the staff currently works on various aspects of the process (Interview A, 23 May 2016). The Commission as a whole invested a lot of effort into co-ordinating the European Semester by establishing a so-called 'Core Group' composed of the Secretariat General, DG Economic and Financial Affairs (ECFIN), DG EMPL, and DG Internal Market. A Commission official explained that DG ECFIN, which is paired with the EFC/EWG/EPC trio of committees, has always played quite an important role in the process, although other DGs participate at the same level. The involvement of DG EMPL, which is linked to the work of the EMCO/SPC duo, grew over time, especially since the crisis (COM2). There was definitely more emphasis within the Commission on social aspects, which were merged together with economic aspects in the MIP as a more binding procedural instrument in an attempt to increase compliance by member states (EPC).

Though formally the reverse qualified majority voting procedure has made it very difficult for member states to change CSRs proposed by the Commission, enforcement is another question altogether. A Commission official described that views within the institution are generally negative when it comes to assessing the impact of the European Semester, especially in terms of the human and financial investment made into the decision-making process. After all, member states can send a simple comment to the responsible committee explaining why a CSR cannot be implemented at the domestic level (COM2). There is so much effort invested in the European Semester within the Commission that one official confessed that:

> In the end the CSRs are Council recommendations, even if we [in the Commission] sometimes forget that. (COM3)

## Conclusions

Deliberative intergovernmentalism provides important conceptual access to contemporary developments in the European Semester by understanding the co-ordination framework as an expression of the post-Maastricht integration paradox: member states seek closer integration in order to address undeniable policy interdependencies, but they are reluctant to empower supranational actors. Instead, they prefer collective agreement on co-ordination objectives. This leads to an enhanced quest for consensus, as policy co-ordination is inherently fragile and is not backed up by centralized enforcement mechanisms. Yet, the generation of high-level policy consensus is not trivial. EU socioeconomic governance implies controversial engagement with existing policy paths and has repercussions for domestic politics. Consensus requires institutional engineering, notably an adjustment of working methods so as to enable policy-makers at *all* levels of decision-making, including the most senior representatives of national governments, to engage in frequent, informal, frank and open policy debates. Previous research relating to the period immediately before the European Semester showed that this is the case in settings such as the European Council, the Eurogroup and the ECOFIN Council. The research presented here demonstrates that the European Semester triggered institutional engineering aimed at enhancing the consensus generation capacity at all levels of decision-making. Yet, institutional engineering directed at the European Semester has been incomplete and partially counter-productive. It has been uneven when it comes to comparing different actors. Most importantly, the institutional asymmetry between economic governance actors and social policy actors remains.

The European Council has become the most senior forum for policy dialogue in the field of economic governance. The heads exercised an interventionist role during the euro crisis and have been able to repeatedly forge high-level consensus. Agenda data confirms the argument by deliberative intergovernmentalism that there is highly frequent and extensive discussion related to economic governance issues. The heads also called on multiple occasions for a more integrated socioeconomic governance approach and launched comprehensive processes to this end – the original Lisbon process and the European Semester. The latter is part of an entire set of institutional reforms which were endorsed in the context of the euro crisis. However, the heads have been pressed by other economic governance issues, notably financial assistance programs. This diverted attention away from the European Semester. By the end of the 2010–2015 period investigated in this contribution, the European Council had retreated from a closer engagement with the European Semester. This retreat comes at the expense of social and employment policies, which gradually featured less on the agenda of the heads in comparison to economic issues, and is indicative of an underlying institutional asymmetry.

The Eurogroup and the ECOFIN Council have developed a track record of conducting intensive policy dialogue, and they use informal working methods which facilitate consensus generation. Finance ministers meet very frequently and show the highest engagement with European Semester issues when it comes to the absolute number of meetings during which this portfolio is debated. That they ultimately determine the overall direction of the European Semester process confirms the expectation by deliberative intergovernmentalism. Their position is the most consolidated. Yet, when it comes to overall attention to the European Semester more recently, finance ministers tend to spend less time on this portfolio. Instead they focus consensus-building efforts on pressing political issues, such as excessive deficits and assistance programmes. This, however, does not imply that finance ministers have conceded ground to other actors. Essentially, the EFC/EWG/EPC trio acts as their gatekeeper.

The European Semester has become central to the agenda of EPSCO. This finding echoes Zeitlin and Vanhercke's analyses of the European Semester (Vanhercke *et al.* 2015; Zeitlin and Vanhercke 2014). There have been important changes to the role of the EPSCO Council and its working practices. This again confirms the expectation by deliberative intergovernmentalism. Social and employment affairs ministers seek to level their influence by placing a stronger emphasis on policy deliberation. There is evidence of institutional engineering. They devote more time to co-ordination owing to the lack of legislative work, yet they still lag behind finance ministers. Policy dialogue among EPSCO ministers is constrained by the choice of working methods. The format of public debates runs counter to the idea of frank discussions. Moreover, unlike the ECOFIN/Eurogroup tandem, EPSCO suffers from a disconnect with the European Council. Social issues are thus not debated at all levels of decision-making.

Senior expert committees provide the bureaucratic backbone of European Semester, together with the Commission. However, there is a remarkable disconnect with political decision-makers who thus may feel little ownership in relation to individual CSRs. Senior expert committees are efficient consensus-generating forums. Yet, the roles of the EFC/EWG/EPC trio, on the economic side, and the EMCO/SPC duo, on the social and employment side, are asymmetric. The integration of social provisions into the MIP has rather strengthened the role of the EFC/EWG/EPC trio. There is little doubt about the central role of the Commission in the European Semester. However, this role is in line with the expectations of new intergovernmentalism. The supranational administration retreated from ambitions to have more social policy legislation and reallocated administrative resources in support of co-ordination. The procedural logic of the MIP ultimately refers the Commission back to the powerful ECOFIN/Eurogroup tandem, which can easily overcome the reverse qualified majority threshold, given its track record in consensus decision-making. The frustration of interviewees with how easily governments can circumvent policy guidance is telling.

Thus, deliberative intergovernmentalism can help to better understand the diverging interpretations of the European Semester framework in the literature. There is indeed a socialization of the European Semester to the extent that the Commission and the social committees have made advances in anchoring social issues more firmly in the co-ordination process. There is also institutional engineering regarding EPSCO. Deliberative intergovernmentalism also speaks to arguments that the conditions are not favourable for social actors. The co-ordination framework of those actors who put a greater emphasis on fiscal consolidation and structural reform is by far more developed and their working consensus is the ultimate reference point which they can articulate in relation to lower level actors, the committees, and high-level actors, the European Council. Deliberative intergovernmentalism is mute on the impact of party politics on this asymmetry but rather emphasizes the institutional evolution of co-ordination among finance ministers. These two perspectives are not mutually exclusive. A shift in focus towards social issues is unlikely to be sustainable without direct oversight on part of the European Council and a further reform of EPSCO. Sceptics may invest little hope in the European Council playing the role of a social policy advocate, though. This is ultimately a question of political majorities within the Union. The point here was to reveal the institutional mechanisms can work either as facilitators or obstacles in relation to how individual groups of ministers or the heads may gain influence over the policy process. With regard to possibilities for policy change, the difference in the way the European Council Presidents Van Rompuy and Tusk addressed the socioeconomic governance portfolio may serve as an illustration for how the focus on social policy issues may be enhanced or diminished in the context of the European Semester. Earlier initiatives of the European Council in the field of socioeconomic governance prior to the introduction of the European Semester in the late 1990s and the early 2000s, notably the Luxembourg and Lisbon European Council meetings, illustrate the potential for political momentum being created by the heads.

## Notes

1. COM, COUNCIL, EPC, EUCO indicate interviewee affiliations. For the list of interviews see the Online Appendix.
2. Press release, Belgian Presidency of the Council, 8 July 2010, http://www.eutrio.be/pressrelease/informal-council-epsco-employment-central-new-economic-governance (accessed 2 June 2016).
3. Press release, Irish Presidency of the Council, 28 February 2013, http://eu2013.ie/news/news-items/20130228post-epscodjei/ (accessed 2 June 2016).
4. Agence Europe, 28 February 2013.

## Acknowledgements

The authors would like to thank Jonathan Zeitlin and Amy Verdun as well as the anonymous reviewers for their valuable comments and suggestions.

## Disclosure statement

No potential conflict of interest was reported by the authors.

## References


Bekker, S. (2015) *European socioeconomic governance in action: coordinating social policies in the third European Semester*, OSE Research Paper No. 19, Brussels: European Social Observatory.

Bickerton, C., Hodson, D. and Puetter, U. (2015a) 'The new intergovernmentalism and the study of European integration', in C. Bickerton, D. Hodson, and U. Puetter (eds), *The New Intergovernmentalism: States and Supranational Actors in the Post-Maastricht Era*, Oxford: Oxford University Press, pp. 1–48.

Bickerton, C., Hodson, D. and Puetter, U. (2015b) 'The new intergovernmentalism: European integration in the post-Maastricht era', *Journal of Common Market Studies* 53(4): 703–722.

Borrás, S. and Jacobsson, K. (2004) 'The open method of co-ordination and new governance patterns in the EU', *Journal of European Public Policy* 11(2): 185–208.

Costamagna, F. (2013) 'The European Semester in action: strengthening economic policy coordination while weakening the social dimension?' *LPF Working Paper* (5): 1–25.

Crespy, A. and Menz, G. (2015) 'Introduction: the pursuit of social Europe in the face of crisis', in A. Crespy and G. Menz (eds), *Social Policy and the Euro Crisis: Quo Vadis Social Europe*, London: Palgrave Macmillan UK, pp. 1–23, available at http://link.springer.com/10.1057/9781137473400 (accessed November 2016).

Darvas, Z. and Leandro, Á. (2015) 'The limitations of policy coordination in the euro area under the European Semester', *Bruegel Policy Contribution* (19): 1–29.

Dawson, M. (2015) 'The legal and political accountability structure of "post-crisis" EU economic governance', *Journal of Common Market Studies* 53(5): 976–993.

European Commission (2015) *Press release - Better regulation agenda: questions & answers*, 19 May 2015, available at http://europa.eu/rapid/press-release_MEMO-15-4989_en.htm (accessed June 2016).

European Council (2010a) *European Council 17 June 2010: Conclusions*, available at http://ec.europa.eu/eu2020/pdf/council_conclusion_17_june_en.pdf (accessed February 2016).

European Council (2010b) *Strengthening economic governance in the EU. Report of the task force of the European Council*, available at http://www.consilium.europa.eu/en/press/press-releases/2010/10/pdf/strengthening-economic-governance-in-the-eu-report-of-the-task-force-to-the-european-council/ (accessed February 2016).

Graziano, P. and Hartlapp, M. (2015) 'The end of social Europe? Assessing the role of political and organizational change in the EU political system', conference paper, UACES 45th Annual Conference, Bilbao, 6-9 September 2015, available at http://www.uaces.org/documents/papers/1501/Graziano.pdf (accessed June 2016).

Hermann, C. (2017) 'Crisis, structural reform and the dismantling of the European social model(s)', *Economic and Industrial Democracy* 38(1): 51–68.

Jacobsson, K. and Vifell, Å. (2007) 'Deliberative transnationalism? Analysing the role of committee interaction in soft co-ordination', in I. Linsenmann, C.O. Meyer, and W.T.

Wessels (eds), *Economic Government of the EU: A Balance Sheet of new Modes of Policy Co-ordination*, Houndmills, Basingstoke: Palgrave Macmillan, pp. 163–186, available at http://link.springer.com/chapter/10.1057/9780230625723_9 (accessed November 2016).

Pochet, P. and Degryse, C. (2012) 'The programmed dismantling of the "European social model"', *Intereconomics: Review of European Economic Policy* 47(4): 212–217.

Puetter, U. (2006) *The Eurogroup: How a Secretive Circle of Finance Ministers Shape European Economic Governance*, Manchester: Manchester University Press.

Puetter, U. (2012) 'Europe's deliberative intergovernmentalism: the role of the Council and European Council in EU economic governance', *Journal of European Public Policy* 19(2): 161–178.

Puetter, U. (2014) *The European Council and the Council: New Intergovernmentalism and Institutional Change*, Oxford: Oxford University Press.

Vanhercke, B. and Zeitlin, J., with Zwinkels, A. (2015) *Further socializing the European Semester: Moving forward for the social triple A?*, report for the Luxembourg Parliament and Presidency of the European Union, Brussels: European Social Observatory.

Zeitlin, J. and Vanhercke, B. (2014) *Socializing the European Semester: Economic governance and social policy coordination in Europe 2020*, SIEPS Report 2014:7, Stockholm: Swedish Institute for European Policy Studies.

Zeitlin, J. and Vanhercke, B. (2017) 'Socialising the European Semester: EU social and economic policy coordination in crisis and beyond' doi:10.1080/13501763.2017.1363269.

# Enforcing the European Semester: the politics of asymmetric information in the excessive deficit and macroeconomic imbalance procedures

James D. Savage and David Howarth

**ABSTRACT**

The European Semester is an information-driven surveillance system that relies upon budgetary and economic statistics collected from the European Union's memberstates and analyzed by the European Commission. This is true for both the Excessive Deficit Procedure (EDP) and the Macroeconomic Imbalance Procedure (MIP). This article employs Principal–Agent theory to analyze the politics of asymmetric information in the EDP and MIP. The study explores how the statistical requirements of the Six-Pack have been enforced by the Commission and the Economic and Financial Affairs Council to strengthen the EDP, even as the statistical integrity of the MIP received less protection. The article examines how the misrepresentation of statistics by Spain's Autonomous Community of Valencia provoked the first financial sanction in the history of Economic and Monetary Union, as well as the Commission's unsuccessful efforts to strengthen the reliability of MIP statistics.

## Introduction

The European Semester was created in response to the Greek and Euro crises to strengthen and deepen the fiscal and economic coordination of the European Union (EU). At the center of the Semester is an information-driven surveillance process that relies heavily upon fiscal and economic information collected from the member states and analyzed by the European Commission (Commission). This is true for both the Stability and Growth Pact's (SGP) Excessive Deficit Procedure (EDP) and the Macroeconomic Imbalance Procedure (MIP). The EDP relies on deficit and debt statistics to determine member

This study incorporates interviews conducted with 16 senior Commission officials in the Secretariat-General, ECFIN, Eurostat, and the Cabinet of the Commissioner for Employment, Social Affairs, Skills and Labor Mobility.

state compliance and the application of sanctions. The MIP relies on 11 headline and 28 auxiliary statistical indicators as part of the EU's economic alert mechanism to determine whether to activate In-Depth Reviews and the application of sanctions (Essi and Stiglbauer 2011; Moschella 2014; Zeitlin and Vanhercke 2014). As stated in the Six-Pack, 'The availability of fiscal data is crucial to the proper functioning of the budgetary surveillance framework of the Union', and 'Reliable statistical data is the basis for the surveillance of macroeconomic imbalances' (Council Directive 2011/85/EU; Council Regulation 1174/2011). Both procedures function in the context of asymmetrical information relationships where supranational organizations must obtain statistical information generated by the member states that may ultimately serve as the basis for corrective sanctioning through the EDP and the Excessive Imbalance Procedure (EIP).

Despite the significance of the Semester's asymmetric information for EU economic governance, with few exceptions, little scholarly attention has been paid as to how the rules governing the Semester's procedures for administering these data affect the political relations between EU institutions and the member states (Savage 2005; Schelkle 2009; Mabbett and Schelkle 2014; Gandrud and Hallerberg 2016). This paper addresses this deficiency in the literature by analyzing through a Principal–Agent (PA) framework the politics of asymmetric information in the EDP and MIP. As a result of the Greek and Euro crises, member states agreed to long-standing Commission initiatives to change the information and date gathering requirements of the surveillance process from one characterized by a fire-alarm to a police-patrol system of monitoring. The layering of new rules and administrative practices significantly expanded the scope of economic EU surveillance in the form of the Semester (Chang 2013a; Verdun 2015). In the context of the Semester's extensive information requirements, this paper first explores how the Commission and the Economic and Financial Affairs Council (ECOFIN) required member state compliance with the statistical provisions of the Semester to strengthen the EDP. For the first time in the history of the Economic and Monetary Union (EMU), a member state has been subjected to the ultimate sanction: a financial penalty. This fine was imposed not for a member state's violation of the EDPs deficit and debt thresholds, but for the failure to provide accurate statistical information to the Commission. This paper next examines a similar, but less successful initiative by the Commission to strengthen the accuracy of its MIP statistics. Because of these decisions taken by both principals and agents, in the context of ensuring the credibility of member state statistics the EDP resembles an enhanced police-patrol monitoring system while the MIP resembles the less rigorous fire-alarm approach to surveillance.

Finally, this paper places the politics of EDP/MIP asymmetric information within the context of the current debate over the rise of intergovernmentalism since the onset of the Euro crisis. As anticipated by PA theory, the creation and enforcement of the EU's surveillance procedures reflect the ebb and flow of power relationships between multiple principals and supranational agents that are dynamic and contested over time. Most recently, the member states through the European Council have reasserted their authority over EU economic governance as a result of the Euro crisis (Puetter 2012; Hodson 2013; Bickerton *et al* 2015; Schimmelfennig 2015). The Euro crisis has also witnessed the rise of the European Parliament (EP) as an additional principal in the surveillance process (Dinan 2014; Rittberger 2014). This paper argues that this intergovernmentalist turn occurred even as ECOFIN approved the Commission's entrepreneurial initiatives for enhanced authority over the member states in the effort to control asymmetric information (Ellinas and Suleiman 2011; Chang 2013b; Bauer and Becker 2014a, 2014b; Dehousse 2015; Savage and Verdun 2016). Yet, at the same time, as will be shown here, the member states have withheld approval for the Commission's proposed regulation over the quality of MIP statistics that they view as counter to their interests (da Conceição-Heldt 2016; Bauer and Becker 2016).

## The dynamics of principal–agent theory and asymmetric information

This study employs a PA framework to analyze the surveillance relationships between and among member states and EU institutions, especially the Commission. In PA theory, principals delegate authority and functional tasks to agents because of their organizational capacities and technical competencies. PA relationships may be cooperative, but they are frequently contested and even adversarial. Tensions exist because agents often have their own agendas and organizational imperatives that may result in opportunistic behavior that runs counter to the interests and intent of their principals. This opportunistic behavior often takes the form of agency loss in the form of drift and shirking, where agents pursue their own preferences rather than those of the principals. Agents possess privileged asymmetric information that they may misrepresent or hide from principals to advise their interests (Kiewiet and McCubbins 1991; Miller 2005). Principals respond to the presence of this asymmetric information asymmetry through monitoring and sanctioning. Classic PA theory expresses a clear preference for the monitoring system that principals should employ to control their agents. The strongest expression of this is found in the difference between 'police-patrol' and 'fire-alarm' surveillance. PA theorists reason that decentralized fire-alarm systems produce greater political benefits for principals than centralized police-patrol systems. Where police-patrol systems require administratively burdensome and costly direct oversight by principals of their agents, fire-alarm systems rely upon constituents and vested interests to complain, or sound the alarm, about dysfunctional, unresponsive agents. Although monitoring systems often include elements of the two methods of surveillance, PA theorists argue that surveillance regimes that 'predominantly' employ fire-alarm systems are more politically effective in controlling agents than police-patrol systems, and are more 'likely to secure compliance with legislative goals' (McCubbins and Schwartz 1984: 171).

This paper argues that the classic PA model is inverted in the context of European economic governance. Rather than principals monitoring agents, member state principals delegate to supranational agents the task of monitoring the budgetary and economic behavior of the principals themselves (Schuknecht 2004; Hodson 2009; Chang 2013a; Gren, Howarth, and Quaglia 2015). The member states exercise final authority over their agents in the design and implementation of the surveillance procedure. The member states ultimately determine how intrusively and in what manner the Commission may conduct its monitoring, and in this way determine whether the surveillance system reflects a police-patrol or fire-alarm framework. The principals approve the rules the Commission must enforce, and they ultimately determine whether they themselves should be sanctioned. The Commission may, for example, propose how often and under what circumstance member states should be visited, and whether member state budgets should be audited. Yet these initiatives must be approved by the member states. The principals identify which supranational agents participate in the surveillance procedure, and they adjudicate when multiple agents compete for the right to administer various monitoring tasks, in what constitutes supranational 'bureaucratic politics' (Pollack 1997; Schelkle 2005; Hawkins *et al.* 2006). To promote the integrity of the surveillance procedure, the member states may also delegate discretionary authority to its agents, granting them some of the prerogatives of a trustee (Majone 2001; Tallberg 2002).

The EU's PA relationships are further complicated by the structure of some member state governments, especially those that are extensively federated or jurisdictionally segmented. The Treaty on European Union (TEU) and allied legislation apply to 'general government', the aggregated levels of government within a member state, not simply the national government. So, for example, in the case of Spain, there are 17 Autonomous Communities (AC), 50 provinces within those communities, and seven of those ACs are considered to be both an AC and a province. Madrid is one of these single province communities while the AC of Valencia contains three provinces. There are some 5,000 units of government and publicly funded agencies that report budgetary information that eventually constitute Spain's aggregate deficit and debt figures.

Prior to the Euro crisis, the member state principals preferred a monitoring procedure analogous to the fire-alarm system. Through the TEU's Article 104 (2), its Protocol on the Excessive Deficit Procedure, and Council Regulation 3605/93, the member states delegated to supranational agencies the fiscal surveillance of the EMU. Yet, member states limited the Commission's authority to employ all of the monitoring tools available to conduct a penetrating surveillance of the member states' fiscal actions. First, for example, the TEU's Article 126 limited the Commission's surveillance only 'to identifying gross errors' in the budgetary statistics submitted by the member states in their biannual reports to the Commission. Second, the TEU did not call upon the European Court of Auditors, the one EU institution familiar with analyzing member state budgets, to deploy its auditors to review these budgets. Third, Eurostat, the Commission's statistical agency responsible for certifying the biannual reports was greatly restrained in making country visits and precluded from conducting audits of member state accounts. To a great extent, the surveillance process relied on the fire-alarms of external sources, including the media and private rating services such as Moody's to identify egregious member state budgetary activity (Savage 2006).

Furthermore, it is important to recall that sanctions play a critical role in PA theory. Although the process of collecting information itself may produce disciplinary effects through the systematic use of surveillance techniques, the compliance of agents ultimately depends upon the application of meaningful sanctions. In the history of EMU, prior to the Spanish case described in this study, no member state had been subjected to a financial penalty, despite widespread noncompliance with the EU's deficit and debt requirements. Member states have instead been sanctioned by a host of soft sanctions that take the form of repeated reports, recommendations, and guidelines drafted by the Commission calling for compliance. The softness of these sanctions is exemplified by the Commission's Broad Economic Policy Guidelines issued during the EMU convergence process. This fire-alarm styled arrangement changed in reaction to the economic crises that soon gripped Europe.

## The Six-Pack: controlling information evasion after the Greek and Euro crises

If PA theorists prefer fire-alarm systems, then why did the EU's principals move towards a police-patrol system? Because contrary to theory, the fire-alarm system failed to 'secure compliance with [the EU's] legislative goals' (McCubbins and Schwartz 1984: 171). The Greek and Euro crises served as critical junctures in the evolution of the surveillance process, as previously reluctant member states increasingly strengthened the EU's supranational institutions' centralized police-patrol capabilities. The Greek statistical crises of 2004 and 2009, during which Greece submitted falsified statistics regarding the size of its budget deficit to gain entry into the EMU and that later contributed to the Euro crisis, resulted in numerous rules that highlighted the importance of transparent and credible statistics (Savage and Verdun 2016). As a senior official in Employment Commissioner Marianne Thyssen's Cabinet, to whom

Eurostat reports, noted, 'Greece made countries very determined on making sure the data were correct, and gave Eurostat invasive powers it never would have got otherwise, and that was obvious'.[1] After multiple requests, ECOFIN granted Eurostat auditing powers through Council Regulations 479/2009 and 679/2010. Of the five regulations and one directive that constitute the Six-Pack, one regulation and the directive focus on the problem of asymmetric information. Council Regulation 1173/2011 outlines the policing of member states engaged in the 'misrepresentation, whether intentional or due to serious negligence' of government fiscal data. The regulation establishes the basis for detecting, investigating, and financially sanctioning duplicitous member state behavior. The Commission is empowered to conduct surveys for 'detecting and exposing' statistical manipulations, and for conducting 'any investigations necessary' if there are indications of statistical manipulation. The regulation permits the Commission to interview anyone involved in the creation of data, if that person agrees to the meeting. Significantly, the regulation authorizes the Commission to recommend that the egregious member state that 'intentionally or by serious negligence misrepresents deficit and debt data' be fined for this violation in a manner that 'shall be effective, dissuasive and proportional to the nature, seriousness and duration of the misrepresentation'. Although the total amount of the fine shall not exceed .2 percent of the member state's GDP, the reference amount for the penalty shall be equal to 5 percent of the misrepresentation of either the member state's deficit or debt covered by the notification period of the EDP. The Six-Pack's provisions soon came into play when the Commission sought sanctions against Spain for the misrepresentation of its EDP statistics.

## The politics of asymmetric information in the EDP: the case of Valencia

The Valencia case is the first of two analyzed in this study that exemplify how the politics of asymmetric information play a critical role in EU economic governance. In reaction to Greece and the Euro crisis, the EU reinforced the SGP in a centralized police-patrol-like manner, to the extent that both principals and agents agreed for the first time in EMU history to impose financial penalties against a member state for misrepresenting its data for the EDP's surveillance procedure.

### *The institutional framework of Spanish EDP reporting*

To appreciate the Valencia case, it is first necessary to understand that the EU's challenge of managing asymmetrical information begins with the TEU's requirement that member states report their fiscal and economic data to Eurostat on a biannual basis, in March and October. These data must be submitted in a manner consistent with the European System of National Accounts (ESA). Eurostat exercises trustee-like authority to interpret the ESA, which is the overall accounting system that harmonizes member state deficit and debt figures and determines their calculation for the EDP and the MIP. The collection and analysis of these data reflect a long chain of interlaced institutional PA relationships, first emanating from member state approved treaties and secondary rules, through supranational agencies, to the member state national governments, to regional and local government and public units, all of which must be managed effectively to overcome the presence of asymmetric information in the surveillance process. The Spanish case suggests how this chain of PA relationships produces the budgetary and economic statistics that are employed in the European economic governance.

In the case of Spain, the provision of budgetary information to the EU begins with Spanish law (Ministerial Order ORDEN HAC/2283/2003) that requires the National Audit Office, which is a unit in the national Ministry of Finance (MOF), to collect budgetary data from the 17 ACs. Each AC through its ministry of finance is responsible for producing a set of public financial accounts. Each regional ministry of finance contains a regional audit office charged with that task. Spanish law delegates to the National Audit Office the power to audit central government and social security accounts, but restricts the auditing of regional accounts to these regional auditing offices. In the AC of Valencia, this unit is the Valencia Audit Office, which gathers data from the various government and publicly funded units in the region, such as the regional Ministry of Health. There also exists a National Court of Auditors and regional courts of auditors that are responsible for ensuring the credibility of the data generated by the national and regional ministries of finance audit offices. The Valencia Audit Office submits its data four times a year to the National Audit Office, which then translates these public accounts figures into the ESA national accounts framework. Finally, EU Council Regulation 2011/85/EU and Spain's General Public Accounting Plan require that these public accounts figures include expenditure data that reflect accrual accounting principles. These data are next submitted to the National Statistical Institute, which reviews and enters the data in the Commission's biannual reporting forms, and then advances these forms to Eurostat. Nevertheless, these formal rules and procedures proved to be insufficient to prevent severe irregularities from emerging in the statistics reported to Eurostat.

### *'Severe irregularities' in Spanish statistics*

In May 2012, Spain's National Statistical Institute informed Eurostat that the 2011 deficit figure of 8.5 percent of GDP it submitted in Spain's March 2012 biannual report needed to be increased by .4 percent. The Institute indicated that it had identified unreported budget expenditures in the ACs of Madrid and Valencia. Eurostat incorporated this revision in the October 2012 biannual report, which helped increase Spain's 2011 deficit to 9.4 percent of GDP. In June 2012, Eurostat initiated a series of on-site 'methodological' visits to investigate the cause of the revisions, as authorized by Regulations 479/2009 and 679/2010, and Commission Delegated Decision 2012/678/EU. Eurostat found that Madrid's accounts were inaccurate, but accepted that these errors were unintentionally entered. In the case of Valencia, however, Eurostat discovered extensive intentional misreporting and underreporting of health expenditures of €1.893 billion between 2007 and 2011.

Eurostat's investigation revealed numerous 'severe irregularities' that contributed to the breakdown in the PA monitoring system that Spain established to meet its EDP reporting requirements (Commission 2015a). The Valencia Audit Office failed to record health expenditures in their proper accounts, in a manner consistent with Spanish and regional accrual accounting principles. The Audit Office ignored recommendations from the regional audit office and the regional ministry of health and failed to record expenditures in their proper accounts for five years, during which time none of these obligations were paid. The Audit Office then submitted its falsified information to the National Statistics Institute, which reported inaccurate expenditure and deficit figures to Eurostat. Oversight national and regional institutions were either ignored, uninformed, or powerless to control Valencia's behavior. Reflecting upon Spain's broken surveillance process, an official in the Directorate-General for Economic and Financial Affairs (DG ECFIN) declared that 'when it comes to budgetary statistics, the national statistical institutes are in the position of gathering asymmetric information *vis-à-vis* the government. So a government determined to cheat, could at least for a time, get away with it'.[2]

Valencia's motivation for hiding its expenditures was rooted in the TEU's requirement that a member state's deficit and debt figures would be based on a general government calculation. This created adversarial PA relations over asymmetric information within the member states, as central governments necessarily began monitoring their subunits with greater attention. In 2001, Spain enacted an internal stability pact, followed by the Organic Law of 2012 on Budgetary Stability and Financial Sustainability, and the addition of Article 135.1 to Spain's constitution in 2012 created in compliance with Treaty on the Functioning of the European Union. These laws progressively attempted to constrain AC spending through spending, deficit, and debt ceilings, enforced by sanctions, though analyses of these rules indicate that they have been ineffective in controlling AC deficits (Almendral 2013a, 2013b). Valencia's manipulations of statistics represented an attempt to evade these restrictions.

The Spanish government discovered the Valencia Audit Office's misreporting in 2012. That year, the government created a Special Payment Mechanism (SPM) to assume the collected commercial payments in arrears to suppliers for of all of Spain's ACs and municipal governments. The ministries of finance of these governments were required to disclose their fiscal deficiencies by submitting invoices of their unpaid bills to the central Ministry of Finance, in exchange for relieving them of these payments. As the Valencia Audit Office was a unit in Valencia's regional ministry of finance, the ministry was aware of these unpaid expenditures and included them in the AC's invoices sent to the national MOF for funding through the SPM. Consequently, in order to benefit from the central government's payment of its outstanding obligations, the AC of Valencia was required to reveal its long-term, unpaid expenditures. As the SPM process progressed and Valencia's errors became known to the MOF, the MOF informed the National Statistical Institute that Spain's budgetary figures that were incorporated into its EDP reports to Eurostat were inaccurate. The Institute then notified Eurostat that the 2011 deficit needed to be revised upwards.

The discovery of these statistical discrepancies led the Commission in July 2014 to authorize Eurostat's formal investigation of Spain's deficits and debt figures. The Six-Pack Directive 2011/85/EU outlined the new investigatory procedures the Commission could apply, including its right to interview 'any person directly or indirectly involved in compiling deficit and debt data, who agrees to be interviewed', at any level of government. According to the Commissioner then responsible for Eurostat and European statistics, Algirdas Ŝemeta, 'The quality and credibility of European Statistics is not something the Commission is willing to compromise on. We depend on sound data to make sound decisions, and reliable statistics for evidence-based policy making' (Commission 2014). Subsequently, a detailed report drafted by Eurostat and submitted by the Commission to ECOFIN declared that the Valencia Audit Office actively engaged in the misrepresentation of Valencia's expenditures.

### *Spain's response and ECOFIN's financial sanction of Valencia*

Spain defended itself against the Commission's investigation and reports by filing an action on 14 September, 2014 with the General Court of the European Court of Justice and by submitting its own rejoinder report to ECOFIN (Curia 2014; Commission 2015b). Spain argued that Eurostat never questioned the data the National Statistical Institute submitted for the March EDP, and that Spain and the Institute should receive credit for immediately alerting Eurostat to the statistical discrepancies existing in the statistics. The data reflected neither grave negligence nor intent on the part of the Spanish government. More importantly, under the terms of Decision 2012/678, Eurostat lacked the authority to review data prior to December 2011. Eurostat's 'covert' investigation constituted an act of 'retroactivity', by examining data dating to 1998, far beyond the period covered in the 2012 EDP reports. This meant that the legitimate investigation was necessarily limited in scope and that penalties could only be imposed for the National Statistical Institute's 2011 data. Furthermore, member states often revised their data, so Spain should not be punished for what 'is standard practice in the majority of countries' (Commission 2015b: 15). Finally, Spain's notification to Eurostat came in sufficient time to avoid any compromise to the EDP process applied to Spain; there was no 'detrimental effect at all', none that would affect the Commission's surveillance ability 'to identify gross errors', as called for the TEU. Of the €1.893 billion in missing expenditures identified by Eurostat covering the period 2007–2012, only €862 million could be attributed to 2011, the year in question, or just 0.08 percent of that year's GDP.

On 13 July, 2015, ECOFIN acted on the Commission's reports and issued Council Decision 2015/1289 that imposed a fine of €94.65 million on Spain for Valencia's 'serious negligence' leading to the 'manipulation of deficit data'. The fine was set on a reference value that levied the amount equal to 5 percent of the effect on the deficit for the years of the misrepresented data, which totaled of €1.893 billion, up to 0.2 percent of Spain's GDP in 2014. ECOFIN then, on Eurostat's recommendation, began 'taking into account' three extenuating circumstances that reduced the fine: first, the additionally discovered expenditures did not materially alter Spain's deficit for the EDP; second, the official deficit figure reported in the March biannual report was promptly corrected in the October report; and third, the manipulation of statistics represented the act of a regional authority, not Spain's national government. For these reasons, ECOFIN reduced the fine to €18.93 million.

### *The general court's ruling and Spain's reaction*

On 3 September, 2015, the General Court ruled in favor of the Commission (InfoCuria 2015). The Court agreed with the Commission's claim that by itself the investigatory process does not affect the 'legal position' of the member state, and that the Commission conducted the investigation in a manner consistent with Regulation 1173/2011. Spain could only challenge ECOFIN's decision and the fine, not the legality of the investigation. Regarding the fine, the Court ruled that ECOFIN applied the penalty in a manner consistent with TEU Article 261, such that it could 'annul, reduce or increase the fine so imposed' (InfoCuria 2015: 2). The Court rejected Spain's assertion that the penalty should be set aside because this was 'the first decision of the Commission to initiate an investigation on the manipulation of statistics by a Member State' (InfoCuria 2015: 2) under the Six-Pack, and that the investigation created harmful publicity that damaged its standing in international financial markets. The Court dismissed Spain's claim and ordered it to pay the fine set by ECOFIN.

Finally, the Commission's investigation, ECOFIN's decision, and the Court's ruling produced political controversy within Spain, and generated accusations between the central government and Valencia. Amid charges of mismanagement and corruption, the People's Party that governed Valencia suffered severe losses during the May 2015 elections. On 11 September, 2015, following the EU's General Court's ruling, the national Ministry of Finance ordered Valencia to pay the fine that had been imposed on the central government within two months. If it did not comply, the MOF would deduct those funds from the budgetary transfers normally sent to Valencia as part of Spain's regional financing.

## Member state pushback: the politics of asymmetric information in the macroeconomic imbalance procedure

The Euro crisis and the Valencia case led to a reinforced EDP, but would the member states also permit the Commission to administer a similarly intrusive police-patrol-like surveillance system to ensure the integrity of information submitted for the MIP? This section of the paper examines a Commission initiative to strengthen the statistical accuracy of MIP data through new regulations that would clarify and enhance Eurostat's authority over MIP statistics. The Commission's proposal to monitor asymmetric information, however, faced opposition from its member state principals in ECOFIN and the EP, as well as from and opposition from another surveillance agent, the European Central Bank.

### *Eurostat's proposed regulations for 'quality' MIP statistics*

In 2011, ECOFIN declared that the MIP 'must rely upon sound official statistics for inclusion in the scoreboard' (Council of the European Union, 2011: 3). Following this declaration, Commissioner Algirdas Ŝemeta directed Eurostat to draft regulations that would grant the agency authority over MIP statistics similar to what it excised over EDP statistics. Ŝemeta, whose portfolio also included Taxation, Customs, Audit, and Anti-Fraud as well as European statistics, was well-known in the Commission for being a strong enforcer of EU rules and ensuring the transparency of financial transactions. The resulting proposed regulation, COM(213)342, assigned Eurostat the police-patrol powers to receive and assess the quality of the MIP data provided by the member states, conduct mission and investigatory methodological visits, express reservations on the quality of these data to the member state and ECOFIN's Economic Policy Committee, provide the data used for the MIP, amend the data, and, acting through the Commission, recommend fines against a member state not exceeding 0.05 percent of its GDP for the intentional or seriously negligent manipulation of statistics. Eurostat learned from its experience with Greece and other member states that without enhanced investigatory authority even country visits failed to reveal bad statistics. Though this new regulation, Eurostat would effectively receive the same authority over MIP data that it exercised over EDP statistics. As a senior Commission official with responsibility for Eurostat observed,

> Eurostat believes if the data can lead to fines it must be of the utmost quality, and therefore it must be controlled by Eurostat. If we put our stamp on it, we must have the power to check that it is good. So now if you introduce the MIP that can also lead to fines, then that data should also be subject to the same level of control and invasiveness that's in the EDP.[3]

Ŝemeta successfully championed the proposal within the Commission, arguing that reliable and credible MIP statistics advanced the Commission's administration of the Semester. As an ECFIN official concluded, 'It is difficult to take the position "I am against good statistics"'.[4]

Despite Commission approval, the proposal met opposition from another agent in the MIP surveillance procedure, the European Central Bank (ECB), which viewed the proposed regulations as infringing on its administrative autonomy. Although the ECB plays no role in generating EDP statistics, it does produce statistics for the MIP's Net International Investment indicator and the Net External Debt auxiliary indicator (Hartlapp *et al.* 2013). There are two major statistical data systems in Europe: the European Statistical System (ESS) administered by Eurostat, and the European System of Central Banks (ESCB) administered by the ECB under the authority of Regulation 2533/98. This regulation authorizes the ECB to oversee the statistics generated by the various member state National Central Banks (NCB) and private financial institutions. Thus, the working relationships are more frequent and the institutional loyalties stronger between Eurostat and the national statistical institutes on the one hand, and the ECB and the NCBs on the other. The TEU and all subsequent statistics required for the EMU convergence process, the SGP, and the EDP rely upon the ESS. The MIP also relies heavily on the ESS, but the Net International Investment headline indicator and the Net External Debt auxiliary indicator rely on ESCB data.

After gaining approval from within the Commission, the regulation was submitted to the European Parliament and ECOFIN for their consideration in June 2013. In its 'Opinion' to the EP, the ECB declared that the Commission's proposal threatened the central bank's independence in governing ESCB statistics (European Central Bank 2013). The ECB argued that the proposal 'seems to establish parallel quality assessments' (European Central Bank 2013: 2), while calling instead for preserving 'the already existing quality assurance arrangements of the ESS and the ESCB' (2013: 2), which 'should also be applied to the statistical data for the MIP' (2013: 2). Noting that the responsibility for generating MIP statistics are 'shared,' the ECB recommended that the coordination for the 'close cooperation' between the two systems should take place in the Committee on Monetary, Financial, and Balance of Payments Statistics (CMFB). The CMFB is the only institution where all of Europe's statistical units, Eurostat, the national statistical institutes, NCBs, and the ECB come together. Established in 1991, the CMFB is the premier body for setting policy on statistical requirements and methodologies. The ECB suggested that a memorandum of understanding (MOU) could be created in the CFMB to clarify the 'practical operational arrangements' between the two systems in the production of MIP statistics.

The EP Committee on Economic and Monetary Affairs' amendments to the draft regulation echoed concerns expressed by both the member states and the ECB. Adopted by the EP during the first reading of the legislation in March 2014, the amendments directed that the 'the institutional separation of the [ESCB] and the independence of [NCBs] should be respected' (European Parliament 2014: Amendment 9), added the ECB to the ESS Group of Directors of Macroeconomic Statistics, called for 'close cooperation' between the ESCB and the ESS, recommended that the 'practical operational arrangements' be set by an MOU, and required consultation between the national statistical institutes with the NCBs in the production of member state MIP data. The amendments reflected member state interests by calling for the Commission's 'closer and more timely involvement' of the national parliaments and the EP in MIP statistical surveillance, with NSIs potentially called to participate in EP committee hearings (European Parliament 2014: Amendment 11). Eurostat would be required to provide the EP with provisional reports on investigatory missions, and final findings would be sent to the EP as well as ECOFIN. Significantly, the process for fining member states was extended and made more difficult to impose. The fine would consist of an interest-bearing deposit not exceeding 0.05 percent of GDP in the preceding year, and it would be 'a last resort', and, in an important revision, require that the offending member state be proved to be one that 'has acted intentionally to misrepresent the MIP relevant data' (European Parliament 2014: Amendment 34). When the EP considered the proposal said a Eurostat official, 'they have it in their minds that the same sanctions [employed in the EDP] will be applied in the MIP'.[5] Furthermore, this misbehavior must be one that 'as a consequence has impacted on the ability of the Commission to make a true and fair assessment' (European Parliament 2014: Amendment 34). Thus, these amendments would greatly strengthen the EP's role as a principal overseeing Eurostat's monitoring of the member states' asymmetric information.

For its part, ECOFIN has 'taken note' of the regulation and it 'welcomes close cooperation' of the ESS and the ESCB, yet has not formally read the proposal (Council of the European Union 2015). Nevertheless, as Thyssen's cabinet officer noted, the member states view the EDP and MIP data as serving different purposes.

> [The proposal] is mostly blocked at the level of the member states in the Council. Their argument is that [unlike the EDP's deficits and debt targets] ... the MIP is more open. You have the alert mechanism and the in-depth review; it's not just that number that leads to the opening of a procedure that can lead to a fine. Thus, there is no particular reason why these data should be subject to that level of invasiveness.[6]

As a consequence, the member states support a surveillance system that offers less rigorous controls over their statistical information.

### *Current status of the proposal*

The Commission is reluctant to press the legislation forward with either the EP or ECOFIN. In lieu of the regulation, Eurostat responded by entering into an MOU with the ECB in 2015, while creating a CMFB task force on statistical quality on MIP indicators involving the member state NSIs and NCBs (Eurostat 2015). These arrangements encourage cooperation in the development of MIP data, but they reify the ECB's institutional role in overseeing its separate data stream employed in the MIP. The MIP data, therefore, lack the regulatory protection and enforcement granted SGP/EDP statistics.

## Discussion and conclusion

These research findings illustrate the challenges of managing the multilevel PA aspects of asymmetric fiscal, economic, and social information in the EU. This study argues that prior to the Greek and Euro crises the member states preferred a looser fiscal surveillance regime, similar to the PA notion of fire-alarm. Having some surveillance system in place suggested their credible commitment to controlling the negative spillover effects of noncompliant behavior, with relatively limited intrusion on member state budgetary autonomy. The Greek crisis that stemmed from hidden information and its association with the debt crisis significantly altered the member states' willingness to adopt Commission recommendations to create an enhanced police-patrol type of surveillance procedure for the SGP and EDP. Council regulations enacted in 2009 strengthening the Commission's authority to visit member states and scrutinize member state fiscal statistics were significantly augmented by the Six-Pack. This legislation promotes deeper Europeanization and enhances the authority of the Commission in confronting the member states (Knill 2001; Featherstone and Radaelli 2003).

These crises strengthened the Commission's role in economic governance, specifically as analyzed here in its role in managing and ensuring the transparency of critical asymmetric member state information (Ellinas and Suleiman 2011; Chang 2013b; Bauer and Becker 2014a, 2014b, 2016; Savage and Verdun 2016). The Six-Pack granted the Commission the right to conduct investigations of member state administrative practices as they applied to fiscal statistics, the right to review the fiscal data and transactions of all levels of government within a member state, and the right to sanction member states with financial penalties. As a DG Secretariat-General official observed,

> If you look at it from a sovereignty perspective, we're interfering with what you could consider to be national governance. Here comes a supranational authority and does not address the central state, which is the main interlocutor with the EU, but can interfere directly with regional authorities.[7]

A DG ECFIN official involved with the case concurred, saying, 'We have established a precedent ... The extent of potential cases is huge'.[8] Using this authority based on the experience of the Valencia case, the Commission launched an investigation in March 2016 into the possible manipulation of statistics by the Austrian province of Salzburg (Commission 2016).

In addition, in March 2015, ECOFIN amended Regulation 223/2009 to enhance the independence of member state NSIs that worked closely with Eurostat in the European Statistical System that governs EU statistics. This legislation promotes Europeanization, offers the Commission the opportunity to scrutinize the statistical activities of the member states, and helps build networks and epistemic communities among European statisticians. In the Valencia case, it was Spain's National Statistics Institute that alerted Eurostat to the discrepancies in that country's statistics. The ruling against Valencia advanced Eurostat's authority with the member states regarding their statistics. Because of Valencia, as a senior Eurostat official deeply involved in the case explained,

> We now have the power to investigate and recommend fines. Member states have realized they can be fined. Now they comply. After Valencia, everyone understood this can happen to them as well. So they are much more cooperative in giving even confidential data to the statistical offices.[9]

Nevertheless, even as the Valencia case represents the assertiveness of supranational agencies, the politics of asymmetric information also reflect the assertion by the EU's principals to exert their intergovernmental authority to restrict the Commission's initiatives when they regard it in their interests to do so (Puetter 2012; Hodson 2013; Rittberger 2014; Dinan 2014; Bickerton *et al* 2015; Schimmelfennig 2015). The MIP presented the Commission with an important opportunity to expand its prerogatives through Eurostat's oversight of the asymmetric information it obtained from the member states. A Eurostat official recalled, "We would like to allow for the possibility of methodological visits or sanctions ... With this proposal, we have more elements to strengthen the process and make sure the data are credible'.[10] The Parliament, however, revised Eurostat's proposal by reducing its investigatory powers, limiting its ability to recommend financial penalties, and by requiring Eurostat to report to the Parliament. In the bureaucratic competition between the two agents, Eurostat and the ECB, the Parliament ruled in favor of the ECB, permitting it to maintain its separate control over statistical information. ECOFIN has yet to act formally on the proposal, but has signaled its lack of interest in strengthening Eurostat's authority over member state statistics. Thus, while the member states supported a stronger police-patrol monitoring of asymmetric information for the EDP, they expressed their preference for a relatively less restrictive fire-alarm monitoring of member state information for the MIP.

In terms of economic governance, the politics of asymmetric information reflect the current status of the shifting power relationships between the member states and EU institutions as a result of the Euro crisis. ECOFIN approved the Commission's entrepreneurial initiatives for greater authority over the member states in the effort to overcome asymmetric information barriers. The member states conceded that obtaining credible statistical information serves as a necessary condition for an effective EDP surveillance system. The member states and the Parliament's experiences with the MIP differ from those of the EDP. The MIP has yet to be viewed as contributing to the type of economic and political crises created by the breakdown in Greek statistics. Consequently, the member states and Parliament relied upon an MIP surveillance process that operates without the assurance of statistics as reliable as those in the EDP. What remains to be seen is whether at some point the MIP's alert mechanism and In-Depth Reviews may be compromised by this decision on asymmetric information, leading the EU's principals to delegate more authority to their agents in the Commission.

## Notes

1. Interview with official in Commissioner Thyssen's Cabinet, 16 October 2015.
2. Interview with DG ECFIN official, 15 October 2015.
3. Interview with official in Commissioner Thyssen's Cabinet, 16 October 2015.
4. Interview with DG ECFIN official, 15 October 2015.
5. Interview with Eurostat official, 2 October 2015.
6. Interview with official in Commissioner Thyssen's Cabinet, 16 October 2015.
7. Interview with DG Secretariat-General official, 23 September 2015.
8. Interview with DG ECFIN official, 15 October 2015.
9. Interview with Eurostat official, 7 September 2015.
10. Interview with Eurostat official, 7 September 2015.

## Acknowledgements

The authors thank Luca Ascoli for his generous assistance with this research. We thank the Fonds National de la Recherche Luxembourg's Intermobility Programme for its support. We thank Caroline de la Porte and Emmanuelle Schön-Quinlivan for their helpful comments.

## Disclosure statement

No potential conflict of interest was reported by the authors.

## References

Almendral, V.R. (2013a) 'Curbing the deficit in Spain and its autonomous communities: a constitutional conundrum', *Bij De Buren TvCR* January: 68–77.

Almendral, V.R. (2013b) 'The spanish legal framework for curbing the public debt and the deficit', *European Constitutional Law Review* 9: 189–204.

Bauer, M. and Becker, S. (2014a) 'The unexpected winner of the crisis: the European Commission's role in policy execution', *Journal of European Public Policy* 12(2): 217–36.

Bauer, M. and Becker, S. (2014b) 'Debate: from the front line to the back stage—How the financial crisis has strengthened the European commission', *Public Money & Management* 34(3): 161–3.

Bauer M. and Becker, S. (2016) 'Absolute gains are still gains: why the European Commission is a winner of the crisis, and unexpectedly so. A rejoinder to Eugénia da Conceição-Heldt', *Journal of European Integration* 38(1): 101–6.

Bickerton, C.J., Hodson, D. and Puetter, U. (2015) 'The new intergovernmentalism: European integration in the post-maastricht era', *JCMS: Journal of Common Market Studies* 53(4): 703–22.

Chang, M. (2013a) 'Constructing the commission's six-pack proposals: political leadership thwarted?' in M. Change and J. Monar (eds) *The European Commission in the Post-Lisbon Era of Crises*, Brussels: Peter Lang Publishers, pp. 147–69.

Chang, M. (2013b) 'Fiscal policy coordination and the future of the community Method', *Journal of European Integration* 35(3): 255–69.

da Conceição-Heldt, E. (2016) 'Why the European Commission is not the "unexpected winner" of the Euro crisis: a comment on Bauer and Becker', *Journal of European Integration* 38(1): 95–100.

Council of the European Union. (2011) 'Council conclusions on an early warning scoreboard for the surveillance of macroeconomic imbalances', 8 November.

Council of the European Union. (2015) 'Council conclusions on EU statistics', 8 December.

Curia. (2014) 'Action brought on 22 September 2014, Spain v. Commission', 22.9.24, Case T-676/14.

Dehousse, R. (2015) 'The new supranationalism', Paper Prepared for ECPR General Conference, Montreal.

Dinan, D. (2014) 'Governance and institutions: the unrelenting rise of the European Parliament', *JCMS: Journal of Common Market Studies* 52(Annual Review): 109–24.

Ellinas, A. and Suleiman, E. (2011) 'Supranationalism in a transnational bureaucracy: the case of the european Commission', *JCMS: Journal of Common Market Studies* 49(5): 923–47.

Essi, S. and Stiglbauer, A. (2011) 'Prevention and correction of macroeconomic imbalances: the excessive imbalance procedure', *Monetary Policy & the Economy* Q4/11: 99–113.

European Central Bank. (2013) 'Opinion of the European Central Bank', 10.10.13, CON/ 2013/72).

European Commission. (2014) 'Commission opens investigation into statistical reporting in Valencia', 11.7.2014, IP/14/822.

European Commission. (2015a) 'Report from the Commission', 7.5.2015, COM(2015)211 Final.

European Commission. (2015b) 'Annex to the Commission report', 7.5.2015, COM (2015)211 Final.

European Commission. (2016) 'Commission decision on the launch of an investigation of statistics in Austria', 3.5.2016, C(2016)2633 Final.

European Parliament. (2014) 'Amendments adopted by the European Parliament', 11.3.14. http://www.europarl.europa.eu/sides/getDoc.do?pubRef=-//EP//TEXT+TA+P7-TA-2014-0181+0+DOC+XML+V0//EN.

Eurostat. (2015) 'ESS-ESCB quality assessment report on statistics underlying the macroeconomic imbalance procedure', 24 August.

Featherstone, K. and Radaelli, C. (eds) (2003) *The Politics of Europeanization*, New York: Oxford University Press.

Gandrud, C. and Hallerberg, M. (2016) 'Statistical agencies and responses to financial crises: Eurostat, bad banks, and the esm', *West European Politics* Forthcoming.

Gren, J., Howarth, D. and Quaglia, L. (2015) 'Supranational banking supervision in Europe: the construction of a credible watchdog', *JCMS: Journal of Common Market Studies*, 53(1): 1–17.

Hartlapp, M., Metz, J. and Rauh, C. (2013) 'Linking agenda setting to coordination structures: bureaucratic politics inside the European Commission', *Journal of European Integration* 35(4): 425–41.

Hawkins, D., Lake, D., Nielson, D., and Tierney, M. (eds) (2006) *Delegation and Agency in International Organizations*. New York: Cambridge University Press.

Hodson, D. (2009) 'Reforming EU economic governance: a view from (and on) the principal-agent approach', *Comparative European Politics* 7(4): 455–75.

Hodson, D. (2013) 'The little engine that wouldn't: supranational entrepreneurship and the Barroso Commission', *Journal of European Integration* 35(3): 301–14.

InfoCuria. (2015) 'Order of the General Court', 3.9.15, Case T-676/14. http://curia.europa.eu/juris/document/document.jsf?text=&docid=167541&pageIndex=0&doclang=EN&mode=lst&dir=&occ=first&part=1&cid=625246

Kiewiet, R. and McCubbins, M. (1991) *The Logic of Delegation*, Chicago: University of Chicago Press.

Knill, C. (2001) *The Europeanization of National Administration: Patterns of Institutional Change and Persistence*. New York: Cambridge University Press.

Mabbett, D. and Schelkle, W. (2014) 'Searching under the lamp-post: the evolution of fiscal surveillance', London School of Economics European in Question Paper Series, No. 75.

Majone, G. (2001) 'Two logics of delegation: agency and fiduciary relations in EU governance', *European Union Politics* 2(1): 103–22.

McCubbins, M. and Schwartz, T. (1984) 'Congressional oversight overlooked: police patrols versus fire Alarms', *American Journal of Political Science* 28(1): 165–79.

Miller, G.J. (2005) 'The political evolution of principal-agent models', *Annual Review of Political Science* 8: 203–25.

Moschella, M. (2014) 'Monitoring macroeconomic imbalances: is EU surveillance more effective than IMF surveillance?' *JCMS: Journal of Common Market Studies* 52(5): 1273–89.

Pollack, M. (1997) 'Delegation, agency, and agenda setting in the European Community', *International Organization* 51(1): 99–134.

Puetter, U. (2012) 'Europe's deliberative intergovernmentalism: the role of the council and European council in EU economic governance', *Journal of European Public Policy* 19(2): 161–78.

Rittberger, B. (2014) 'Integration without representation? The european parliament and the reform of economic governance in the EU', *JCMS: Journal of Common Market Studies* 52(6): 1174–83.

Savage, J. (2005) *Making the EMU: The Politics of Budgetary Surveillance and the Enforcement of Maastricht*. Oxford: Oxford University Press.

Savage, J. (2006) 'Member state budgetary transparency in the economic and monetary union', in C. Hood and D. Heald (eds), *Transparency: The Key to Better Governance?* New York: Oxford University Press, pp. 145–63.

Savage, J. and Verdun, A. (2016) 'Strengthening the European commission's budgetary and economic surveillance capacity since Greece and the Euro area crisis: a study of five directorates-General', *Journal of European Public Policy*, 23(1): 101–18.

Schelkle, W. (2005) 'The political economy of fiscal policy Co-ordination in EMU: from disciplinarian device to insurance arrangement*', *JCMS: Journal of Common Market Studies* 43(2): 371–91.

Schelkle, W. (2009) 'The contentious creation of the regulatory state in fiscal surveillance', *West European Politics* 32(4): 829–46.

Schimmelfennig, F. (2015) 'Liberal intergovernmentalism and the Euro area crisis', *Journal of European Public Policy* 22(2): 177–95.

Schuknecht, L. (2004) 'EU fiscal rules: issues and lessons from political economy', *European Central Bank Working Paper*, No. 421.

Tallberg, J. (2002) 'Delegation to supranational institutions: why, how, and with what consequences?' *West European Politics* 25(1): 23–46.

Verdun, A. (2015) 'A historical institutionalist explanation of the EU's responses to the Euro area financial crisis', *Journal of European Public Policy* 22(2): 219–37.

Zeitlin, J. and Vanhercke, B. (2014) 'Socializing the European semester?: economic governance and social policy coordination in Europe 2020', *Swedish Institute for European Policy Studies*, Report 7.

# Cherry-picking external constraints: Latvia and EU economic governance, 2008–2014

Edgars Eihmanis

**ABSTRACT**

The paper analyses Latvian economic policy during the period 2008–2014 when the country was simultaneously subject to three European Union (EU) economic governance frameworks – the European Semester, the Balance-of-Payments programme and the Maastricht convergence criteria (for euro adoption). Through in-depth process tracing based on public policy documents, interviews with senior officials in Riga and Brussels and the press, the paper finds that the Latvian government cherry-picked and instrumentalized EU economic policy targets and overachieved in them. In contrast to the literature depicting the European Commission as a neoliberal actor which systematically undermines social protection, the paper shows that against the backdrop of fiscally austere national authorities, the Commission instead played the role of social policy advocate, repeatedly calling for stronger measures to help the poor. Shedding light on the limits of one-size-fits-all governance, the findings of the Latvian case have significant implications for EU economic governance more generally.

## Introduction

Since the onset of the economic crisis, European Union (EU) economic governance has become increasingly complex. The European Commission initiated a set of new economic governance tools, considerably narrowing the discretionary powers of individual member states. Besides strengthening and enforcing fiscal discipline, frameworks such as the Fiscal Compact, the Two-Pack, the Six-Pack and the Euro-Plus Pact controlled for macroeconomic imbalances in a range of policy areas, such as housing, current account balance and labour competitiveness, among many others. All these initiatives were incorporated into the European Semester – itself a framework designed to enhance the effectiveness of economic governance (Bekker 2013; Laffan and Schlosser 2016). However, over the course of the crisis, the Commission's management of the crisis in general and the EU economic governance architecture in particular has been criticized as fundamentally neoliberal, operating to undermine the welfare state (cf. Joerges 2014).

Some critics are concerned that European social security systems have become a mere adjustment variable for Economic and Monetary Union (EMU) (Degryse *et al.* 2013; Pochet and Degryse 2012; Scharpf 2014: 143), and/or that the crisis might even lead to the end of the European Social Model (Hacker 2012). Others have argued that 'governing by the rules and ruling by the numbers', the 'new EU economic governance' framework exacerbated the social problems created by the crisis, as budget deficit reductions with pressure for structural reforms came at the expense of labour protection (Crespy and Menz 2015: 10; Schmidt 2015a, 2015b). Finally, the Commission has been heavily criticized for its management of the Balance-of-Payments (BoP) and Economic Adjustment programmes. The overwhelming focus on austerity as a means to regain economic growth and – as a consequence – the neglect of social policy has even been lambasted by its in-house auditors and the International Monetary Fund (IMF) (European Court of Auditors 2015; Spiegel *et al.* 2015). According to Lütz and Kranke (2014), the conditionality imposed on Hungary, Latvia and Romania amounted to a 'European rescue of the Washington Consensus' (Lütz and Kranke 2014: 310). Specifically focusing on crisis resolution in the Baltic countries, Woolfson and Sommers (2016: 90) argue that the undeviating commitment to strictly neoliberal disciplinarian terms by the current European Commission and the international financial community has been an ultimate social and economic failure.

Analysing Latvia's economic governance simultaneously under the BoP programme, euro convergence and the European Semester, the paper aims to provide a more balanced view of the Commission's stance on social policy. Drawing on interviews with senior officials in the Latvian government and Commission, public policy documents and the press, I find that against the backdrop of national authorities pursuing radical market-oriented policies, the Commission played the role of social policy advocate. In fact, the Latvian government cherry-picked and instrumentalized EU fiscal rules, achieving them well beyond the targets set by the Commission. Avoiding any additional spending even when allowed by the Fiscal Compact and the BoP programme, the authorities instead focused on early payment of the bailout loans. Similarly, in order to increase the chances of meeting the Maastricht inflation criterion, the government cut value added tax (VAT), thus postponing a long-pending social reform.

While endorsing the excessive fiscal consolidation pursued by the national authorities, as it helped to securitize against uncertainty, the Commission also consistently expressed social concerns. Together with the World Bank and the IMF, the Commission repeatedly called for stronger measures to help the poor and vulnerable. Moreover, besides showing how the Commission advocated for additional targeted measures, the paper shows several instances where the Commission economists called for more social spending in absolute terms. First, the Commission opposed the government decision to cut VAT (to curb inflation), as this eliminated the fiscal space to help lower income earners. Second, the Commission economists stated that they were ready to accept more social spending from any windfall revenue in the budget – as was allowed by the memorandum of understanding in the first place.

Finally, the paper shows how the Commission together with the World Bank and the IMF triggered a progressive change in Latvia's social policy. When the national authorities wanted to phase out the state co-financing of guaranteed minimum income (GMI) benefits on the assumption that due to dependence on welfare benefits people were unwilling to work, the lenders – the largest of whom was the Commission – demanded evidence and forced the government to commission a study by the World Bank. The subsequent report significantly challenged the common wisdom on social policy among the Latvian élites, and served as a basis for policy change. A key contribution to the literature is thus that the Commission's persistent stance on Latvian social policy clearly goes beyond the sort of neoliberalism which is commonly assumed by many accounts of EU socio-economic governance since the crisis.

The Latvian case provides us with a unique opportunity to analyse the simultaneous operation of three distinct EU governance frameworks. First, facing a default in 2008, Latvia became subject to the BoP programme. Subsequently, from January 2012 to January 2015, Latvia entered the post-programme surveillance phase, still subject to Commission scrutiny in order to 'closely monitor risks that could jeopardize macro-economic stability and hence affect the repayment capacity' (European Commission 2012c). Second, by 2011, as the BoP programme expired, the European Semester and Country-specific Recommendations (CSRs) started to apply to Latvia.[1] Finally, not wanting to renounce its commitment to join the euro area in 2014, Latvia sought to comply with the Maastricht convergence requirements on inflation, budgetary deficit, long-term interest rates and public debt.

Analysis of the Latvian case contributes to several important debates on EU post-crisis governance. First, it shows that the Latvian government was able to cherry-pick policy targets from various governance frameworks, justifying non-compliance in some areas with over-compliance in others. Second, in contrast to the literature that calls for a more enforceable social dimension at the EU level (e.g., Schoukens 2013; Vandenbroucke *et al.* 2013), the evidence from the Latvian case does not support the view that more hierarchical governance would necessarily lead to better results. In fact, the Latvian authorities exercised considerable discretion not only in 'soft' policy areas, such as social assistance, but also in 'hard' fiscal policy areas such as taxation, budgeting and spending as well. Moreover, the Latvian case shows that hierarchically imposed ready-made rules not only fail to address adequately local needs and challenges, but can also be strategically misused by the governing élites.

The paper is organized as follows. First, I briefly review evaluations of EU economic governance since the crisis and introduce the analytical framework. Then, after reviewing the background to the economic crisis, I explore the Latvian fiscal and social policy-making process as the country was converging to the euro. I conclude by briefly drawing out the broader implications of the Latvian case for EU economic governance more generally.

## EU economic governance and 'usages of Europe'

A central criticism of the enforced economic governance architecture has concerned the imbalance between fiscal and macroeconomic surveillance, on the one hand, and broader social policy, on the other (de la Porte and Heins 2016). While the macroeconomic governance tools are based on pre-set numerical indicators and sanctions in the case of non-compliance, social policy continues by and large with the soft governance approach established by the open method of co-ordination (Vandenbroucke *et al.* 2013: 5). However, the conceptual line between 'soft' and 'hard' governance may not be so sharp in practice. As argued by Trubek and Trubek (2005), with increased emphasis on experimentation, deliberation and discursive diffusion, 'soft' law may be 'harder' than it seems at first glance. In addition, due to implementation problems, 'hard' law on the books does not necessarily correspond to law in action (Trubek and Trubek 2005: 361). Thus, Bekker (2013) finds that since the crisis the 'hardness' from the fiscal policy domain has to some extent spilled over to the social policy domain – for instance, employment and social policy are increasingly evaluated from an economic or financial perspective (Bekker 2013: 9). The opposite dynamic is also visible. According to Schmidt (2015a), rather than lending 'hardness' to the social domain, economic and fiscal governance itself has become more flexible and interpretation-based – if not admitted openly, then 'by stealth'. For instance, within the excessive deficit procedure, public deficits were increasingly considered on a 'structural' rather than 'cyclical' basis, thus allowing for more fiscal space (Schmidt 2015a: 27–9). However, beyond these enforcement dynamics, there is no doubt that in substantive terms EU economic governance has become increasingly socially balanced since the beginning of the crisis. If the 2011 Annual Growth Survey (AGS) prioritized rigorous fiscal consolidation, labour market reforms and growth enhancing measures, its successors provided a broader and more socially balanced set of priorities, which was further reflected in the European Semester (European Commission 2011, 2012a). The subsequent rounds of CSRs proposed a variety of reforms in social security, pension, education and healthcare systems. Together with the intensification of social monitoring, multilateral surveillance and an enhanced role for social and employment policy actors, this has resulted in the 'progressive socialization' of the European Semester (Zeitlin and Vanhercke 2017.

The paper shows how the national authorities in Latvia cherry-picked and instrumentalized various EU rules and recommendations by using them as external constraint(s) (cf. Woll and Jacquot 2010). A classic example of governing by external constraint or what Dyson and Featherstone (1996) call a *vincolo esterno* is Italy in the 1990s. In order to overcome the problem of obstructive party dominance, the Italian technocratic élite shared a belief in the need for externally imposed economic discipline, and found it in the euro conditionality (Dyson and Featherstone 1996). The EU anchor served a double function for Italy. First, it offered incentives for the reorientation of economic, social and political attitudes from below (related to the four freedoms of labour, goods, capital and services). Second, it gave the élite precious resources from above to legitimize difficult policy measures. The combination of carrots (accession to EMU) and sticks (higher interest rates and currency depreciations whenever the markets expected Italy to devalue) led to significant upgrades in the organization of Italy's labour market, as well as in the fiscal and social policy domains (Ferrera and Gualmini 2004). I show that the Latvian authorities used similar 'hand-tying' strategies to pursue their preferred policies.

In order to establish the causal mechanisms involved, I trace the policy-making process on the basis of three broad data sources (George and Bennett 2005). First, I conducted élite interviews with four economists at the Commission's Directorate-Generals for Economic and Financial Affairs (ECFIN), Employment, Social Affairs and Equal Opportunities (EMPL), three senior officials at the Latvian Ministries of Economics, Finance and Welfare, as well as Ilze Viņķele, former minister of welfare (2011–2014). Second, I draw extensively on official documents from different policy co-ordination frameworks. For instance, within the European Semester, I analyse CSRs, National Reform Plans and Commission staff working documents. I also examine euro convergence reports (programmes), as well as the BoP programme reviews. Finally, I rely on the relevant press sources to follow the public debates.

## Economic crisis in Latvia

On 1 May 2004 Latvia joined the EU, soon after pegging its currency to the euro. Investors' optimism abounded and the country was flooded with foreign capital. In the following years Latvia experienced double-digit real gross domestic product (GDP) and inflation rates. Nominal wages doubled and property prices increased fourfold (European Commission 2012b: 3). However, in 2008, following the freeze of liquidity in the international markets and the collapse of Lehman Brothers, the overheated Latvian economy fell into recession. Needing to nationalize Parex, Latvia's second largest bank with the biggest domestic market share in the EU, the authorities turned to the IMF and the Commission for a bailout (Aslund and Dombrovskis 2011: 33–4). Rejecting advice from various internationally renowned economists and the IMF to devalue the currency (Krugman 2009; Lütz and Kranke 2014: 320; Roubini 2008), the government orchestrated a massive 'internal devaluation'. Framing austerity as 'virtuous pain after the immoral party' (Blyth 2013: 13), a new ethos was constructed: to avoid spending at any cost. A broad range of structural reforms were implemented. Among other things, the government closed half of the 75 government agencies and cut public salaries by 26 per cent (Aslund and Dombrovskis 2011: 72–3). Although Latvian crisis management became a 'success story' in macroeconomic terms, the social costs were immense (Aslund 2013; Austers 2014; Lagarde 2012). In the first two years of the recession, the Latvian economy shrank by approximately a quarter. In 2010, unemployment rose to 20.7 per cent.

In order to push through the reforms, the Latvian authorities relied heavily on 'external constraints'. In his co-authored book *How Latvia came through the Financial Crisis*, Prime Minister (PM) Dombrovskis himself admits that the structural reforms were based on 'an international norm that made sense'. As regards the use of *vincolo esterno*, Dombrovskis is explicit:

> Luckily, the government did not have to invent these reforms hastily. They were well prepared and documented, primarily through studies the government had done with the World Bank. The government basically had to take these reform proposals off the shelf and start implementing them, and it did. (Aslund and Dombrovskis 2011: 72–3)

Relatedly, as I show below, the bailout conditionality and the Fiscal Compact were welcomed by the Latvian government as tools for more rapid budget consolidation.

The economic recession, however, had limited electoral effects on the distribution of political power. Despite the hardship imposed on Latvian society, PM Dombrovskis was re-elected in 2010 and 2011. To a large extent this can be explained by the well-established 'ethnic cleavage with a corruption divide'. In brief, ethnic Latvians vote mostly for the centre-right Latvian parties depending on their stance of fighting corruption, while ethnic Russians vote for the centre-left Russian parties – which have so far been kept out of government (Auers 2013: 94). Latvia's politics during the recession closely follows these lines. Replacing the allegedly corrupt and profligate previous government, PM Dombrovskis formed a centre-right cabinet with a twofold agenda of fiscal consolidation and euro accession. Capitalizing on the established political divisions over ethnicity and corruption, the ruling coalition could pursue extremely radical austerity policies. Meanwhile, economic policy alternatives, mostly articulated by either Russian and/or oligarchic parties, remained politically unrealistic (Eihmanis 2017). The same applies to euro accession. Aiming to integrate further in the EU and obtain security against the perceived threat of Russia, the Latvian authorities did not abandon their ambition to adopt the euro throughout the crisis (Dandashly and Verdun 2015: 5; Milne 2013). In economic terms, the authorities emphasized the significance of financial stability and market confidence, which would probably lead to lower borrowing costs, increased investment and economic growth (Traynor 2012). Politically, euro accession was bundled together with Latvia's 'success story' of internal devaluation, where one continued the other.

## Governance in fiscal policy

Latvia's fiscal policy during the crisis consisted of a chain of overachievements. The government voluntarily set more ambitious fiscal policy targets than required by the EU frameworks and the bailout conditionality, thus minimizing its spending options. Reviewing three major instances of self-imposed austerity, I show that the Latvian government pursued a more austere approach to fiscal consolidation than the lenders. First, the government repeatedly used the positive growth dynamics in its trade partners' economies to revise the budget targets; second, the government instrumentalized the most stringent version of the Fiscal Compact to maximize fiscal discipline; and third, the government did not take the advantage of windfall revenue as would have been permitted by the BoP programme.

In late 2010, the government projected a 2011 budget deficit at 5.4 per cent of GDP – a considerably lower target than the previously planned 6 per cent. By April 2011, adopting additional fiscal consolidation measures, the government reduced the deficit even further to 4.5 per cent of GDP. The budget deficit target for 2012 was then set at 2.5 per cent of GDP, thus overachieving the 3 per cent threshold required by the excessive deficit procedure (Ministry of Economics 2011: 10). By early 2012, the budget deficit target for 2012 was further reduced to 2.1 per cent of GDP (Ministry of Economics 2012: 24). To a considerable degree, overachieving of the fiscal targets was enabled by 'better-than-expected economic growth', as Latvia took the advantage of the positive economic conditions in its main trading partners' economies and the slower development of some planned investment projects. To put it in the words of an ECFIN economist: 'to some extent, Latvia was just lucky' (Interviews 2013a, 2013f).

The setting of excessive budget targets served several purposes. First, it provided a safety margin against the unpredictability of Latvia's political process. According to a national official, tying politicians' hands simply made the budget drafting process much easier: 'Nobody really knows how one or another political power would behave before or after the budget adoption. Therefore, everything is planned with a certain reserve margin' (Interview 2013g). That the excessive fiscal stringency also helped the government's commitment to comply with the Maastricht deficit criterion for joining the euro was confirmed by both the officials at the Commission and the government: 'All these plans on the euro made it possible to put the ruling powers in a kind of frame because there are always desires and needs ... ' (Interviews 2013a, 2013g).

For the same 'hand-tying' reasons, the national authorities warmly welcomed the introduction of the Treaty on Stability, Coordination and Governance (the Fiscal Compact), and voluntarily overachieved its targets. In fact, Finance Minister Vilks had already argued for the need to secure fiscal discipline in the constitution in 2010 – before the adoption of the Fiscal Compact in 2012 and the Fiscal Discipline Law in 2013.[2] Commenting on the Latvian Constitutional Court decision (2009) to repeal the planned pension cuts as they violated the pensioners' right to social security, Vilks was concerned that the Constitutional Court 'limited the scope of austerity' (tvnet.lv 2010).

As the Fiscal Compact stipulates, a country's medium-term objective (MTO) budgetary deficit can be −1 per cent of GDP, provided that its public debt is significantly below 60 per cent of GDP. With 46.0 per cent of GDP in 2011 and 40.7 per cent of GDP in 2012, Latvia complied with this provision; however, the authorities chose to set the MTO at −0.5 per cent of GDP. Exercising a completely free choice in the matter, the Latvian government simply wanted to be 'more ambitious' (Interviews 2013a, 2013b, 2013f). Its rationale was to maximize the discipline imposed by an external constraint to save the authorities from any 'unnecessary' disputes and arguments, particularly from the opposition. According to a high-ranking official at the Ministry of Welfare, 'Before the Fiscal Discipline Law nobody really knew what the actual fiscal space was. Budgeting was a total chaos. Now you simply look at the number. Certainty is the most important thing' (Interview 2013g). According to a high-ranking Finance Ministry official, the Fiscal Compact guaranteed that 'the state would not return to "fiscal blackguardism" anymore' (Interview 2013f).

The Latvian government, however, did not use all the fiscal spending options allowed by the EU frameworks and the bailout conditionality. As stipulated by the 2010 memorandum of understanding, after the regular payback of the bailout loan all 'unexpected' windfall revenue should have been used for three purposes: first, to achieve a lower-than-targeted budget deficit; second, to accelerate EU funds expenditure; and third, to increase funding for active labour market policies and social safety net measures (European Commission 2009, 2010: 6). Nonetheless, rather than taking the opportunity for additional spending, the government chose to concentrate on early payback of the bailout loans.

Regarding the excessive austerity measures, the Commission's position seems ambivalent. On the one hand, it endorsed the excessive fiscal policy targets pursued by the national authorities, as this helped to securitize against uncertainty (Interview 2013c). On the other hand, the Commission worried about the social costs of the consolidation measures: 'We have been emphasizing that more resources have to be allocated for social needs, and training for the unemployed ... However, the government did not listen to us. Rather, they were looking forward to getting better budget numbers' (Interview 2013b).

It has to be noted that, while overachieving the targets in some fiscal areas, the government breached them in others. Special attention should be given to the fact that these derogations occurred while Latvia was subject to post-programme surveillance. In mid-2012, inspired by Latvia's unexpected economic growth – at the time the highest in the EU – the authorities reopened the state budget. Additional spending amounting to 0.5 per cent of GDP was allocated to a range of sectors, including healthcare, transport infrastructure, agriculture, demography and culture. According to PM Dombrovskis, this was the first time in five years that the government allowed itself to spend on priorities other than fiscal consolidation. However, in order to maintain fiscal discipline, the additional spending covered only a fraction of the windfall revenue (Dārziņa 2012; European Commission 2013c). The government also set a three-year strategy to cut the flat personal income tax rate from 25 to 20 per cent. As these measures ran counter to both the National Reform Programme and the CSRs (European Commission 2012c: 4; Ministry of Economics 2012: 28), they were strongly disapproved by the Commission (European Commission 2013c: 2).

Finally, taking advantage of the 'structural reform clause', which provided flexibility within the EU fiscal rules (European Commission 2015b: 10), Latvia exercised significant discretion in managing its pension system. In 2009, responding to the rapidly decreasing levels of social security contributions in the first pension pillar, the government had reduced the contribution rate to the second pillar from 8 to 2 per cent (Volskis 2012: 9). Initially, it was planned that from 2013 contributions at a rate of 6 per cent to the second pillar would be restored (Ministry of Economics 2012: 13). However, in order to accumulate additional assets in the social budget, the government restored the contributions at a rate of only a 4 per cent. Although the Commission noted that the policy ran 'contrary to previous commitments by the authorities under the (BoP) program as well as more recent Country-Specific Recommendations', eventually it not only accepted this move, but also allowed Latvia to derogate from the pre-set MTO of budget deficit of 0.5 per cent of GDP for the amount needed to continue the pension reform (European Commission 2013c: 9; Interview 2013b). The above provides another example showing how the Commission compromised fiscal targets for the sake of a socially significant reform.

## Convergence towards the euro

In order to the join the euro area, Latvia had to comply with the Maastricht convergence criteria with regard to the budget deficit, government debt, long-term interest rate and inflation.[3] Since the other targets had already been covered by the consolidation programme, the main challenge was inflation – especially due to its dependence on a variety of factors beyond the control of the government. Lithuania's failure to qualify for the euro in 2006, by missing the inflation target by just 0.1 per cent, served as an effective reminder. Committed to avoiding a similar scenario by any means possible, the Latvian government had already started to plan a range of measures in 2010. According to the finance minister, the control of inflation was a strategic priority and, compared with the other convergence targets, the most elusive one:

> The sooner we can push inflation down to a certain level, the better for all. Unless there is a strong tripartite collaboration and agreement between the government, employers, and employees, Latvia will not succeed in decreasing inflation to the level needed to introduce the euro. (Vilks 2010, 2011)

Most notably, inflation curbing involved *ad hoc* manipulations of the VAT rate. In 2010, aiming to increase the budget revenue, the government considered increasing VAT by one percentage point. Finance Minister Vilks proposed that VAT should be raised in 2011, as raising it in 2012 could endanger compliance with the inflation target (Vilks 2010). Accordingly, from January 2011 the standard VAT rate was raised from 21 to 22 per cent, while the lower VAT rate was raised from 10 to 12 per cent. In mid-2012, as predicted, the risk of missing the inflation target increased substantially, as Latvia had become one of the most rapidly growing economies in the EU. The government intervened again, cutting the VAT rate from 22 to 21 per cent. That the tax cut was euro-motivated was later confirmed by staff at the Commission and the Ministry of Economics (Interviews 2013b, 2013e). Eventually, Latvia met the inflation target with a 1.4 per cent reserve; thus, the estimated 0.5 percentage point effect of the VAT cut was not decisive for Latvia's qualification for the euro (European Commission 2013b: 30). However, as observed by two ECFIN economists, if the inflation benchmark had been met only with the help of the VAT cut, Latvia's euro application could have been rejected (Interviews 2013a, 2013c). Meanwhile, the Commission was concerned that the VAT cut limited opportunities to raise non-taxable thresholds and thus help low earners: 'There are too many low wages, and the tax wedge on labour is the highest for people with the lowest income. That was a good opportunity to help them a bit already then' (Interview 2013b).

## Governance of social policy: before and after accession to the euro

Throughout the budget consolidation process, social policy was subordinated to the early payment of the bailout loans and accession to the euro. The authorities constantly ignored the Commission's social recommendations. Responding to lenders' criticisms, Latvia sought in its 2011 National Reform Programme to reduce the personal income tax burden on the economically active population and the population at risk of poverty, to raise the personal income allowance for dependants, to introduce a differentiated personal income tax, to provide social protection for families with children, and to encourage participation in the labour market (Ministry of Economics 2011). However, little of this was achieved in practice within the relevant time frame (European Commission 2012c; Interviews 2013a, 2013b).

The few successful social measures valued by the Commission included active labour market policies and training for the unemployed, initiatives to reverse the declining demographic trends (relaxing caps on maternity/paternity allowances, increasing minimum paternal benefits, childcare benefits and personal income tax [PIT] allowance for dependants), as well as the temporary public job programme 'Workplaces with stipends', financed by the European Social Fund. Although the programme was successful in helping the unemployed to mitigate the impact of the crisis (World Bank 2013a: 10), the Commission was concerned that it was used as a substitute for social assistance and did not address the main barriers to employment (European Commission 2013a: 17). Overall, Latvia's progress in social policy reforms remained unsatisfactory (European Commission 2013a: 4).

The picture changed after the government paid the lenders – and was admitted into the euro area (mid-2013). As the first Latvian budget drafted in the euro currency, the 2014 budget was also 'historic' in the sense that it prioritized reducing inequality and poverty, as well as improving the demographic situation (The Baltic Course 2013). Various social goals remained high on the political agenda over the coming years (Latvia.eu 2015; The Baltic Course 2014a, 2014b). Subsequently, several long-pending social policy reforms were adopted. The government introduced and extended a range of support measures for families with children, including maternity and paternity allowances, minimum monthly paternal and childcare benefits and a PIT allowance for dependants. Partial indexation of pensions resumed and disability benefits were increased. The minimum wage was raised from EUR 320 to EUR 360 in 2015 and to EUR 370 in 2016.

Notably, the social policy turn was not due to changes in the government. In fact, Unity (*Vienotība*) remained the main ruling party throughout the crisis. Even when PM Dombrovskis resigned after the Zolitūde shopping centre collapse in early 2013, the next prime minister, Laimdota Straujuma (also from the Unity party), kept largely the same cabinet both before and after the 2014 elections (Ikstens 2015: 185).

At a general level, the social policy turn was a response to the far- and wide-reaching hardships imposed by the recession (Interviews 2013d, 2013g). Looking more closely, however, evidence suggests that the critical juncture was the negotiation process on GMI benefits and housing allowances between the lenders and the government. At the onset of the recession, following recommendations by the Commission and the World Bank, the GMI payment was taken over from the local municipalities by the government and the amount was increased substantially from LVL 27 to 45 (EUR 64) for children and to LVL 40 (EUR 57) for adults. However, as the economy improved the government wanted to return to the previous arrangement. As admitted by Ilze Viņķele, then minister of welfare, in a personal interview, all the lenders were strictly against phasing-out of the state financing and the decrease in the benefit amount. In turn, the municipalities that would have to take over the payments ardently protested that the GMI benefit had to be eliminated altogether. According to the city mayors, people were 'becoming recipients of benefits over generations' and therefore did not want to work. As recalled by Minister Viņķele:

> Since we lacked any credible data as to what was actually going on with the GMI benefit recipients, I came up with an offer that if our current proposal was accepted, the government would study the GMI recipients, and then on the basis of the findings, would change the benefit system (Interview 2016).

However, the lenders responded with a unanimous 'ultimatum' that the research had to be done by the World Bank, since the government allegedly lacked the skills, experience and methodology to make such a study credible (Interview 2016).

In the meantime, despite the lenders' fierce objections, the government proceeded on its own. As from 2013, the authorities decreased the GMI to LVL 35 for all recipients and returned its administration to the municipalities. As a 'significant reversal of gains achieved during and following the crisis', this policy was criticized by the World Bank (World Bank 2013a: 8, 2013b), the IMF and the Commission. The latter was concerned that the decision would 'maintain an uneven system with negative impact on benefit coverage and adequacy' (European Commission 2013c: 10; IMF 2013: 48).

The subsequent World Bank report 'Who is unemployed, inactive or needy?', partially financed by the European Social Fund, plainly refuted the common wisdom in Latvian government and business circles that there was a large-scale dependence on social welfare benefits, which, in turn, made the poor unwilling to work (World Bank 2013c). As publicly admitted by Minister Viņķele, the study challenged the government's view on welfare, shifting it away from 'stereotypes, emotional opinions and "even phobias"' (Tapiņš 2013). Shortly after its publication, the Ministry of Welfare announced plans to increase the non-taxable income threshold, tax credits for dependants and the disabled, as well as the minimum wage (Dārziņa 2013). The Latvian government continued this progressive policy course even after the end of the Commission's close monitoring in 2014 – notably, in taxation. While the wave of tax credits and allowances for the poor and unprotected represented progressive taxation 'by stealth', the measures adopted from 2016 did so more openly (The Baltic Course 2015; Vanags and Zasova 2015).

## Conclusion

This case study of Latvia's economic governance, first, gives in-depth insight into how EU rules may be cherry-picked and instrumentalized by national authorities. The Latvian government took advantage of all three governance frameworks to which it was subject – the BoP programme, the Maastricht convergence criteria and the European Semester, according to its priorities at the time. Initially, the government mainly focused on fiscal consolidation and early payback of the loans. In order to do this, the BoP programme and the Fiscal Compact were instrumentalized by pushing fiscal targets to the extreme. However, once the authorities had accomplished the early loan repayment to the IMF and paid 75 per cent of the loan back to the Commission (thus entering the post-programme surveillance phase with a significantly reduced level of monitoring), the government shifted its reform focus to euro convergence. In order to push down inflation and comply with the Maastricht price stability criterion, the government cut VAT. Meanwhile, against a backdrop of self-imposed austerity, the authorities constantly ignored the Commission's advocacy to take care of the poor and vulnerable groups.

Nonetheless, in 2013, as Latvia received the green light to join the euro area, the Commission's social policy recommendations finally started to gain traction – without major changes in government. During the subsequent years, Latvia adopted a range of progressive reforms targeted at reducing poverty and inequality. As the paper shows, to a considerable extent this progress in Latvia's social policy was a result of the advocacy by the international lenders – notably, the Commission, the World Bank and the IMF. In response to the government's plans to phase out the state financing of social benefits, the international lenders – of whom the Commission was by far the largest – unanimously forced the government to commission a study by the World Bank. The subsequent report effectively refuted the common wisdom on welfare provision among the Latvian élites, and served as a basis for far-reaching social reforms.

'Harder' social policy governance, however, does not always lead to more compliance. In fact, the government continued the progressive policy reforms even after 2014 when close monitoring ended. In addition, the authorities exercised substantial discretion in 'soft' social policy, as well as in 'hard' fiscal policy areas, such as budgeting, pensions, taxation and spending – even when subject to the BoP programme and post-programme surveillance. Yet, to the extent that the formal overachievements in some policy areas were used implicitly as a justification for the derogations in others, the limited effectiveness of social policy governance might be a consequence of the one-size-fits-all operation of the fiscal and euro-related governance frameworks, as these were pushed to the extreme by the national authorities.

This case study has significant implications for EU economic governance as a whole. As the evidence shows, hierarchical governance structures suffer not only from an inability to address local needs and challenges, but also from ineffectiveness in operation. When designing one-size-fits-all fiscal rules or the convergence criteria, EU policy-makers could not have anticipated either the socio-economic conditions of the specific member state, or the preferences of its governing élites. Additional uncertainty came about as a result of opportunistic cherry-picking and instrumentalization of the frameworks on the part of the government. Meanwhile, the Commission's advocacy of social policy in Latvia serves as a positive example of how its governance approach can be dynamically adjusted according to experience on the ground. Responding to the fiscal radicalism pursued by the authorities, the Commission became a social policy advocate even before the broader social agenda of the European Semester was first formalized in the 2012 AGS (European Commission 2012a). Latvia's social policy still falls significantly short of the European Semester benchmarks. The Commission has concluded that little progress had been made on a number of big-ticket 'quality-of-life-improving' reforms to tackle high social inequality and poverty (European Commission 2014, 2015a). Nonetheless, social policy in Latvia has become increasingly progressive since the economic crisis – to a large extent because of the Commission's pressure. The Latvian experience may send a positive signal to other countries in the EU's periphery, struggling with malfunctioning social policy systems, whether in terms of poor targeting or low spending – such as the other neoliberal Baltic countries and the weak states in south-eastern Europe (i.e. Romania, Bulgaria and Croatia) (Bohle and Greskovits 2012). As the Latvian case shows, if electoral support for economic redistribution is low, pressure from external institutions can play an important role to instigate change.

## Notes

1. The European Semester is an annual cycle of economic policy co-ordination, according to which the Commission undertakes a detailed analysis of the member states' reform programmes.
2. Latvia adopted the Fiscal Compact through the Fiscal Discipline Law that entered into force in March 2013.
3. The inflation rate may not exceed 1.5 percentage points above the rate of the three best performing member states. Budget deficit may not exceed 3 per cent, while government debt – 60 per cent of GDP. The long-term interest rate on government bonds may not be higher than two percentage points the rate of the three best performing member states. Finally, a member state must participate in the ERMII mechanism for at least two years without severe tensions.

## Disclosure Statement

No potential conflict of interest was reported by the author.

## References


Aslund, A. (2013) 'Why austerity works and stimulus doesn't', 7 January, Bloomberg View, available at http://www.bloombergview.com/articles/2013-01-07/why-austerity-works-and-fiscal-stimulus-doesn-t (accessed January 2016).

Aslund, A. and Dombrovskis, V. (2011) *How Latvia Came Through the Financial Crisis*, Washington, DC: Institute of International Economics.

Auers, D. (2013) 'Latvia', in S. Berglund, J. Ekman, K. Deegan-Krause, and T. Knutsen (eds.), *The Handbook of Political Change in Eastern Europe*, 3rd ed. Cheltenham, UK: Edward Elgar Publishing, pp. 85–123.

Austers, A. (2014) 'How great is Latvia's success story?', *Intereconomics* 49(4): 228–38.

Bekker, S. (2013) *The EU's Stricter Economic Governance: A Step Towards More Binding Coordination of Social Policies?*

Blyth, M. (2013) *Austerity: The History of a Dangerous Idea*, New York: Oxford University Press.

Bohle, D. and Greskovits, B. (2012) *Capitalist Diversity on Europe's Periphery*, Ithaca and London: Cornell University Press.

Crespy, A. and Menz, G. (2015) 'Commission entrepreneurship and the debasing of social Europe before and after the Eurocrisis', *JCMS: Journal of Common Market Studies* 53(4): 753–68.

Dandashly, A. and Verdun, A. (2015) 'Boarding the euro plane: euro adoption in the Czech Republic and Slovakia', *Review of European and Russian Affairs* 9(2): 1–26.

Dārziņa, L. (2012) 'Budžeta grozījumi: palielinot izdevumus, visus virsplāna ieņēmumus netērēs', Latvijas Vēstneša portāls, available at http://www.lvportals.lv/visi/likumi-prakse/250540-budzeta-grozijumi-palielinot-izdevumus-visus-virsplana-ienemumus-neteres/ (accessed March 2016).

Dārziņa, L. (2013) 'Pasaules Bankas pētījumu Labklājības ministrija izmantos sociālās drošības politikas pilnveidei', Latvijas Vēstneša portāls, available at http://www.lvportals.lv/visi/likumi-prakse/255607-pasaules-bankas-petijumu-labklajibas-ministrija-izmantos-socialas-drosibas-politikas-pilnveidei/ (accessed September 2016).

de la Porte, C. and Heins, E. (2016) 'Game change in EU social policy: from optional recalibration to coercive retrenchment', in E. Xiarchogiannopoulou and M. Rodrigues (eds.), *The Eurozone Crisis and the Transformation of EU Governance: Internal and External Implications*, Routledge: London, pp. 157–170.

Degryse, C., Jepsen, M. and Pochet, P. (2013) 'The Euro crisis and its impact on national and European social policies', *Working paper, May*, Brussels: European Trade Union Institute, available at https://www.etui.org/Publications2/Working-Papers/The-Euro-crisis-and-its-impact-on-national-and-European-social-policies (accessed July 2016).

Dyson, K. and Featherstone, K. (1996) 'Italy and EMU as a "Vincolo Esterno": empowering the technocrats, transforming the state', *South European Society and Politics* 1(2): 272–99.

Eihmanis, E. (2017) 'An ever wider gap: the ethnic divide in Latvian party competition', in S. Hutter and H. Kriesi (eds), *European Party Politics in Times of Crises*. Forthcoming.

European Commission (2009) *First Addendum to the Memorandum of Understanding Between the European Union and the Republic of Latvia*, Brussels: Directorate General for Financial and Economic Affairs, available at https://ec.europa.eu/info/sites/info/files/ecfin_mou_add1_bop_latvia_en.pdf (accessed July 2016).

European Commission (2010) *Second Addendum to the Memorandum of Understanding Between the European Union and the Republic of Latvia*, Brussels: Directorate General for Financial and Economic Affairs, available at https://ec.europa.eu/info/sites/info/files/ecfin_mou_add2_bop_latvia_en.pdf (accessed July 2016).

European Commission (2011) 'Annual growth survey: advancing the EU's comprehensive response to the crisis', *COM(2011) 11 final*, January 12, Brussels, available at http://ec.europa.eu/europe2020/pdf/en_final.pdf (accessed April 2016).

European Commission (2012a) 'Communication from the commission: annual growth survey', *COM(2011) 815 final, VOL. 1/5*, November 23, Brussels, available at http://ec.europa.eu/europe2020/pdf/ags2012_en.pdf (accessed April 2016).

European Commission (2012b) 'EU balance-of-payments assistance for Latvia: foundations of success', *Occasional Papers 120, ISSN 1725*-3209, Brussels: Directorate-General for Economic and Financial Affairs, available at http://ec.europa.eu/economy_finance/publications/occasional_paper/2012/pdf/ocp120_en.pdf (accessed December 2015).

European Commission (2012c) 'Recommendation for a council recommendation on Latvia's 2012 national reform programme and delivering a council opinion on Latvia's convergence programme for 2012–2015', *SWD(2012) 320 final*, May 30, Brussels, available at http://ec.europa.eu/europe2020/pdf/nd/csr2012_latvia_en.pdf (accessed January 2016).

European Commission (2013a) 'Commission staff working document: assessment of the 2013 national reform programme and convergence programme for Latvia', *SWD(2013) 364 final*, Brussels, available at http://ec.europa.eu/europe2020/pdf/nd/swd2013_latvia_en.pdf (accessed March 2016).

European Commission (2013b) 'Convergence report 2013 on Latvia', *ISSN 1725*-3217, European Economy 3, Brussels, available at http://ec.europa.eu/economy_finance/publications/european_economy/2013/pdf/ee3_en.pdf (accessed December 2015).

European Commission (2013c) 'EU BoP assistance to Latvia – second review under post-programme surveillance', January 15, Brussels: Directorate General, Economic and Financial Affairs, available at https://ec.europa.eu/info/sites/info/files/ecfin_lv_efc_note_2nd_pps_mission_en.pdf (accessed July 2016).

European Commission (2014) 'Recommendation for a council recommendation on Latvia's 2014 national reform programme and delivering a Council opinion on Latvia's 2014 stability programme', *COM(2014) 415 final*, June 2, Brussels, available at http://ec.europa.eu/europe2020/pdf/csr2014/csr2014_latvia_en.pdf (accessed April 2016).

European Commission (2015a) 'Commission staff working document: country report Latvia 2015', *COM(2015) 85 final*, February 26, Brussels, available at http://ec.europa.eu/europe2020/pdf/csr2015/cr2015_latvia_en.pdf (accessed March 2015).

European Commission (2015b) 'Making the best use of the flexibility within the existing rules of the stability and growth pact', *COM(2015) 12 final*, Strasbourg, available at http://eur-lex.europa.eu/legal-content/EN/TXT/PDF/?uri=CELEX:52015DC0012&from=EN (accessed April 2016).

European Court of Auditors (2015) 'Financial assistance provided to countries in difficulties', *Special Report No 18*, Luxemburg, available at http://www.eca.europa.eu/Lists/ECADocuments/SR15_18/SR_CRISIS_SUPPORT_EN.pdf (accessed March 2016).

Ferrera, M. and Gualmini, E. (2004) *Rescued by Europe?: Social and Labour Market Reforms in Italy From Maastricht to Berlusconi*, 1 edition, Amsterdam: Amsterdam University Press.

George, A. L. and Bennett, A. (2005) *Case Studies and Theory Development in the Social Sciences*, London: MIT Press.

Hacker, B. (2012) 'The end of the European Social Model as we have envisioned it? Political economy principles in Europe may be changed by the economic crisis governance', University of Sheffield, 1-3 July, available at http://speri.dept.shef.ac.uk/wp-content/uploads/2013/06/SPERI_Paper_Hacker.pdf (accessed July 2016).

Ikstens, J. (2015) 'Latvia', *European Journal of Political Research Political Data Yearbook* 54(1): 181–9.

IMF (2013) *'Republic of Latvia: ex post evaluation of exceptional access under the 2008 stand-by arrangement', IMF Country Report No. 13/30*, Washington, DC: International Monetary Fund, available at https://www.imf.org/external/pubs/ft/scr/2013/cr1330.pdf (accessed July 2016).

Interview (2013a) *Economist at the European Commission.*

Interview (2013b) *Economist at the European Commission.*

Interview (2013c) *Economist at the European Commission.*

Interview (2013d) *Economist at the European Commission.*

Interview (2013e) *Official at the Ministry of Economics of the Republic of Latvia.*

Interview (2013f) *Official at the Ministry of Finance of the Republic of Latvia.*

Interview (2013g) *Official at the Ministry of Welfare of the Republic of Latvia.*

Interview (2016) *Ilze Viņķele, Minister of Welfare of the Republic of Latvia 2011–2014.*

Joerges, C. (2014) 'Law and politics in Europe's crisis: on the history of the impact of an unfortunate configuration', *Constellations* 21(2): 249–61.

Krugman, P. (2009) 'Latvia is the new Argentina (slightly wonkish)', Paul Krugman Blog, available at http://krugman.blogs.nytimes.com/2008/12/23/latvia-is-the-new-argentina-slightly-wonkish/ (accessed December 2015).

Laffan, B. and Schlosser, P. (2016) 'Public finances in Europe: fortifying EU economic governance in the shadow of the crisis', *Journal of European Integration* 38(3): 237–49.

Lagarde, C. (2012) 'Latvia and the Baltics—a story of recovery', Washington DC: International Monetary Fund, available at https://www.imf.org/en/News/Articles/2015/09/28/04/53/sp060512 (accessed July 2016).

Latvia.eu (2015) 'Budget for 2016 approved by the Saeima', 1 December, available at http://www.latvia.eu/news/budget-2016-approved-saeima (accessed March 2016).

Lütz, S. and Kranke, M. (2014) 'The European rescue of the Washington consensus? EU and IMF lending to central and Eastern European countries', *Review of International Political Economy* 21(2): 310–38.

Milne, R. (2013) 'Latvia: reaching for the Euro', *Financial Times* 23 April, available at http://www.ft.com/intl/cms/s/0/5df14d34-a776-11e2-bfcd-00144feabdc0.html#axzz436nUHu2w (accessed March 2016).

Ministry of Economics (2011) 'National reform programme of Latvia for the implementation of the 'Europe 2020' strategy', available at http://ec.europa.eu/europe2020/pdf/nrp/nrp_latvia_en.pdf (accessed March 2016).

Ministry of Economics (2012) 'Progress report on the implementation of the national reform programme of Latvia within the 'Europe 2020' strategy', Riga, available at http://ec.europa.eu/europe2020/pdf/nd/nrp2012_latvia_en.pdf (accessed February 2016).

Pochet, P. and Degryse, C. (2012) 'The programmed dismantling of the 'European Social Model'', *Intereconomics* 47(4): 212–7.

Roubini, N. (2008) *EconoMonitor*, available at http://www.economonitor.com/nouriel/2009/06/10/latvias-currency-crisis-is-a-rerun-of-argentinas/ (accessed December 2015).

Scharpf, F. (2014) 'Legitimacy intermediation in the multilevel European polity and its collapse in the Eurocrisis. Comment', in J. E. Fossum and A. J. Menéndez (eds), *The European Union in Crises or the European Union as Crises?*, ARENA Report No 2/14, Oslo: ARENA, pp. 93–157.

Schmidt, V. (2015a) 'The Eurozone's crisis of democratic legitimacy: can the EU rebuild public trust and support for European Economic Integration?' *Discussion paper 015, ISSN 2443*-8022, Brussels: European Commission, available at https://ec.europa.eu/info/sites/info/files/file_import/dp015_en_2.pdf (accessed July 2016).

Schmidt, V. (2015b) 'Changing the policies, politics, and processes of the Eurozone in crisis: will this time be different?', in D. Natali and B. Vanhercke (eds), *Social Policy in the European Union: State of Play 2015*, Brussels: European Trade Union Institute, pp. 33–64.

Schoukens, P. (2013) 'From soft monitoring to enforceable action: a quest for new legal approaches in the EU Fight against social exclusion', *Euroforum policy paper 5*, available at https://lirias.kuleuven.be/handle/123456789/404634 (accessed April 2016).

Spiegel, P. et al. (2015) 'IMF criticises Greece bailout deal with EU', *Financial Times* 15 July, available at http://www.ft.com/intl/cms/s/0/444a0bc8-2a46-11e5-8613-e7aedbb7bdb7.html#axzz45sq5PFOr (accessed April 2016).

Tapiņš, A. (2013) 'The government prepares to tackle inequality after years of ignoring advice', Re:Baltica, available at http://www.rebaltica.lv/en/important/a/949/the_government_prepares_to_tackle_inequality_after_years_of_ignoring_advice.html (accessed September 2016).

The Baltic Course (2013) 'Latvia's PM calls 2014 budget 'historic'', available at http://www.baltic-course.com/eng/finances/?doc=82199 (accessed March 2016).

The Baltic Course (2014a) 'Reirs names fiscal discipline and reducing inequality as his priorities in Latvia', available at http://www.baltic-course.com/eng/finances/?doc=98493 (accessed April 2016).

The Baltic Course (2014b) 'Vilks: budget priorities in 2015 will focus on defense, healthcare and social inequality', available at http://www.baltic-course.com/eng/finances/?doc=97642 (accessed March 2016).

The Baltic Course (2015) 'Solidarity tax to be charged on high salaries in Latvia as of 2016', available at http://www.baltic-course.com/eng/legislation/?doc=113639 (accessed January 2016).

Traynor, I. (2012) 'Latvia still keen to join single currency despite euro crisis', *The Guardian*, 19 September, available at http://www.theguardian.com/world/2012/sep/19/latvia-keen-join-euro (accessed December 2015).

Trubek, D. and Trubek, L. (2005) 'Hard and soft Law in the construction of social Europe: the role of the open method of co-ordination', *European Law Journal* 11(3): 343–64.

tvnet.lv (2010) 'Vilks: Satversmes tiesa ierobežo iespēju taupīt', *Financenet*, available at http://financenet.tvnet.lv/viedokli/358745-vilks_satversmes_tiesa_ierobezo_iespeju_taupit (accessed June 2016).

Vanags, A. and Zasova, A. (2015) 'Latvia stumbling towards progressive income taxation', *BICEPS Policy Brief*, available at http://freepolicybriefs.org/2015/11/16/latvia-stumbling-towards-progressive-income-taxation-2/ (accessed March 2016).

Vandenbroucke, F. et al. (2013) 'Excessive social imbalances and the performance of welfare states in the EU', *Euroforum policy paper 3*, available at https://www.kuleuven.be/euroforum/viewpic.php?LAN=E&TABLE=DOCS&ID=855 (accessed July 2016).

Vilks, A. (2010) 'PVN jāpalielina no nākamā gada, nevis 2012. gadā', *Leta video*, available at https://www.youtube.com/watch?v=1HHQObjkLkA (accessed December 2015).

Vilks, A. (2011) 'A.Vilks: Inflācijai gada otrajā pusē vajadzētu samazināties', *LTV Panorāma*, available at https://www.youtube.com/watch?v=5kB8Kbv5zEk (accessed December 2015).

Volskis, E. (2012) 'Reforms of Baltic States pension systems: challenges and benefits', Tallin: Estonian Ministry of Finance, EBRD, 7 December, available at http://www.ebrd.com/downloads/news/pension-system.pdf (accessed April 2016).

Woll, C. and Jacquot, S. (2010) 'Using Europe: strategic action in multi-level politics', *Comparative European Politics* 8(1): 110–26.

Woolfson, C. and Sommers, J. (2016) 'Austerity and the demise of social Europe: The Baltic Model versus the European Social Model', *Globalizations* 13(1): 78–93.

World Bank (2013a) 'Expenditure and performance of welfare benefits and employment programs', in 'Latvia: 'Who is Unemployed, Inactive or Needy? Assessing Post-Crisis Policy Options'', available at http://www.lm.gov.lv/upload/aktualitates/lv_expenditure_and_performance.pdf (accessed December 2015).

World Bank (2013b) 'Latvia GMI program: main design characteristics and comparison with minimum', in 'Latvia: 'Who is Unemployed, Inactive or Needy? Assessing Post-Crisis Policy Options'', available at http://www.lm.gov.lv/upload/aktualitates/lv_gmi_note_270513.pdf (accessed December 2015).

World Bank (2013c) 'Latvia: who is unemployed, inactive or needy?', available at http://www.worldbank.org/en/news/feature/2013/05/17/latvia-who-is-unemployed-inactive-or-needy (accessed June 2016).

Zeitlin, J. and Vanhercke, B. (2017) 'Socialising the European Semester: EU Economic and Social Policy Coordination in Crisis and Beyond', *Journal of European Public Policy*, doi:10.1080/13501763.2017.1363269

# Explaining the evolving role of national parliaments under the European Semester

Mark Hallerberg, Benedicta Marzinotto and Guntram B. Wolff

**ABSTRACT**

This contribution examines and explains the role of national parliaments in the European Semester process. It builds on original survey-based evidence and traces whether national parliaments discuss and vote on Stability/Convergence and on National Reform Programmes; how their involvement changed over time; and what might condition national varieties of parliamentary scrutiny over European Union (EU) affairs. We find significant cross-country variation in whether the debate is taking place at the parliamentary level; whether it is European Affairs or finance committees that are involved; and whether there is involvement *ex ante* (before submission) and/or *ex post* (after country-specific recommendations). From 2012 to 2015, finance committees played an increasingly prominent role. Traditional measures of the strength of parliament do not explain what we observe. We do find that non-euro area member states were most likely to monitor EU recommendations under the European Semester and that this effect increased over time.

## 1. Introduction

The institutional reforms introduced at the European Union (EU) level in response to the debt crisis have expanded the potential for national parliaments to take active part in European economic governance. The Lisbon Treaty had already empowered national parliaments to 'contribute actively to the good functioning of the Union' (Art.12 of the Treaty on the Functioning of the European Union [TFEU]). The deepening of the co-ordination of EU economic policy following the approval of the Six-Pack in 2011 and of the Two-Pack in 2013 calls for a fresh assessment of whether/how national parliaments are truly involved in the process and of what factors might condition their involvement (Kreilinger 2016). Ultimately, information on parliamentary

Supplemental data for this article can be accessed at https://doi.org/10.1080/13501763.2017.1363273.

scrutiny of EU affairs allows one to draw conclusions on the democratic (input) legitimacy of EU economic governance.

The existing literature on the impact of EU politics and policies on national parliaments is divided in two. Some see a diminishing role for national parliaments on the back of more intense inter-state relations (see, for example, Crum 2017; De Wilde and Raunio forthcoming), while others recognize new opportunities for national parliaments (see, for example, Goetz and Meyer-Sahling 2008, Jancic 2016). Beyond judgement, there is an extensive empirical literature on the factors that affect the extent to which domestic legislatures become 'Europeanized', with the most common finding that parliamentary scrutiny of EU affairs rises with the institutional strength of parliaments (e.g., Auel and Höing 2014) and with the Euroscepticism of élites or the public opinion or both.

This contribution adds to this literature by using the specific case of the European Semester to assess parliamentary scrutiny of EU affairs and to isolate the factors that condition the response of national legislatures to an exogenous source of Europeanization. We define 'scrutiny' as the degree to which parliamentary committees discuss reform commitments in the EU context and the timing for doing so, whether *ex ante* – when national governments prepare reform plans – or *ex post* – after the EU has provided feedback to national plans. While we are aware that having the topic on the agenda does not necessarily come with genuine involvement and that it is likely to mean different things for different countries, this dependent variable offers the most transparent and immediate way of comparing the involvement of national parliaments across countries.

Through the European Semester, national governments submit jointly Stability or Convergence Programmes and National Reform Programmes, on the basis of which they will receive specific policy recommendations. To gather comparable information on national parliaments' involvement in the European Semester, we rely on an original survey, which we submitted to national parliaments in the EU in different rounds between 2011 and 2015. The survey provides information on what parliaments do at each stage of the European Semester and on how their role might have changed over time.

Our results are as follows. Member states that are not part of the euro area are, on average, more involved in the European Semester in both 2012 and 2015, and more so in *ex post* monitoring of country-specific recommendations. In each of these member states outside the euro area, there is an electoral cleavage concerning the EU; debates in parliament on European matters can raise the profile of parties before electorates that care about European issues. Moreover, we find that by 2015 parliamentary committees in all EU countries are more active than in 2012, with budget committees playing a more prominent role than EU affairs committees.

## 2. Literature on the Europeanization of national parliaments

Existing studies on the impact of EU politics on domestic parliaments are divided into two opposing views. On the one hand are those who suggest that state-level negotiations have diminished the importance of national parliamentary bodies (Crum 2017). On the other hand, there are those for whom the process of European integration is providing national parliaments with an opportunity to engage in international affairs in ways that may have been unthinkable in its absence (Goetz and Meyer-Sahling 2008). Jančić (2016) argues that national parliaments have acquired various rights of approvals in the European Semester. Rittberger and Winzen (2015) find that 'strong' parliaments prior to the crisis were the most active during and after the crisis concerning European economic and financial matters. De Wilde and Raunio (forthcoming) contend that national parliaments still need to re-direct more resources to important decisions that are being taken in the European Council. Another strand of literature distinguishes between forms of their involvement. Rozenberg and Hefftler (2015) provide a useful framework for thinking about the functions of parliamentary scrutiny. They discuss whether parliament engages as a (1) policy shaper, (2) government watchdog, (3) public forum, (4) EU expert, or (5) European player.

Finally, there is an empirical literature on the factors that might explain cross-country variation in parliamentary scrutiny of EU affairs, which is the one to which this contribution relates. A common finding in the literature is that stronger parliaments will succeed in assuming a greater oversight role for themselves. Raunio (2005) finds that one important determinant of whether a national parliament engages with the European level is the strength and quality of intervention rights of national parliaments in the domestic balance of power. Auel and Höing (2014) argue that parliamentary institutional strength is positively correlated with the level of parliamentary crisis activity.

The position of national political parties on European integration and the role of public opinions are important factors in explaining the involvement of national parliaments in EU policy-making. Bergman (1997) contends that less supportive public opinions towards European integration are associated with greater parliamentary control over governments. Raunio (2005) shows that the combination of a powerful legislature and a more Eurosceptic public opinion leads to higher levels of parliamentary control over government. By contrast, Auel and Höing (2014) posit that the stronger Eurosceptic parties in parliament are associated with more parliamentary scrutiny, but they do not find evidence for this in their data.

We build on the existing literature to isolate key determinants of parliamentary involvement, focusing on the institutional strength of parliament and on the Euroscepticism of publics. We expect strong parliaments to engage more with the European Semester process. Euroscepticism should condition the behaviour of parliamentarians who want to score points with voters. We anticipate that countries with more Eurosceptic populations have parliamentarians more willing to debate opinions on national policy that come from Brussels than parliamentarians in member states where 'Europe' is not a relevant political cleavage.

While the existing literature offers guidance on factors that condition parliamentary scrutiny, we adapt our hypotheses to the specific case of the European Semester. EU recommendations concerning public finances are binding for euro area members, but not for the others. Only euro area countries are subject to possible fines. This aspect is likely to bear an impact on the behaviour of parliaments. We should find more scrutiny from euro area parliaments. Moreover, we would expect the budget committee to be most active.

Nevertheless, we argue that non-euro area countries are not all the same. We distinguish between two categories of non-members. Some have made a conscious decision not to join – they either have opt-outs (Denmark and the United Kingdom), have had referenda where the voters opted against membership (again Denmark and also Sweden), or have signalled that they have no intention of joining over the medium term (the Czech Republic). There are others that have not joined because they do not meet the formal convergence criteria, but their governments do foresee eventual membership. This second group is certainly more diffuse than the first – whether the Bulgarian government really intends to push for euro membership is anyone's guess. But in the first group there is a conscious decision not to join, and this aspect may condition the extent to which non-membership comes with less parliamentary involvement. The opposite could occur – such parliaments could be especially concerned with the encroachment of the EU into domestic affairs in such countries, which is best epitomized by the 'European Scrutiny Committee' of the House of Commons in the United Kingdom. This is where the divide between euro area and non-euro area members crosses with issues of Euroscepticism and more specifically with Eurosceptic élites. By distinguishing between definite euro-outs and those that simply do not qualify, we discriminate between two competing explanations for involvement, i.e., euro membership and the Euroscepticism of national establishments. Less involvement probably means that countries outside the monetary union do not perceive EU fiscal recommendations as binding upon them, while greater involvement is likely to come from some form of Euroscepticism and more generally from the politicization of EU issues at the level of élites and possibly also of the public opinion.

## 3. Survey-based evidence on the role national parliaments in the European Semester process

### *3.1. The survey's sample*

To collect comparable information, we conducted surveys over the period 2011–2015. Initially, in April 2011, a pilot survey was submitted to national parliaments in six EU member states. The European Semester had been activated only few months earlier, in January 2011, before being inserted in binding regulation under the Six-Pack of December 2011. Between March and April 2012, we addressed all 27 member states and received responses from all member states but Bulgaria.[1] We then sent out a third wave to all member states' parliaments between March and June 2013.[2] Of the 27, 18 replied while another two arrived after the intended window. The 2013 survey was used to confirm the results from 2012, and they matched in the surveys for the year 2012 except for Denmark and Ireland, which were in the process of increasing national parliamentary involvement.[3] The final wave was returned after the 2015 European Semester was complete, between October 2015 and April 2016. We received replies from all lower houses except the Czech Republic.[4] Our empirical analysis therefore compares 2012 and 2015, namely the first full year of the European Semester under the Six-Pack and the most recent year. This allows us to consider both the initial response to the European Semester and the evolution of parliamentary involvement.

The respondents were usually staff from either the budget or finance (referred to as 'budget' generically below) or European Union affairs committee. In many cases we had responses from both committees.[5] Whilst in some cases we obtained answers both from the upper and lower house, we report lower house responses because this is the chamber that is mostly involved in budget policy-making.

### *3.2. The European Semester: what kind of case study?*

Our evidence is meant to capture the reaction of member states' parliaments to the creation of the European Semester. While the introduction to this collection provides further details, we offer a quick sketch of the Semester's most important facets.

National governments are obliged to submit their European plans to the European Commission by 30 April every year. The joint submission of the two documents intends to encourage governments to devise consistent reform plans, whilst accounting for complementarities and trade-offs between fiscal adjustment and structural reform. The European Commission delivers country-specific as well as general euro-area recommendations at the end of May every year.[6] These are then discussed at the June European

Council and eventually become binding after the final word by the Council of the European Union. National governments are expected to account for the received country-specific recommendations when drafting the budget law for the consecutive year, which is then typically submitted to national parliaments at the beginning of the parliamentary budget session in the autumn. The period from when the Council issues country-specific recommendations until the final approval of the State budget law at the end of each year is normally referred to as the 'National Semester.'

In terms of parliamentary involvement, the Six-Pack provides the European Parliament the power to intervene in the process by means of the newly established Economic Dialogue, through which the European Parliament is entitled to question EU institutions on issues related either to the Annual Growth Survey (AGS) or the country-specific recommendations, as well as to invite national representatives to discuss the received country-specific recommendations. The Six-Pack regulation also formally encourages governments to seek a dialogue with their respective national parliaments before submitting the documents to Brussels. We consider this possible discussion in parliament as an *ex ante* consideration of what the government proposes; that is, a consideration of the government's plans before they leave the respective capital city. Parliaments can also provide *ex post* consideration; that is, a debate of the county-specific recommendations that the Council passes.[7]

### *3.3. The survey's main contents and results*

The main purpose of the survey is to identify how national parliaments are involved in the discussion of national medium-term fiscal plans, Stability or Convergence Programmes, and of National Reform Programmes. At the same time, though, we also collect information on the role of national parliaments in the annual budget process to measure their institutional strength. We look at their amendment powers in the discussion of budget laws and at the ways in which they intervene more generally in the discussion of national expenditures and revenues. We also consider the role of national parliaments. The differentiation between domestic and European fiscal documents provides us with leverage to assess whether their potential involvement is indeed the sign of a Europeanization of the legislatures or rather the continuation of a domestic practice of being involved in the discussion of all budget-related issues. We focus on two types of parliamentary surveillance following the European Semester calendar, namely on the *ex ante* monitoring of the Stability/Convergence Programme and of National Reform Programmes that the given member state government submits to Brussels; and on *ex post* monitoring of the recommendations the EU Council makes to the individual member states.

The main stylized facts are as follows. For the formulation of a country's Stability or Convergence Programme as well as its National Reform Programme, we asked where these are prepared in the government. Finance or economics ministries prepared the former in 22 of the member states. National Reform Programmes, however, involved a broader sets of actors, with only 14 prepared exclusively in a finance or economics ministry, five written in a prime minister's office, and the rest written in multiple ministries, such as Austria (drafted jointly by different ministries and co-ordinated by the Federal Chancellery), France (Finance and Prime Minister's Office), and Romania (Finance, Economics, and Prime Minister's Office).

Both plans then could have reached parliament, and the question is whether parliaments debated them before they were formally submitted to Brussels. Rarely did plenaries put the issue on the agenda, but they did debate the Stability or Convergence Programme about a quarter of the time (seven parliaments in 2012, and six in 2015), while they rarely discussed the National Reform Programme (just two parliaments in 2012 – Luxembourg and Italy).[8]

In terms of parliamentary committees, we consider the role of the budget and the European Union affairs committees (see Table 1). In 2012, the pattern was generally on the diagonal, where either none or both were involved – in 10 countries, no committee examined either plan before its government submits it, while in 11 countries both committees discuss the documents. There were no parliaments where a European Union affairs committee considered the SCP but the budget committee did not. In 2015, however, there was a shift towards participation of budget committees, with 18 of 23 in this sample involving regular budget committee review.

The picture for National Reform Programmes is more differentiated in 2012, but it converges to what one observes for the SCP in 2015, with the correlation between the consideration of the two plans in finance committees at about 0.9.[9] In nine countries in 2012, which overlap to some extent with the same group for Stability or Convergence Programmes, neither committee was involved. In only six member states did both committees participate. But the relevant committee changed – in a third of the member states it was the European Union affairs committee that debated the National Reform Programme, and in all but one of these it did so exclusively.[10] By 2015, however, there is the same movement to the budget committee, with 19 of 26 budget committees discussing the *ex ante* plans of the NRPs.

The results are different when we consider the involvement of parliament in *ex post* monitoring, which comes after the European Commission first issues its recommendations and then the Council approves the formal recommendations to the member states. These recommendations are country-specific under the European Semester, and they represent commentary on the two plans the government submitted to Brussels in April. They could also put

**Table 1.** Different forms of committee involvement.

| | Committee involvement in Stability or Convergence Programmes | | |
|---|---|---|---|
| | Budget Committee Debate SCP? | EU Affairs Committee Debate SCP? | |
| 2012 | | No | Yes |
| | No | AT, CY, DK, ES, IE, MT, NL, PL, RO, SK, UK | |
| | Yes | FR, LU, PT, SE | BE, CZ, DE, EE, FI, IT, LV, LT, HU, SI |
| 2015 | | No | Yes |
| | No | DE, HU, MT, NL, SI, RO, UK | |
| | Yes | AT, BU, FR, ES, IE, LT, PT, SE | BE, DK, EE, FI, LV, LU, IT, PL, SI, SK |
| | Committee involvement in National Reform Programmes | | |
| | Budget Committee Debate NPR? | EU Affairs Committee Debate SCP? | |
| 2012 | | No | Yes |
| | No | AT, DK, EL, ES, FI, IE, MT, NL, PL | BE, CY, CZ, EE, LV, PT, RO, SK, UK |
| | Yes | LU, SE | DE, FR, IT, LT, HU, SI |
| 2015 | | No | Yes |
| | No | CY, EL, MT, NL, RO, UK | DE |
| | Yes | AT, BU, ES, LT, PT, SE, SI | BE, DK, EE, FI, FR, HU, IE, IT, LU, LV, PL, SK |
| | Committee involvement in *ex post* Monitoring | | |
| | Budget Committee Debate? | EU Affairs Committee Debate SCP? | |
| 2012 | | No | Yes |
| | No | **AT**, **DE**, **ES**, **FR**, **IT**, **MT**, **PL**, **PT**, **RO**, **SI**, SK, *FI* | **DK**, **EE**, **HU**, **NL**, **UK**, *CY*, *CZ*, *SK* |
| | Yes | **LU**, IE, CY, *LT*, LV | **BE**, **SE**, CZ, FI, LT |
| 2015 | | No | Yes |
| | No | **AT**, *CY*, **DE**, FR, **IT**, *EL*. **IE**, **MT**, *LU*, *SI* | |
| | Yes | **BG**, **EE**, **ES**, *FR*, LU, **NL**, **PT** | **BE**, **DK**, **FI**, **HU**, **LV**, **LT**, **PL**, **RO SE**, **SK**, SI |

pressure on governments to respond to Council recommendations in terms of the proposed budget or in terms of various reform proposals. The last part of Table 1 considers whether the same two committees debated Council recommendations either on the Stability/Convergence Programme or on the National Reform Programme. Those that appear in bold indicate that the same committees considered both; those in normal type the consideration of the SCP; and those in italics the consideration of the NRP. There is some consistency in the answers. In 2012, nine member states did not discuss the Council recommendations. These included the four largest member states in the euro area – France, Germany, Italy and Spain.[11] Once again, the EU affairs committee was most important in the remaining group. In seven member states it considered recommendations on both plans, while it played a role in another six member states. The budget committee played a role in nine states, and it was more important in debating SCP than NRP.

By 2015, however, budget committees had again come to the fore. There were no cases where a European Union affairs committee evaluated the country-specific recommendations while the budget committee did not in

2015, whereas in 16 member states budget committees debated one and/or the other programme. At the same time, the move towards debate is less complete. Germany and Italy continue to avoid debates on the recommendations in their parliamentary committees, with the German response notable – while the recommendations appeared on the agenda of its Budget Committee in the Bundestag, they were not debated.

In the next section, we try to explain these patterns; that is, why some parliaments are active under the European Semester and why at one stage rather than another, while others are not.

## 4. Analysis: possible explanations of parliamentary involvement in the European Semester

What explains the patterns in parliamentary involvement under the European Semester?

First, we are interested in determining whether the strength of parliament has any bearing on the extent and nature of the scrutiny it may exercise over EU affairs both *ex ante* and *ex post*. A common finding in the literature discussed above is that stronger parliaments will succeed in assuming a greater oversight role for themselves. Rittberger and Winzen (2015), looking at a broader set of dependent variables that includes the European Semester but also European Stability Mechanism packages and Article 13 of the Fiscal Compact, argue that strong parliaments are the most likely to react to European-level events. We test whether there is any relationship between the strength of individual parliaments and their involvement in the European Semester and whether the procedural requirements of the European Semester alter this relationship compared with earlier, more general findings regarding scrutiny over EU affairs. The prediction is that stronger parliaments/committees are more active. Compare with existing studies, we constructed separate measures for the strength of budget and European Affairs committees respectively and indeed expect stronger committees to be more likely to participate in the European Semester. Moreover, we account for the institutional power of national parliaments over different agendas, distinguishing between budget and European affairs.

For budget strength, we generate these data ourselves using data from the 2012 survey. It is based on the formulation in Hallerberg *et al.*'s (2009) study of fiscal governance in EU member states. We assess the relative strength of parliaments along the following dimensions and give it a score of 1 for each of the following rights/competences: (1) a parliament can propose a budget independently of government; (2) it can propose amendments to the government's budget plan; (3) the amendments that it can propose are unlimited; (4) amendments do not face an offset rule on spending, which means that any suggested rise in spending need not be matched by with spending cuts; (5)

it does not face an offset rule relative to the budget balance; and (6) amendments to the government's budget plan can cause the fall of government. We update the Hallerberg *et al.* (2009) dataset with results from our surveys. The highest possible score is six, whilst the lowest is zero. The average in our sample is two and half, but there is a high dispersion of parliamentary budget powers, with either strong or weak national parliaments. The strongest national parliaments are those in Austria, Finland and Romania with a score of five, while seven other parliaments have a score of four. At the other extreme, 12 national parliaments have a score of one. They include the traditionally weak parliaments of France, Ireland, and the United Kingdom, but they also include some parliaments in the new member states in Central and Eastern Europe, Greece and Sweden.

The second institutional measure focuses on parliamentary strength in European Union affairs, and it comes from Auel *et al.* (2015). Their OPAL score of institutional strength measures the respective parliament's access to information, the processing of that information, and enforcement. It is therefore a measure of *potential* strength. Based on an analysis of documents from the 40 parliaments, they also measure the activity of parliaments in EU matters. The authors collected the data in approximately the same period as the data collected on budget/finance committees.[12] The strongest national parliament is in Finland, with a score of 0.84, while the weakest is in Belgium, with a score of 0.24. The Spearman rank correlation between the two indices is only 0.17, which suggests that they are measuring different dimensions.

The main statistical measures we use are a Spearman rank correlation. Spearman rank correlations measure the strength of association between two ranked variables such as, for example, reform outcomes and individual conditioning factors. In other words, it assesses if and how well the relationship between two ranked variables can be described by a monotonic function – a Spearman correlation of +1 means that each of the considered variables is a perfect monotone function of the other. The rank correlation approach is notably well suited for use with small samples (Tompson, 2009). In an Online Appendix, we provide a probit analysis. We have only approximately 50 observations, which means that the multivariate analysis is only suggestive.

Comparing the strength of parliament in the budget process to both *ex ante* and *ex post* measures, Table 2 indicates that only the institutional strength of European affairs has some effect. There are no statistically significant relationships for budget strength, with the correlations all quite low. In contrast, the institutional strength in the field of European affairs is relevant in the initial year. In 2012, those countries with stronger pre-existing parliaments in this matter were more likely to have both their EU affairs and their budget committee review their SCP *ex ante*, and to have their EU affairs committee scrutinize the country-specific recommendations *ex post*. However, this relationship weakens considerably by 2015. We know the reason from the

**Table 2.** Strength of parliament in the budget process and *ex ante* and *ex post* parliamentary monitoring – 2012 and 2015.

| | Strength of parliament – budget | | Strength of parliament – EU affairs | |
|---|---|---|---|---|
| | 2012 | 2015 | 2012 | 2015 |
| *Ex ante* | | | | |
| Budget – SCP | 0.09 | 0.00 | 0.42* | 0.11 |
| EU affairs – SCP | 0.1 | −0.05 | 0.40* | 0.21 |
| Budget – NRP | −0.09 | −0.05 | 0.34 | 0.25 |
| EU affairs – NRP | −0.08 | −0.01 | −0.03 | 0.34 |
| *Ex post* | | | | |
| Budget – SCP | 0.25 | 0.05 | 0.06 | −0.1 |
| EU affairs – SCP | 0.05 | −0.03 | 0.44* | 0.22 |
| Budget – NRP | 0.03 | −0.05 | −0.22 | 0.19 |
| EU affairs – NRP | −0.16 | 0.01 | −0.07 | 0.24 |

Notes: The column with numbers provide the Spearman rank correlation. Those starred are significant at the 0.05 level.

previous tables – budget committees are supplanting European Union affairs committees in some countries. Even there, however, the overall strength of the parliament in budgetary matters does not predict where budget committees will be most active.[13]

Second, we are interested in whether membership in the euro area makes a difference (see Table 3). We generally expect that parliaments in euro area members pay more attention to EU recommendations that are binding on them. In this case, the role of national parliaments may be conditioned by the fact that the government could be subject to possible fines if it does not correct an 'excessive deficits.' This procedure suggests more scrutiny from budget committees.

**Table 3.** Role of euro area membership, definite euro-outs, and population Euroscepticism.

| | Euro area out | | Definite euro-out | | Euro-scepticism (Eurobarometer) | |
|---|---|---|---|---|---|---|
| | 2012 | 2015 | 2012 | 2015 | 2012 | 2015 |
| *Ex ante* | | | | | | |
| Budget – SCP | 0.07 | −0.11 | 0.04 | −0.12 | −0.1 | −0.31 |
| EU affairs – SCP | 0.01 | −0.18 | −0.04 | −0.08 | 0.15 | −0.16 |
| Budget – NRP | 0.14 | 0.07 | 0.09 | 0.12 | 0.2 | −0.34 |
| EU affairs – NRP | 0.1 | −0.13 | 0.06 | 0.07 | 0.01 | −0.2 |
| *Ex post* | | | | | | |
| Budget – SCP | 0.37 | 0.48* | 0.16 | 0.26 | 0.15 | −0.34 |
| EU affairs – SCP | .42* | 0.35 | 0.67* | 0.49* | 0.05 | 0.3 |
| Budget – NRP | 0.29 | 0.52* | −0.26 | 0.28 | −0.07 | −0.41* |
| EU affairs – NRP | 0.43 | 0.45* | 0.36 | 0.54* | 0.19 | 0.04 |

Notes: The numbers indicate the Spearman rank correlation. A 'euro area-out' is any country not in the euro area. A definite euro-out is one of five member states: Czech Republic, Denmark, Hungary, Sweden, and United Kingdom. The measure for population for population Euroscepticism comes from the Eurobarometer.

At the same time, the group of non-members cannot be considered to be a unitary actor, which implies that it is not obvious that all non-euro-area parliaments are inactive during the Semester process. Some member states have made a conscious decision not to join ('definite euro-out') – they either have opt-outs (Denmark and the United Kingdom), have had referenda where the voters opted against membership (Denmark and Sweden), or have not signed the Fiscal Compact and/or the Euro-Plus Pact (Czech Republic and Hungary). There are others that have not joined because they do not meet the formal convergence criteria, but their governments do foresee eventual membership. This second group is certainly more diffuse than the first. These varieties of non-membership can be considered as a reflection of a cleavage on the European Union on its own – government choose not to participate in Economic and Monetary Union because they would otherwise lose office if they did. Our expectation is that parliaments are more concerned with the encroachment of the EU into domestic affairs in define euro-outs countries, which is best epitomized by the 'European Scrutiny Committee' of the House of Commons in the United Kingdom.

Table 3 provides the main results. 'Definite euro-out' are member states where any expansion of European competence on economic matters is contested.[14] There are then five member states in total, and they constitute a subset of euro-outs.[15] Finally, we contrast this with the relative popularity of the European Union in Eurobarometer surveys among populations.[16] The result that jumps out is the importance of the European affairs committee in the review of Council recommendations. In 2012, these reviews are followed more in non-euro area member states than in those participating in the common currency. An explanation for this correlation comes from the 'definite euro-outs': in both 2012 and 2015 every one had its European Union affairs committee debate conclusions on both its Convergence Report and its National Reform Programme.[17] There is less parliamentary involvement in the euro area countries in *ex post* debates. In 2015, this result is clear for three of the four categories for member states outside the euro area – parliaments in countries outside of the euro area have more active parliamentary committees. This is consistent with an argument that the euro area 'outs' are more actively scrutinizing what the European Union is saying about their governments.

Third, another determinant of parliaments' involvement could be their positioning on EU affairs, which may be a function of the governing party's position on Europe and of public opinion. We test whether more 'Eurosceptic' populations, as measured through Eurobarometer surveys, indicate the potential for domestic parliamentarians to score points with voters. The data come from European Commission (2012) and European Commission (2015), which refer to the 'fall' versions of the Eurobarometer. We look at whether the public opinion thinks the country would be better if it were outside the EU, which we consider the most extreme measure of Euroscepticism, as it makes it more likely that parties, whether explicitly anti-European or not, feel a need to respond to an anti-European streak in their populations. The prediction here is that more Eurosceptic member states have more active parliaments under the European Semester and especially in the *ex post* phase when reviewing country-specific recommendations.[18]

The one unexpected finding is that the more Eurosceptic the population, the less likely that its budget committee reviews the NRP (Table 3). Notably, the result is the opposite of the one whether a member state is a euro area out. In fact, there is no correlation between whether a country is a euro area out and whether its population is Eurosceptic. An explanation for this finding may be idiosyncratic. The programme member states of Cyprus and Greece submit NRPs only, and these countries had increases in those who thought it would be better off outside the European Union, with Cyprus in 2015 having the highest percentage of its population that voiced this opinion (55 per cent). But it also indicates the changing nature of what it means to be 'Eurosceptic' and the effects on the formal powers of parliament.

These results contrast with non-findings concerning *ex ante* debates, where the measure of Euroscepticism does not predict whether a given committee has a debate.

## 5. Conclusions

This contribution explored parliamentary scrutiny of EU affairs through the European Semester process. It built on original survey-based evidence summarizing whether/how national parliaments in the EU are involved in the discussion of reform plans and of the feedback they receive from Brussels. We considered the *ex ante* role of the budget and European Union affairs committees in the discussion of Stability/Convergence Programmes and the National Reform Programmes. We also discussed the role these committees play in *ex post* monitoring of Council recommendations.

Having summarized the main results, we have attempted to provide an indication of what might affect cross-country variation in the participation of national parliaments in European economic governance. More traditional measures of the 'strength' of parliament played a role in 2012. The strength of European Union Affairs committees in *ex ante* monitoring mattered in 2012. One general finding for 2012 is that European Union affairs committees played a more important role than Budget/Finance in *ex post* scrutiny. There was a certain irony to this. An intention of the European Semester was to increase co-ordination across the Euro Area. Scrutiny of member state-specific recommendations would put pressure on governments to adopt the recommendations, or at least to respond to them. This, in turn, would lead to economic reforms that benefit all euro area members. The evidence for 2012 suggested that where the scrutiny would potentially be most useful in economic terms is where it was least practised.

This changed, however, by 2015, as Budget/Finance committees played an increasingly prominent role. The strength of European Union Affairs committees was no longer a good predictor of whether a given committee *ex ante* called debates. The increased role of Budget/Finance mirrors the rise of finance ministries domestically under the European Semester (see Maricut and Puetter 2017). It also mirrors developments in the social realm – Zeitlin and Vanhercke 2017 find that there has been a partial 'socialization' of the Semester over time, with more social goals appearing in the country-specific recommendations and more treatment of social topics at both the national and European levels. While these authors pose the question of an 'Economic vs Social Europe', our results suggest that domestic economic specialists in parliaments at least know more about the European Semester and debate it more in 2015 than in 2012. These results suggest a sort of deepening of 'Economic Europe' to match the partial deepening of 'Social Europe' these authors describe.

If one takes our results together, they indicate that whether a member state was a euro area out is the strongest predictor of whether there will be *ex post* evaluation of the country-specific recommendations. In the early years of the Semester, the parliaments in such member states found the Council's recommendations of most interest. Over time, those in member states outside the euro area became even more active than those inside the euro area. Our prior is that parliamentary committees became more active as recommendations touched upon more politically controversial topics, and the very involvement of 'Europe' in recommending domestic reforms under the country-specific recommendations was more controversial in euro area 'outs', which led to more active parliamentary committees in these member states. This argument would suggest that parliamentarians care most electoral incentives – controversial topics are ones that resonate with voters. We do not have transcripts of debates within committees, however, which would provide evidence for this argument to explain the difference between euro area 'outs' and 'ins', nor other types of evidence such as interviews with parliamentarians. There are other plausible explanations, such as institutional factors, as well as perhaps the greater orientation of Eastern European members towards EU institutions owing to their recent accession. The question of what explains this divergence according to membership in the euro area remains for further research.

## Notes

1. The staff from the Bulgarian Parliament wrote to us in 2012 that they refused to answer the survey, and the staff from the respective committees did not answer at all in 2013.
2. The countries included in the pilot project were Estonia, Finland, France, Germany, Hungary and Ireland. See Hallerberg *et al.* (2011).
3. We discussed the Danish case in the introduction. In Ireland, in 2013, the Finance and European Affairs committees respectively participated in *ex ante* discussions for the first time, with the former debating its Stability Programme and the latter its National Reform Programme.
4. We did not have data for 2012 for Croatia, when it was not a member state, and we did not include it in the 2015 survey.
5. On some occasions, a member of parliament on the respective committee answered a questionnaire instead of, or in addition to, a committee staff member.
6. The European Commission also delivered detailed country reports prior to the release of its country-specific recommendations, as two separate documents prior to 2015 and as a Country Report released in February as of 2015 (for more details, see the introduction to this collection 2017). We did not ask national parliaments about these documents.
7. The European framework also encourages national parliamentary involvement through the Treaty on Stability, Co-ordination and Governance in the Economic and Monetary Union (known as the Fiscal Compact) where all EU governments recognize the importance of a stronger co-operation between the European and national parliaments on budgetary issues making use of the Interparliamentary Co-operation (Art.13), as well as stress that any fiscal corrective action should be put in place in full respect of the prerogatives of national parliaments (Art.3).
8. Maatsch (2017) notes, however, that the plenaries in three of her four cases in 2014 did discuss country-specific recommendations when a given party disputed them. This contestation was not repeated in these countries in 2015.
9. Note that member states submit one document that includes both the SCP and NRP. There remain, however, key differences *ex post* in the consideration of the two.
10. The exception is Italy, where four committees – Budget, Economics, Labour/Employment, and European – debated the National Reform Programme. In addition to Italy, only in Germany (Economics) and Luxembourg (Labour) were other committees involved.
11. Spain held a plenary debate on the Commission response to the SCP (only) in 2011.
12. Auel *et al.* (2015) also measure the activity of national parliaments on EU matters and combine this information into a more general score, or the 'OPAL EU score'. Because we wish to check whether stronger parliaments are more active, we rely only on their institutional score. More on the OPAL project may be found at http://www.opal-europe.org.
13. One can also define 'strength' as whether parliament already debates the government's domestic multi-annual fiscal plans. This is a narrower definition of 'strength' that focuses only on debate rather than action, but it accords well with the information we have on debates in the plenary and in committee on European Semester matters. In 2012, only five countries had plenary debates

on domestic as well as on European multiannual plans (France, Luxembourg, Slovakia, Spain, and the UK). Two countries, Italy and Portugal, did discuss Stability Programmes submitted to the EU even if they did not debate on national plans. As both parliaments were weak on budgetary matters, one can speculate that some weak parliaments may exploit EU procedures to gain access to issues they would not otherwise have a chance to discuss. Eleven countries that discussed government multi-annual plans in plenary ignored Stability/Convergence Programmes. Clearly, this is not a good predictor, and we did not pursue this argument further in the 2015 survey.

14. See also Dandashly and Verdun (2016), who discuss the views among the Czech, Hungarian and Polish populations. They note that Hungary began as the most positive towards euro adoption and the Czech Republic as the least, but the euro crisis meant that support for the euro also decreased in Hungary.
15. The five are the Czech Republic, Denmark, Hungary, Sweden and the United Kingdom.
16. We use the percentage of respondents who agreed with the following statement: '(OUR COUNTRY) could better face the future outside the EU.'
17. Note, however, that there are two missing in 2015, with the UK not holding hearings because there were no parliamentary committees yet formed after May 2015 elections in the US to host them and because the Czech Republic is the one missing survey for the 2015 cohort.
18. Baerg and Hallerberg (2016) used the question 'Taking everything into consideration, would you say that (your country) has on balance benefited or not from being a member of the European Community (Common Market)? But the European Commission did not ask this question under the Eurobarometer in 2012.

## Acknowledgments

We would like to thank participants at the ACCESS EUROPE workshop, 11–12 December 2015, at the University of Amsterdam, for their helpful comments. Our anonymous reviewers checked each draft and pushed us to improve the text. Amy Verdun and Jonathan Zeitlin have been terrific, and patient, co-editors. Lola Mueller and Dayna Sadow provided needed editorial assistance. Finally, we thank the many respondents to our surveys.

## Disclosure statement

No potential conflict of interest was reported by the authors.

## ORCID

*Mark Hallerberg* http://orcid.org/0000-0002-4617-9929

## References

Auel, K. and Höing, O. (2014) 'Parliaments in the euro crisis: Can the losers of integration still fight back?', *JCMS: Journal of Common Market Studies* 52(6): 1184–1193.

Auel, K., Rozenberg, O. and Taccea, A. (2015) 'Fighting back? And if yes, how? Measuring parliamentary strength and activity in EU Affairs', in C. Hefftler, C. Neuhold, O. Rozenberg and J. Smith (eds), *The Palgrave Handbook of National Parliaments and the European Union*, Basingstoke: Palgrave Macmillan, pp. 60–93.

Baerg, N. and Hallerberg, M. (2016) 'Explaining instability in the stability and growth pact: The contribution of member state power and euroskepticism to the euro Crisis', *Comparative Political Studies* 49(7): 968–1009.

Bergman, T. (1997) 'National parliaments and EU affairs committees: notes on empirical variation and competing explanations', *Journal of European Public Policy* 4(3): 373–387.

Crum, B. (2017) 'Parliamentary accountability in multilevel governance: What role for parliaments in economic governance?' *Journal of European Public Policy*. doi:10.1080/13501763.2017.1363270.

Dandashly, A. and Verdun, A. (2016) 'Euro adoption in the Czech Republic, Hungary and Poland: laggards by default and laggards by choice', *Comparative European Politics* 56: 697. advance online publication 8 February 2016; doi:10.1057/cep.2015.46

European Commission (2012) Public opinion in the European Union. *Eurobarometer* 78 (Autumn).

European Commission (2015) Public opinion in the European Union. *Eurobarometer* 84 (December).

Goetz, K.H. and Meyer-Sahling, J.-H. (2008) 'The europeanisation of national political systems: parliaments and executives', *Living Reviews in European Governance* 3(2): 1–30.

Hallerberg, M., Marzinotto, B. and Wolff, G.B. (2011) 'An Assessment of the European Semester', Bruegel.

Hallerberg, M., Strauch, R. and von Hagen, J. (2009) *Fiscal Governance: Evidence From Europe*, Cambridge: Cambridge University Press.

Jančić, D. (2016) 'National parliaments and EU fiscal Integration', *European Law Journal* 22(2): 225–249.

Kreilinger, V. (2016) 'National parliaments, surveillance mechanisms and ownership in the euro area', Jacques Delors Institute, Berlin (March).

Maatsch, A. (2017) 'Effectiveness of the European Semester: Explaining Domestic Consent and Contestation', *Max Planck Institute for the Study of Societies Discussion Paper*, 17/6.

Maricut, A. and Puetter, U. (2017) 'Deciding on the European Semester: the European Council, the Council and the enduring asymmetry between economic and social policy issues', *Journal of European Public Policy*. doi:10.1080/13501763.2017.1363271.

Raunio, T. (2005) 'Holding governments accountable in european affairs: explaining cross-national variation', *The Journal of Legislative Studies* 11(3/4): 319–342.

Rittberger, B. and Winzen, T. (2015) 'Parlamentarismus nach der krise: Die vertiefung parlamentarischer asymmetrie in der reformierten wirtschafts- und Währungsunion', *Politische Vierteljahresschrift* 56(3): 430–456.

Rozenberg, O. and Hefftler, C. (2015) 'Introduction', in C. Hefftler, C. Neuhold, O. Rozenberg and J. Smith (eds), *The Palgrave Handbook of National Parliaments and the European Union*, Basingstoke: Palgrave Macmillan, pp. 1–39.
Tompson, W. (2009) *The Political Economy of Reform*, Paris: Organisation for Economic Cooperation and Development.
de Wilde, P. and Raunio, T. (Forthcoming) 'Redirecting national parliaments: setting priorities for involvement in EU affairs', *Comparative European Politics*.
Zeitlin, J. and Vanhercke, B. (2017) 'Socialising the European Semester: EU social and economic policy coordination in crisis and beyond', *Journal of European Public Policy*. doi:10.1080/13501763.2017.1363269.

OPEN ACCESS

# Parliamentary accountability in multilevel governance: what role for parliaments in post-crisis EU economic governance?

Ben Crum

**ABSTRACT**

How has the new structure of European Union (EU) economic governance affected the ability of parliaments (national and European) to scrutinize and control economic policy? Departing from the premise that executive power needs to be matched by appropriate parliamentary control, this contribution argues that parliamentary powers have been compromised in EU economic governance. Although budgetary powers remain formally at the national level, governments' decisions have become constrained and national parliaments find themselves on the losing side of a reinforced two-level game. This loss in parliamentary powers is not compensated at the European level, as at that level political authority is effectively left suspended between the national governments, who are unaccountable as a collective, and the European Commission, which lacks a political mandate of its own. Against this background, a final section identifies guidelines for organizing parliamentary accountability in settings, like EU economic governance, in which executive power has come to be shared across levels.

## Introduction

In the steady stream of reports on the future of Economic and Monetary Union (EMU) that have appeared in recent years, it has become a common habit to reserve the final section for the question of democratic legitimacy (European Commission 2012: Section 4; European Commission 2015b: Section 6; Juncker *et al.* 2015: Section 5; Van Rompuy *et al.* 2012: Section V). These sections tend to remain rather general in character. Typically, they flag that any steps towards further integration in economic affairs 'should go hand-in-hand with greater democratic accountability, legitimacy and institutional strengthening' (Juncker *et al.* 2015: 17). Then, slightly more specifically, it is underlined that parliaments – national parliaments and the European Parliament – are to play a key role in this. Here the 'guiding principle' is that 'democratic control and accountability should occur at the level at which the decisions are taken' (*cf.* European Commission 2012: 35; European Parliament 2015b: 12; Van Rompuy *et al.* 2012: 16). Any more concrete proposals, however, are limited to increasing the efficiency of the ways that parliaments are *consulted* in the European Union's (EU's) economic governance; they stop short of offering parliaments any binding powers.

This contribution seeks to assess how and to what extent the new structure of economic governance of the eurozone has affected the ability of parliaments (national *and* European) to scrutinize and control economic policy. It thus follows the reports mentioned in their normative assumption that parliaments play a key role in ensuring democratic legitimacy and accountability of economic governance. This assumption is developed in the next section, which also underlines the distinctive challenges that emerge once executive power comes to be shared between the national and the supranational level. Against this normative background, the rest of the contribution examines the shifts in economic policy-making power that the new structure of EU economic governance involves and the forms of parliamentary accountability by which these have been matched. Thus, this account offers a holistic view of parliamentary accountability of EU economic governance at both levels, while previous analyses tend to focus on the national (Fasone 2015; Jančić 2016) or the supranational (Fasone 2014) level alone.

In this contribution, I argue that, while the crisis has not led member states to actually transfer economic competences to the European level, it has led them to succumb to a much-reinforced system of surveillance. My central claim is that this system, taken as a whole, undermines parliamentary scrutiny and control. Although the eventual right to adopt the budget is preserved at the national level, governments' economic decisions are increasingly constrained and parliaments thus find themselves at the losing side of a reinforced two-level game. At the same time, this loss in parliamentary powers is not compensated at the European level, as at that level political authority is effectively left suspended between the national governments, who are unaccountable as a collective, and the European Commission, which lacks a political mandate of its own. In light of this two-level diagnosis, a final section identifies guidelines for organizing parliamentary accountability in settings, like the European Semester, in which executive power has come to be shared across levels.

## Theorizing parliamentary accountability in multilevel governance

Parliaments' role in democratic political systems is generally seen as embedded in a chain of delegation in which they act as the intermediary between the electorate and the executive (Strøm 2000). This chain of delegation is exemplified in the fact that elections determine the composition of the parliament and, in parliamentary systems, the composition of parliament in turn determines the composition of the executive. In between elections, processes of parliamentary accountability (information provision, questions, debates, motions etc.) serve to secure that the executive remains aligned with the preferences of the electorate. Thus, parliamentary accountability tracks executive authority.

This understanding of parliamentary accountability relies on a substantial set of normative presuppositions (*cf.* Bovens 2007). It posits parliament as the arena where the exercise of executive power is subject to public justification. The metaphor of an 'arena' is appropriate here, as the executive does not only put forward its justifications, but is likely to find its account critically challenged by alternative accounts from parliament. Depending on the justification offered, parliament usually concedes a certain degree of discretion to the executive. Ultimately, however, the process of parliamentary accountability can be understood as staked on the potential of parliament imposing sanctions on the executive, with the removal from office as the ultimate threat.

This model of parliamentary accountability becomes challenged once states become enmeshed in a multilevel political system like the European Union (Crum and Curtin 2015). If one insists that member states retain ultimate authority within the multilevel system, then accountability can still be offloaded in each of the national parliaments involved. This can be called the 'intergovernmental model'. Its opposite is the 'supranational model' in which executive authority is effectively delegated to the supranational level and is accountable to a corresponding supranational parliament, like the European Parliament (EP).

More complex, however, are the in-between situations in which member states retain a certain level of autonomy but at the same time become constrained by supranational norms. In practice, this seems to be the predominant situation in much of EU policy-making. It is particularly prominent to the extent that states pool powers among themselves rather than that they delegate them to a supranational authority (*cf.* Moravcsik 1998: 67ff.). In doing so, each government retains its own voice, but is eventually bound and constrained by the collective will of all the governments together. Typically, this situation has been addressed by relying on a double-key of parliamentary control, in which European decisions are both directly controlled by the EP as well as indirectly through the controls that national parliaments maintain on their governments in the Council of Ministers. Most importantly, this applies to the standard legislative procedure of the Union (*cf.* Article 10(2) TEU).

Whereas the intergovernmental and the supranational model of parliamentary accountability are rather straightforward, the double-key model raises important conceptual, normative and practical challenges. These concern in particular the interrelation between the two channels of representation (*cf.* Crum and Fossum 2013). In fact, the famous 'democratic deficit' of the European Union may be understood most concretely as a shortfall in the capacity of the supranational parliamentary power to compensate for the reduction of parliamentary powers at the national level (Weiler *et al.* 1995). In contrast, Andrew Moravcsik (2012: 66) has submitted that the superimposition of direct and indirect parliamentary controls actually means that EU decision-making is marked by a 'democratic surplus'. In their conclusion to a recent survey of executive accountability in the EU, Crum and Curtin (2015: 87) assign some credits to both positions as they assert:

> there is a dire need in the EU to align power with responsibility. While it may be true that at present too many EU actors are held responsible for things they do not hold power over, it certainly is also true that there are too many actors exercising EU power for which no one can be held appropriately responsible.

It is in light of these different understandings of parliamentary accountability in the EU that the central question of this contribution – how and to what extent the new structure of economic governance of the eurozone has affected the ability of parliaments to scrutinize and control economic policy – needs to be read. Both understandings share the normative presupposition that executive power should be matched by parliamentary accountability (*cf.* Van Rompuy *et al.* 2012: 16). The empirical question then becomes whether the new structure of economic governance has involved a shift in executive power and, if so, whether that shift has been matched by an appropriate and effective shift in parliamentary prerogatives at the national and/or the European level. Furthermore, if executive powers in economic governance are by now shared between the national and the European level, the case of the new economic governance in the EU (which is mostly non-legislative in character) may offer new pointers as to how parliamentary accountability across the two levels is best co-ordinated.

## EU economic governance – before and after the crisis

Ahead of the crisis, the structure of executive power and accountability in EU economic governance closely resembled the intergovernmental model in which member states remain the main centres of authority and are accountable to their national parliaments. The insistence on the primacy of national macroeconomic policy-making accounts for the well-known asymmetry in the design of EMU. Member states lost control over their exchange rate and much of their ability to manipulate interest rates was moved to the European Central Bank (ECB). However, a complete harmonization of financial and economic policies was considered unnecessary. All that was provided for was the Stability and Growth Pact (SGP) (Heipertz and Verdun 2010), which defined a few parameters within which the public finances of the eurozone countries were to operate, most importantly a maximum cap on the budget deficit of 3 per cent of gross domestic product (GDP). At the same time, supranational powers in economic governance were limited and severely constrained. The European Commission was tasked with monitoring the economic performance of the member states, but its powers remained subject to the political instructions and approval of the national governments (Savage and Howarth 2017).

Obviously, this structure of governance was severely shaken up as the financial crisis erupted in late 2008 and gradually morphed into a sovereign debt crisis in the eurozone. Beyond the bail-outs of individual governments and the adoption of new treaties, the most structural EU policy response to the euro crisis has been the build-up of the European Semester. Essentially, the European Semester involves the systematic reviewing of national budget plans and economic outlooks by the EU in the spring (semester) ahead of their formal adoption in the autumn. As such, the European Semester builds upon the multilateral surveillance of economic policies as it already took place before the crisis through the SGP and the Broad Economic Policy Guidelines.

Through a number of EU laws (the so-called 'Six-Pack' and 'Two-Pack'), macroeconomic surveillance has been stepped up (*cf.* Verdun and Zeitlin 2017). For one, with the addition of a Macroeconomic Imbalance Procedure (MIP), the scope of European surveillance has been broadened beyond public finance to also include macroeconomic indicators (e.g., about private debt, liabilities in the financial sector and unemployment). The most visible feature of the European Semester is that it harmonizes the different review procedures in a single co-ordinated calendar. This yearly cycle is organized around several milestones: the publication of the Annual Growth Survey by the Commission in November; the adoption of economic priorities by the March European Council; the submission of financial and economic plans by the governments in April; following which the Commission prepares the Country-Specific Recommendations, which get their eventual political endorsement by the European Council in June. Furthermore, the sanction potential of the procedure is increased by providing that, rather than that Commission recommendations require a qualified majority in the Council to be adopted, they now stand unless there is a qualified majority to reject or amend them.[1]

Crucially, the European Semester is set up as a dialogical process in which the national policy plans are held up against pan-European guidelines but also these guidelines (as for instance contained in the Annual Growth Strategy and the policy guidelines of the European Council) are supposed to adjust reflexively. However, while much of this process can be characterized as 'soft policy', ultimately there remains the threat of penalties. While no financial sanctions have been imposed so far, the more direct threat that countries face is the prospect of more intensive policy scrutiny and ever more detailed prescriptions. Thus, Iain Begg (2013: 60) has aptly characterized the new EU economic governance as 'a system that relies primarily on deterrence'.

The implications that the reforms of EU economic governance have had for the locus and strength of executive power in the Union are severely contested (Schmidt 2016a). On the one hand, there are the advocates of the 'new intergovernmentalism' (Bickerton *et al.* 2015; Fabbrini 2016), who highlight that member states' main responses to crises in the EU have involved intensifying the deliberation and co-ordination among themselves rather than expanding the scope of the Community method and the institutions associated with it (the Commission and the EP). On the other hand, we find proponents of the 'new supranationalism' who submit that supranational institutions, like the ECB and the Commission, have seen a significant expansion of their powers and scope of action (Bauer and Becker 2014; Dehousse 2016).

These two positions may not be as mutually exclusive as is suggested (Schmidt 2016a). It is quite likely that, if the euro crisis has fed a greater centralization of economic governance in the EU, this is reflected in both the intergovernmental and the supranational institutions. However, the question of this contribution is more specific than the question of who has gained power, as it rather asks about executive authority and its accountability to parliament. This is the focus of the more detailed analysis of the following two sections, in which we first look at the relevant changes at the national level and then turn to the European level.

## Sidelining national parliaments: a reinforced two-level game

Formally, the reforms adopted since the crisis have left the primacy of national policy-making in fiscal affairs intact. Above all, this is reflected by the fact that, regardless of all surveillance measures, the final approval of the budget remains in the hands of the national authorities. And while surveillance powers at the supranational level have been increased, member states have been very reluctant to delegate effective decision-power and retain the possibility to reverse the Commission's decisions (*cf.* Schmidt 2015: 99ff.).

Yet there is no denying that governments' fiscal policies have become more constrained (Scharpf 2011). Supranational surveillance has expanded in terms of scope, depth and bite. In practice, the European Semester's constraining influence is very much an effect of the way it has been sequenced. The early start of the European Semester, in the final months of the year preceding the year in which the budget is adopted, means that the European level takes the lead in defining the main policy orientations as well as the scope for national discretion. It is European-level decisions like the Annual Growth Survey, the economic priorities and the Country-Specific Recommendations that set the overarching policy framework. Thus, the supranational constellation of the European Semester pushes governments in a reactive and defensive mode.

Consequently, the effect of the European Semester on the ability of national parliaments to scrutinize their governments' economic policy choices emerges as a reinforced 'two-level game' (*cf.* Benz 2013). Robert Putnam (1988) originally adopted the metaphor of a 'two-level game' to analyse the ways in which governments in international negotiations must navigate between two arenas, that of the international negotiation table and that of the domestic constituency represented by the national parliament. Putnam suggests that governments can use their privileged access to, and knowledge of, one level to increase their leverage at the other. By manoeuvring smartly between the two levels, governments can maximize their standing in the international negotiations while also gaining autonomy from their national constituency.

The European Semester has certainly not strengthened governments' powers. Instead, the qualification of a reinforced two-level game underlines that the Semester has very much tilted the balance of the fiscal two-level game to the supranational level. As governments find their economic policies conditioned by supranational targets and recommendations, their ability to respond to any wishes from their national parliament has become constrained.

Interestingly, however, the very reinforcement of the European reins on national budgets and fiscal policy has provoked an active response among many national parliaments (Fasone 2015; Jančić 2016). Many have used the European Semester to increase their consultation rights in the early stages of budget preparation and on the broader financial and economic frameworks that govern the budgetary process. By 2013, the vast majority of national parliaments in the EU discussed the Stability and Convergence Programmes and the National Reform Programmes that their governments submitted to the Commission (COSAC 2014: 42).

For sure, there is considerable variation in the ways national parliaments have responded to the European Semester. Hallerberg *et al.* (2017) find that it is not in the Euro area but rather in the Eurosceptic countries that are unlikely to ever adopt the euro (the United Kingdom, Sweden, Hungary, Denmark and the Czech Republic) where parliaments are most active in discussing their governments' plans. The scattered evidence on the depth of parliamentary powers (COSAC 2014; European Parliament 2014) suggests furthermore that it is the Nordic parliaments (Latvia, Lithuania, Finland, Estonia), with a tradition of active EU scrutiny (Winzen 2012), where parliaments retain most powers over the government's exchange with the Commission. Beyond Northern Europe, the best-known case is probably the German *Bundestag* whose budgetary authority has been upheld and reinforced by the German Federal Constitutional Court (Hoïng 2015). Also, the traditionally much weaker French *Assemblée Nationale* has seen its involvement in the budgetary process expanded (Jančić 2016: 243). Notably, even parliaments in Mediterranean countries like Italy, Spain and Portugal who have found themselves under severe budgetary pressures have been remarkably assertive in extending their involvement in the budgetary process (Fasone 2015: 20f.; Jančić 2016: 242f.). Still, as Jančić (2016: 225) concludes, on the whole these parliamentary initiatives 'do not outweigh the centralization of the nascent EU fiscal regime' and 'are unlikely substantially to influence EMU policy-making processes'.

In fact, national parliaments display a keen awareness of the limits of their span of control. Most of them are content to be involved in processes of consultation and deliberation with the government without any direct veto powers. Notably, some national parliaments (like the Austrian chambers [COSAC 2014: 43/4]) only get to discuss the government's Stability and Convergence Plans after they have already been sent to the European Commission. Other parliaments, like in the Benelux countries, do debate the plans before they are sent off, but have no powers to reject or amend them (European Parliament 2014: 2). Even the Danish *Folketinget* (2013), which (as so often) was a frontrunner in adapting to the European Semester, declined to claim a veto over its government's input into the European Semester. In the end, in a survey in 2014, the European Parliament (2014: 2) found that only the Latvian *Saeima* has the power to approve *and* to amend the Stability and Convergence Programme.

Thus, we find that many parliaments have responded to the European Semester by expanding their scrutiny over the national budget, but that they do so only in the lower ranges of accountability mechanisms (information, consultation and debate). When it comes to the substance of the budget, national parliaments tend to cave in as they recognize the Semester as a reinforced two-level game, part of which takes place beyond their span of control. This recognition of economic interdependence in the EU may be regarded as 'a sign of responsibility from the legislatures' (Fasone 2015: 26). Still, it inevitably also means that they recognize their powers to scrutinize and control economic policy to be limited (Laffan 2014). Indeed, the recognition that the European Semester transcends the powers of national parliaments motivates calls for reinforced parliamentary scrutiny at the European level (COSAC 2014: 47f.). Hence, we logically turn to the European Parliament as the parliamentary forum at the supranational level.

## Sidelining the European Parliament: the suspension of supranational political authority

While the European Parliament (EP) has had an important role in the legal establishment of the European Semester, it plays a remarkably marginal role in its actual execution (Fasone 2014; Schmidt 2015: 111). All the European Semester provides for is the 'economic dialogue' that the EP maintains with the Commissioner for Economic and Monetary Affairs, the (rotating) President of the Council and the Eurogroup President. Notably, however, these exchanges are mostly informative and consultative in character, and place the EP in a rather passive, receptive position.

This marginal position of the EP can be justified on the basis of the general principle, already cited in the introduction, that 'democratic control and accountability should occur at the level at which the decisions are taken' (Van Rompuy *et al.* 2012: 16). The presumption is then that the European Semester involves very few binding decisions that are adopted at the supranational level. What is more, as the Semester is an iterative process that moves to its conclusions in a step-by-step fashion, it is very hard to determine the decisive, political moment; at every stage it is possible for the actors involved to refer to the preceding step as conditioning their options. In the words of Mark Dawson (2015: 982): 'Decision-making never crystallizes ... into a "once and for all" agreement but acts as an ongoing series of open-ended "decisions"'. This situation is complicated further by the fact that the European Semester mixes general decisions with country-specific ones, and that these relate to different audiences. In the early phases of the Semester, the pan-EU frameworks are adopted, most notably the Annual Growth Survey and the economic priorities of the European Council, that offer strategic orientations but have no immediate effect. Nevertheless, they condition the subsequent assessments of the national and financial plans, but these are less suitable for supranational scrutiny as they relate to individual countries.

Regardless of the formal status of the positions adopted at the supranational level, they are certainly consequential, especially once one recognizes that, even if actual sanctions are unlikely to materialize, the Semester operates mainly through deterrence (Begg 2013: 60). Then, however, the big issue from a viewpoint of parliamentary accountability is that the structure of the European Semester makes it very difficult to determine the locus of political authority at the supranational level (*cf.* Crum and Curtin 2015: 82f.): while the governments, who are formally responsible, cannot be held accountable as a collective, the Commission that calls most shots in practice operates under the pretence that these are merely administrative decisions. As a consequence, no one is accountable.

For sure, in principle, political authority resides with the member governments. However, the national governments cannot themselves execute the actual supervision of each other's financial and economic policies, as they want to maintain the political neutrality of the process (Savage and Howarth 2017). Hence, the logical solution is to delegate the administration of macroeconomic surveillance to a technical authority, the European Commission (Dehousse 2016: 626).

Indeed, in many respects the European Semester appears to give a particularly strong role to the European Commission, in particular because it is primarily responsible for drafting the recommendations (Bauer and Becker 2014; Dehousse 2016). However, the Commission is not a political institution in its own right; it is to promote 'the general interest of the Union' rather than that it holds a political mandate, its members are appointed rather than elected, and it exercises executive tasks that have been delegated to it by the Council and the EP. The formal primacy of the member states remains reflected in the fact that once the Commission has drafted its Country-Specific Recommendations, they still need the final endorsement of the Council and can, in principle, be recalled, albeit only by a qualified majority.

Since the Commission cannot claim a political mandate of its own, its decisions are guided by rules and benchmarks (Schmidt 2015). The most famous example is the original rule in the SGP that precluded EU governments from running a deficit above 3 per cent of their GDP. Further relevant priorities and benchmarks are laid down in the MIP, the Annual Growth Survey, and in the economic priorities adopted by the European Council. As the European Commission (e.g., 2015a: 4) itself is keen to underline, the credibility of the SGP requires it to operate as a 'rules-based system', which forecloses the possibility that the Commission exercises any political judgment for which it has not been authorized.

However, this rules-based understanding of the Commission's assessments is difficult to sustain in practice (Schmidt 2016b). This is evident in the set-up of the MIP where the 'alert thresholds' on the headline indicators do not automatically trigger a policy response but only serve a signalling function, which invites a closer and more holistic review of the relevant economic conditions and the threat they pose for other European economies. But also regarding the SGP, the European Commission has come to a more contextual appraisal of national performance. Step-by-step, the strict 3 per cent norm has been abandoned in favour of a 'Medium-Term Objective' (MTO) for each member state that defines the desired path of budgetary adjustment over time (*cf.* Mabbett and Schelkle 2016: 133/4). Indeed, by the Commission's own admission, some flexibility is indispensable in the way it executes its assessments:

> It is on purpose that the Pact envisages flexibility in the way its rules should be applied, both over time and across countries. It is also on purpose that some discretion is left, within the agreed rules, for the Commission and the Council to

> assess the soundness of public finances in the light of country-specific circumstances, in order to recommend the best course of action based on the latest developments and information. (European Commission 2015a: 4)

Vivien Schmidt (2016b) aptly characterizes this shifting position of the Commission as involving a reinterpretation of the rules 'by stealth'.

However, the recognition of the indispensability of context-sensitive judgments exposes a gap in supranational political authorization, as with this sphere of discretion the Commission inevitably moves beyond the instructions from the Council (*cf.* Dawson 2015; Schmidt 2015: 99). In practice, the two institutions aim to play down the 'disjunction between discourse and action' (Schmidt 2016b: 1033). The Commission threads cautiously in issuing its recommendations and seeks to anticipate as much as possible the will of the (majority of the) member states. In turn, the member states have actually been quite happy to leave the lead to the Commission and to adopt its proposals as a rallying point. Typically, even when it comes to the adoption of the political priorities at the March European Council, the Heads of Government tend to simply endorse the priorities of the Commission's Annual Growth Survey rather than to formulate their own (e.g., European Council 2016: 3).

All in all, it is undeniable that the European Semester involves the making of political judgments at the European level, which are consequential in that they constrain member states' financial and economic decisions and are backed up by close surveillance and, ultimately, the threat of financial sanctions. Naturally, these political judgments should be subject to parliamentary control. However, while an extensive web of economic dialogue has developed at the European level, any effective powers to intervene have been withheld from the EP. The deeper problem is that it is not clear who should be held accountable because the locus of supranational political authority has been left suspended. The Commission lacks a political mandate of its own and hence presents all its decisions as mere executions of the rules set by the member states (often with endorsement of the EP). The member states are not politically accountable as a collective at the European level and, in the absence of a coherent political orientation of themselves, tend to rally behind the positions adopted by the Commission.

## (Re)parliamentarizing EU economic governance

Having reviewed parliamentary powers in the European Semester at the national and the European level, the apparent logic of the 'guiding principle' that 'democratic control and accountability should occur at the level at which the decisions are taken' (Van Rompuy *et al.* 2012: 16) turns out to be rather deceptive. Formally, it can be maintained that the ultimate decision power in economic and budgetary affairs remains at the national level, and hence no binding parliamentary powers are necessary at the supranational level. Yet, in practice, decisions at the national level have become more constrained, while the relevant decisions at the supranational are taken without it being clear who can be held accountable.

The central challenge, then, is whether it is possible to insert political responsibility and accountability into the kind of straddled decision-making structure to which the new economic governance in Europe has given rise. Following on the preceding analyses, four aspects in particular can be identified that can help to ensure that the shift in decision-making power in economic governance that the European Semester involves is met by an appropriate structure of parliamentary control: marking the political moment; embodying political authority; increasing the credibility of the EP; and reinforcing the capacities of national parliaments.

### *Marking the political moment*

Before all else, it is essential to identify the key political moments in the iterative process of the European Semester. In principle, the critical political moment at the European level is the setting of the economic priorities by the March European Council. This is the moment for the member states to claim political control over the process and adjust the priorities depending on their appreciation of the political and economic conditions. What is more, the more the member states elaborate a substantial economic agenda, the less the Commission has to rely on automatic rules and benchmarks in drafting the subsequent policy recommendations.

However, as noted, governments have been reluctant to claim the March European Council as the moment to have a genuine political debate about the economic priorities for Europe. This unwillingness may be explained by the ideological differences within the European Council, which complicates the elaboration of any substantial collective economic strategy. Still, also among the governments (*cf.* Governo Italiano 2016), there are signs of growing frustration with the lack of a substantial and coherent political stance.

Apart from political will, one thing that can help to turn the March European Council into a genuine political moment would be for it to reduce the influence of the Commission's Annual Growth Strategy and to rather invite collectively discussed strategic agendas from the relevant sectoral Councils (i.e., the Councils for Economic and Financial Affairs [Ecofin] and for Employment, Social Policy, Health and Consumer Affairs [EPSCO]). The elaboration of more political agendas for the European Semester would also serve as useful reference points for the subsequent debates on the national plans in the member states.

### *Embodying political authority*

As a complement to the marking of the political moment, for accountability to take place it is essential that political responsibility becomes embodied in some way. Even if the collective political authority of the member states is maintained, there is a need for a proper interlocutor at the European level, who can speak on their behalf and offer public justification of the decisions that the Council adopts, as well as of the ways these are administered. The typical way in which the EU has resolved this kind of situation is by 'double-hatting' executive responsibility between the Council and the Commission, the prime example being the High Representative for the Foreign Affairs and Security Policy (FASP), who is at the same time Vice-President of the European Commission.

Hence, one might envisage the establishment of a 'High Representative' for Economic Affairs who can both act as a special agent of the Council and draw on the Commission's administrative resources (*cf.* Enderlein and Haas 2015). Thus positioned, such a High Representative would play a critical role in reconciling the policy assessments of the Commission with the political backing of the member states. As the example of the High Representative for the FASP illustrates, such a supranational agent remains tied to the mandate that she is given by the national governments. Still, she can be an important policy entrepreneur and agenda setter in moving initiatives forward and in adopting positions that the governments left to themselves would be unlikely to speak out on. Crucially, for our purpose, such a High Representative could also act as a spokesperson for the EU's economic policy and offer justifications for it before the public and the parliament. Indeed, as a member of the Commission she would be subject to all the scrutiny powers that the EP commands.

### *Increasing the credibility of the European Parliament*

The two preceding steps are actually preconditions for granting the EP more substantial powers in the European Semester. At present, the rights that the EP can claim in the context of the 'economic dialogue' are procedural in character: the right to be informed and to give advice. Notably, the 2015 Five Presidents' Report (Juncker *et al.* 2015: 17) suggests that Commissioners could appear more systematically before the EP, and that they and Council representatives could participate more regularly in interparliamentary meetings.

However, if we take it that ultimate political authority in economic affairs remains with the member states, then the Council rather than the Commission should be the EP's primary port of call. Here the establishment of a High Representative who can speak on behalf of the Council would be of much help in establishing a rapport between the Council and the EP. What is more, once the European Council takes greater political responsibility for the policy priorities, the EP might be given the right to consent to these priorities, possibly through a process of joint decision-making between the Council and the EP modelled on existing conciliation practices (*cf.* the European Parliament's [2015: 13] own proposal for so-called 'Convergence Guidelines').

Inevitably, such steps will bring more politics to the process and reduce its rule-based character. This creates space to set political priorities and to adjust 'alert levels', certainly in the context of the MIP. Also, the flexibility that is now apparent in the interpretation of the SGP would then become subject to public debate, in which all too self-serving interpretations by the member states would need to be balanced by the other members, by the prudence of the Commission and by the political assessment of the EP.

### *Reinforcing the capacities of national parliaments*

Clearly, however, as long as budgetary competences are ultimately exercised at the national level, national parliaments continue to fulfil key scrutiny roles. As indicated, many national parliaments have been remarkably active in responding to the new structure of EU economic governance. Still, most parliaments seem to be reluctant to directly interfere in the exchange between their government and the European Commission. This creates exactly the conditions under which the government can insist that its hand is forced by supranational imperatives.

Hence, if national parliaments want to retain their standing in economic affairs, they need to adopt a two-pronged strategy. On the one hand, depending on the constitutional conditions they face, they can maximize their involvement in the drawing up of the stability and reform national programmes in early spring. For that involvement to have any impact, one would expect them to be involved before the actual submission of the programmes rather than only after it (*cf.* Hallerberg *et al.* 2017; Kreilinger 2016: 32). Ideally, one would even want the programmes to be subject to parliamentary approval, as is already the case in some countries.

On the other hand, it is essential for national parliaments to increase their awareness of and their access to the supranational level. For that, the Interparliamentary Conference on Economic Governance is the natural channel. While this conference has so far disappointed as a forum for substantial political engagement (Cooper 2016; Kreilinger 2015), a more visible political framing of the European Semester – as aimed for by the preceding proposals – should serve to increase the stakes of these European exchanges. It should also encourage national parliamentarians to co-ordinate their input at the national level with the political priorities debated at the European level. What is more, the Interparliamentary Conference should serve to exchange initiatives and best practices in scrutinizing national governments and to co-ordinate, wherever possible, political interventions across parliaments (*cf.* Crum and Fossum 2013).

Obviously, more involvement and awareness of national parliaments will mean that the rules and benchmarks propagated by Brussels will be less taken for granted and subject to greater politicization. Political contestation may well decrease compliance with the Country-Specific Recommendations. However, if such non-compliance is accompanied by a process of political exchange between the national and European level, it is actually in line with the dialogical character that the European Semester is supposed to have. Thus, greater non-compliance with Country-Specific Recommendations may well be the price to pay for the longer-term legitimacy of the European Semester as a process.

## Conclusion

As key national competences become ever more closely co-ordinated at the supranational level, this creates a major challenge for parliamentary accountability. Accountability does not only require that decision-making capacity is matched by adequate parliamentary controls at each level; it also requires taking account of the peculiar ways in which the decision-making processes at the two levels interact. Thus, parliamentary accountability turns out to be particularly vulnerable in a multilevel setting, as its demands at each level may be met by a reference to the constraints at the other.

Concretely, we find that as the experience of the Euro crisis has led national economic policies to become incorporated in a dense web of European surveillance, the capacity of national parliaments to scrutinize the choices of their governments has become severely strained. At the same time, no effective parliamentary accountability has developed at the European level; at that level, political authority remains suspended between the collective of national governments and the (quasi-)technocratic assessments by the Commission, leaving the EP without any authority to hold to account.

A crucial precondition for parliamentary accountability to operate effectively in such a multilevel context is that executive authority can be attributed to a well-specified executive actor. Hence, it is of particular importance in an iterative process like the European Semester that the key political moments are properly marked and that at the European level a political authority is established who can be held answerable for the decisions adopted. Only with these conditions in place can the EP claim a more substantial and consequential role in the process. At the same time, a better readability of the supranational political process can also complement the efforts of national parliaments to engage effectively and to co-ordinate their interventions.

Naturally, effective parliamentary accountability of the European Semester will expose the political choices made to greater contestation and reduce the reliance on rules and benchmarks. While such a shift may indeed reduce member state compliance with the Country-Specific Recommendations, it will reinforce the character of the European Semester as a dialogical process rather than a hierarchical one. At the same time, increasing parliamentary accountability across levels need not necessarily increase the centrifugal tendencies. On the contrary, considered as a package, the suggested guidelines require parliaments to co-ordinate their activities among each other and to more consistently perceive their own role within the broader context of the multilevel system of EU governance as a whole. In that sense, greater parliamentary accountability should eventually contribute to the collective ownership of the European Semester.

## Note

1. The one exception in this regard is the launch of an excessive imbalance procedure under the MIP, which requires the usual qualified majority in the Council.

## Acknowledgements

Previous versions of this contribution have been presented at the ARENA Centre for European Studies in Oslo, the Leuven Centre for Global Governance Studies, the 14th EUSA Conference in Boston, MA, the ACCESS EUROPE Workshop on 'Socio-Economic Governance in the EU since the Crisis', and the University of Bremen. Thanks are due to the participants at these events, and in particular to Kalypso Nicolaïdis, Amy Verdun, Jonathan Zeitlin and three anonymous referees for helpful comments.

## Disclosure statement

No potential conflict of interest was reported by the author.

## ORCID

*Ben Crum* http://orcid.org/0000-0003-4330-295X

## References

Bauer, M. and Becker, S. (2014) 'The unexpected winner of the crisis: the European Commission's strengthened role in economic governance', *Journal of European Integration* 36(3): 213–29.

Begg, I. (2013) 'Are better defined rules enough? An assessment of the post-crisis reforms of the governance of EMU', *Transfer: European Review of Labour and Research* 19(1): 49–62.

Benz, A. (2013) 'An asymmetric two-level game. parliaments in the Euro crisis', in B. Crum and J.E. Fossum (eds), *Practices of Inter-Parliamentary Coordination in International Politics: The European Union and Beyond*, Colchester: ECPR Press, pp. 125–40.

Bickerton, C., Hodson, D. and Puetter, U. (2015) 'The new intergovernmentalism: European integration in the post-maastricht era', *Journal of Common Market Studies* 53(4): 703–22.

Bovens, M. (2007) 'Analysing and assessing accountability: a conceptual framework', *European Law Journal* 13(4): 447–68.

Cooper, I. (2016) 'The interparliamentary conference on stability, economic coordination and governance in the European Union (the 'article 13 conference')', in N. Lupo and C. Fasone (eds) *Interparliamentary Cooperation in the Composite European Constitution*, Oxford: Hart Publishing, pp. 247–68.

COSAC (2014) 'Twenty-first Bi-annual report: developments in European Union procedures and practices relevant to parliamentary scrutiny', Prepared by the COSAC secretariat and presented to the LI conference of parliamentary committees for union affairs of parliaments of the European Union, Athens, 15–17, June 2014.

Crum, B. and Curtin, D. (2015) 'The challenge of making EU executive power accountable', in S. Piattoni (ed.), *The European Union: Democratic Principles and Institutional Architectures in Times of Crisis*, Oxford: Oxford University Press, pp. 63–87.

Crum, B. and Fossum, J.E. (2013) 'Conclusion: towards a *democratic* multilevel parliamentary field?', in B. Crum and J.E. Fossum (eds.), *Practices of Inter-Parliamentary Coordination in International Politics: The European Union and Beyond*, Colchester: ECPR Press, pp. 251–68.

Dawson, M. (2015) 'The legal and political accountability structure of 'post-crisis' EU economic governance', *Journal of Common Market Studies* 53(5): 976–93.

Dehousse, R. (2016) 'Why has EU macroeconomic governance become more supranational?', *Journal of European Integration* 38(5): 617–31.

Enderlein, H. and Haas, J. (2015) 'What would a European finance minister do? A proposal', *Policy Paper 145*, Berlin: Jacques Delors Institute, October.

European Commission (2012) 'A blueprint for a deep and genuine economic and monetary union. Launching a European debate', *COM(2012) 777*. 28 November, Brussels: Commission of the European Communities.

European Commission (2015a) 'Making the best use of the flexibility within the existing rules of the stability and growth pact', *COM(2015)12*, 13 January, Strasbourg: Commission of the European Communities.

European Commission (2015b) 'On steps towards completing economic and monetary union', *COM(2015)600 final*, 21 October, Brussels: Commission of the European Communities.

European Council (2016) 'European council meeting (17 and 18 March 2016) – Conclusions', *Document No. EUCO 12/16*, Brussels: General Secretariat of the Council, 18 March.

European Parliament, Directorate for Relations with National Parliaments (2014) 'Review of Stability and Convergence Programmes by National Parliaments within the framework of the European Semester', *Spotlight on Parliaments on Europe, No. 2*, Brussels, November.

European Parliament (2015) 'Report on the review of the economic governance framework: stocktaking and challenges', EP-Document PE546.753v03-00, Committee on Economic and Monetary Affairs (Rapporteur: Pervenche Berès), 17 June.

Fabbrini, S. (2016) 'From consensus to domination: the intergovernmental union in a crisis situation', *Journal of European Integration* 38(5): 587–99.

Fasone, C. (2014) 'European economic governance and parliamentary representation. what place for the European parliament?', *European Law Journal* 20(2): 164–85.

Fasone, C. (2015) 'Taking budgetary powers away from national parliaments? On parliamentary prerogatives in the Eurozone crisis', *EUI Working Papers LAW 2015/37*. Florence: European University Institute.

Folketinget, European Affairs Committee and the Finance Committee (2013) 'Report on consideration of the European Semester', *Report No. 5 Folketinget – 2012-13*, 21 June.

Governo Italiano (2016) 'A shared European policy strategy for growth, jobs, and stability', Rome, 22 February, available at www.governo.it/sites/governo.it/files/ASharedPolicyStrategy_20160222.pdf (accessed March 2016).

Hallerberg, M., Marzinotto, B. and Wolff, G. (2017) 'Explaining the evolving role of national parliaments under the European Semester', *Journal of European Public Policy*. doi:10.1080/13501763.2017.1363273.

Heipertz, M. and Verdun, A. (2010) *Ruling Europe: The Politics of the Stability and Growth Pact*, Cambridge: Cambridge University Press.

Hoïng, O. (2015) 'With a little help of the constitutional court: the bundestag on its way to an active policy shaper', in C. Hefftler *et al.* (eds), *The Palgrave Handbook of National Parliaments and the European Union*, Basingstoke: Palgrave, pp. 191–208.

Jančić, D. (2016) 'National parliaments and EU fiscal Integration', *European Law Journal* 22(2): 225–49.

Juncker, J.C., in close cooperation with D. Tusk, J. Dijsselbloem, M. Draghi and M. Schulz (2015) 'Completing Europe's economic and Monetary Union', Brussels.

Kreilinger, V. (2015) 'Inter-parliamentary cooperation and its challenges: the case of economic and financial governance', in F. Fabbrini, E. Hirsch Ballin and H. Somsen (eds), *What Form of Government for the EU and the Eurozone?*, Oxford: Hart Publishing, pp. 271–88.

Kreilinger, V. (2016) 'National parliaments, surveillance mechanisms and ownership in the euro area', *Studies & Reports*, Berlin: Jacques Delors Institute, March.

Laffan, B. (2014) 'Testing times: the growing primacy of responsibility in the Euro area', *West European Politics* 37(2): 270–87.

Mabbett, D. and Schelkle, W. (2016) 'Searching under the lamp-post: the evolution of fiscal surveillance', in J. Caporaso and M. Rhodes (eds), *Political and Economic Dynamics of the Eurozone Crisis*, Oxford: Oxford University Press, pp. 122–44.

Moravcsik, A. (1998) *The Choice for Europe*, London: Routledge.

Moravcsik, A. (2012) 'Europe after the crisis: how to sustain a common currency', *Foreign Affairs* 91(3): 54–68.

Putnam, R.D. (1988) 'Diplomacy and domestic politics: the logic of two-level games', *International Organization* 42(3): 427–60.

Savage, J. and Howarth, D. (2017) 'Enforcing the European Semester: the politics of asymmetric information in the excessive deficit and macroeconomic imbalances procedures', *Journal of European Public Policy*. doi:10.1080/13501763.2017.1363268.

Scharpf, F. (2011) 'Monetary Union, fiscal crisis and the pre-emption of democracy', *Zeitschrift für Staats- und Europawissenschaften* 9(2): 163–98.

Schmidt, V. (2015) 'The forgotten problem of democratic legitimacy. "governing by the rules" and "ruling by the numbers"', in M. Matthijs and M. Blyth (eds), *The Future of the Euro*, Oxford: Oxford University Press, pp. 90–115.

Schmidt, V. (2016a) 'The 'new' EU governance: 'new' intergovernmentalism, 'new' supranationalism' plus 'new' parliamentarism', in A. Crespy (ed.), *Issue on The EU Economic Governance*, Cahiers du Cevipol/Brussels Working Papers, n° 5/2016. Brussels: Université Libre de Bruxelles, pp. 5–31.

Schmidt, V. (2016b) 'Reinterpreting the rules 'by stealth' in times of crisis: a discursive institutionalist analysis of the European central bank and the European Commission', *West European Politics* 39(5): 1032–52.

Strøm, K. (2000) 'Delegation and accountability in parliamentary democracies', *European Journal of Political Research* 37(3): 261–89.

Van Rompuy, H. in close collaboration with Barroso, J.M., Juncker, J.-C., and Draghi, M. (2012) 'Towards a genuine economic and monetary union'. Brussels, 5 December.

Verdun, A. and Zeitlin, J. (2017) 'Introduction: the European Semester as a new architecture of EU socio-economic governance in theory and practice', *Journal of European Public Policy*. doi:10.1080/13501763.2017.1363807.

Weiler, J., Haltern, U. and Mayer F. (1995) 'European democracy and its critique', *West European Politics* 18(3): 4–39.

Winzen, T. (2012) 'National parliamentary control of European Union affairs: a cross-national and longitudinal comparison', *West European Politics* 35(3): 657–72.

# Index

*Note*: **Boldface** page numbers refer tables, page numbers followed by "n" denote endnotes

For Product Safety Concerns and Information please contact our EU representative GPSR@taylorandfrancis.com
Taylor & Francis Verlag GmbH, Kaufingerstraße 24, 80331 München, Germany

www.ingramcontent.com/pod-product-compliance
Ingram Content Group UK Ltd.
Pitfield, Milton Keynes, MK11 3LW, UK
UKHW011018180926
475701UK00004B/808
*9780367591212*